Doing Public Journalism

THE GUILFORD COMMUNICATION SERIES

Editors
Theodore L. Glasser, *Stanford University*
Howard E. Sypher, *University of Kansas*

DOING PUBLIC JOURNALISM
Arthur Charity

SOCIAL APPROACHES TO COMMUNICATION
Wendy Leeds-Hurwitz, *Editor*

PUBLIC OPINION AND THE COMMUNICATION OF CONSENT
Theodore L. Glasser and Charles T. Salmon, *Editors*

COMMUNICATION RESEARCH MEASURES: A SOURCEBOOK
Rebecca B. Rubin, Philip Palmgreen, and Howard E. Sypher, *Editors*

PERSUASIVE COMMUNICATION
James B. Stiff

REFORMING LIBEL LAW
John Soloski and Randall P. Bezanson, *Editors*

MESSAGE EFFECTS RESEARCH:
PRINCIPLES OF DESIGN AND ANALYSIS
Sally Jackson

CRITICAL PERSPECTIVES ON MEDIA AND SOCIETY
Robert K. Avery and David Eason, *Editors*

MASS MEDIA AND POLITICAL TRANSITION:
THE HONG KONG PRESS IN CHINA'S ORBIT
Joseph Man Chan and Chin-Chuan Lee

THE JOURNALISM OF OUTRAGE: INVESTIGATIVE
REPORTING AND AGENDA BUILDING IN AMERICA
David L. Protess, Fay Lomax Cook, Jack C. Doppelt, James S. Ettema,
Margaret T. Gordon, Donna R. Leff, and Peter Miller

COMMUNICATION AND CONTROL: NETWORKS
AND THE NEW ECONOMIES OF COMMUNICATION
G. J. Mulgan

STUDYING INTERPERSONAL INTERACTION
Barbara M. Montgomery and Steve Duck, *Editors*

VOICES OF CHINA: THE INTERPLAY
OF POLITICS AND JOURNALISM
Chin-Chuan Lee, *Editor*

CASE STUDIES IN ORGANIZATIONAL COMMUNICATION
Beverly Davenport Sypher, *Editor*

Doing
Public Journalism

✦

ARTHUR CHARITY

Foreword by Jay Rosen

THE GUILFORD PRESS
New York   London

© 1995 The Kettering Foundation

Published by The Guilford Press
A Division of Guilford Publications, Inc.
72 Spring Street, New York, NY, 10012

Printed in the United States of America

This book is printed on acid-free paper.

Last digit is print number: 9 8 7 6 5 4 3 2 1

Library of Congress Cataloging-in-Publication Data

Charity, Arthur
    Doing public journalism / Arthur Charity ; foreword by Jay Rosen ;
  original research into public newspapers by Lisa Austin.
        p.   cm.
    "Part of the literature of the Project on Public Life and the
  Press"——CIP foreword.
    Includes biobliographical references.
    ISBN 1-57230-028-0 (hard). — ISBN 1-57230-030-2 (pbk.)
    1. Journalism—Social aspects.   I.   Project on Public Life and the
  Press (U.S.)   II. Title.
  PN4749.C49   1995
  302.23—dc20   95-34661
                                                           CIP

✦

Foreword

Public journalism is a work in progress, and that is the most important thing anyone can say about it. *Doing Public Journalism* is for everyone who wonders what this work is about and what it means for practicing journalists. As an argument about where the press should be going, as a set of practices that have been tried in real-life settings, and as a movement of people and institutions concerned about the possibilities for reform, public journalism is still quite young, which means that there is room for everyone who wants to get involved. Working journalists who might push into untried territory, writers and scholars who can deepen the rationale, students who can experiment in a campus set-ting—all have contributions to make. Arthur Charity's important con-tribution is to explain the "why" as well as the "how" of public journal-ism: the reason it arose when it did, and the nuts and bolts of how it's been done so far. But the emphasis has to be on the "so far." What public journalism will be in 5 or 10 years no one can say. And that—along with Charity's compelling prose—is what's exciting about this book, the first of its kind.

Doing Public Journalism is part of the literature of the Project on Public Life and the Press, funded by the John S. and James L. Knight Foundation. The Project was launched in 1993 as an expanded version of some early groundwork done by the Kettering Foundation of Dayton, Ohio. Today, the four partners in the Project are the Knight Foundation; the Kettering Foundation, which operates the program; the American Press Institute, which hosts the Project's events; and New York Univer-sity's Department of Journalism, where I teach. In a larger sense, our "partners" have been all the concerned professionals around the country who are beginning to find in the principles of public journalism a renewed sense of mission or simply a practical approach to improving their craft. That includes, of course, university-based teachers of journalism, who are urging their students to take a look at this approach. Ultimately, public journalism will be what all these people decide to make of it. To assist in that decision is the real purpose of the Project on Public Life and the Press.

JAY ROSEN
Director, Project on Public Life and the Press

✦

Acknowledgments

In the early 1990s, a handful of very hard-nosed, pragmatic newspaper editors, considerably less pragmatic critics of the media, and thoroughly intellectual professors in communications, political science, and related fields began to notice that they had something unexpected in common. Down in Kansas, "Buzz" Merritt was busy overhauling the *Wichita Eagle*'s coverage of public affairs, going as far as he could on instinct and reading a divergent array of books to fill in the gaps. In Minnesota, an obscure statewide network of study circles gave *Star Tribune* columnist Jeremy Iggers an idea for changing his paper's way of relating to readers. New York University journalism professor Jay Rosen, meanwhile, was telling surprisingly attentive editors why journalism's livelihood depended on an endangered species of public life. David Broder revealed the flaws of sound-bite politics in his *Washington Post* column. E. J. Dionne and Daniel Yankelovich wrote thoughtful books on how journalists (among others) could make political life work better. Over time people like Merritt, Iggers, and Rosen would read people like Broder, Dionne, and Yankelovich, digest their ideas, and write articles of their own that fertilized the thinking of other editors, media critics, and professors.

The Kettering Foundation of Dayton, Ohio, has an uncanny knack for picking up on these sorts of new social ideas aborning. Kettering is a nonpartisan think tank concerned with the renewal of democracy and housed, not accidentally, on a bucolic wooded lot in a building that looks as if it was airlifted in the night from Thomas Jefferson's University of Virginia. In 1992 its president, David Mathews, invited Rosen, Merritt, Iggers, and an assortment of others to the Foundation to meet one another and discuss how they might create a permanent network to develop the theory and practice of what Rosen had started to call "public journalism"—the journalism, not yet defined, that all of them were struggling to create. Thus the Project on Public Life and the Press was born. Since the second half of 1993 it has been bringing editors, reporters, and journalism scholars together, a few dozen at a time, to compare experiences, to brainstorm ideas for improving journalism, and to marry—as it is too seldom done—the ideals so many of us hold for how American society ought to work with the nuts-and-bolts, necessarily routine actions of our daily lives.

This book grew up with the Project. Jay Rosen hired me to put together a list of sources to which editors and reporters might turn to get ideas for public journalism experiments, and gradually, as the network took off with a momentum that surprised us all, *Doing Public Journalism* expanded into the long practical argument you see here today. Although I wrote the actual words and take credit for most of the book's arguments and many of its tips, I created few of the root ideas. The credit for many of the best should go to Jay, whose name appears frequently in the following chapters, and to someone else whose name does not: Lisa Austin, the Project's research director, who patiently phoned or visited at least twice as many newspapers as are mentioned in this book and who put together the body of knowledge that allows people like Jay, Buzz Merritt, and myself to talk about what public journalism is. She keeps the Project grounded in the real life of newspapering and functioning as an enterprise while Jay thinks, creates, lectures, and visits, and she is in that sense the inadequately sung hero of public journalism.

Virtually all the people whose names are buried in this book's reference section as editors, reporters, directors, founders, and the like gave generously of their time to share ideas and ensure the book's accuracy, as did many others whose names aren't anywhere to be found. A few stand out so much that I ought to mention them now: Ed Arnone, Bob Daley, Sheri Dill, Carol Reese Dykers, Cheryl Gibbs, Jean Johnson, John Marks, Martha McCoy, Buzz Merritt, Hugh Morgan, Chris Peck, Grace Severyn, Martha Steffens, Tom Taschinger, Tom Warhover, Gordon Winters, and Daniel Yankelovich. They either read the entire book at critical stages, or went out of their way to offer help and encouragement, or—in Hugh's case—took *Doing Public Journalism* into the classroom and proved that it had real worth there. Jay Rosen has been wise enough to begin each Project seminar by saying that he isn't the creator of public journalism, that it's a collective creation of every man and woman at every newspaper that's struggling to invent it. I'll borrow his wisdom to say that if *Doing Public Journalism* still reads in many ways like a list of sources and a collaborative effort, that's because it is.

My private thanks go to Peter Wissoker at The Guilford Press, a remarkably calm man.

This book is dedicated to Myra, Art, and Jennifer—the three people to whom anything I write would *have* to be dedicated.

Permission was generously granted to reprint or adapt from the following previously published works:

Pages 4–8: *Coming to Public Judgment: Making Democracy Work in a Complex World* by Daniel Yankelovich (Syracuse, N.Y.: Syracuse University Press, 1991). Copyright 1991 by Syracuse University Press. Permission to adapt Mr. Yankelovich's ideas, described in this book, was granted by Mr. Yankelovich.

Pages 21–23: *Listening Project Training Manual.* (Burnsville, N.C.: Rural Southern Voice for Peace, 1994).

Page 33: *Out of Order* by Thomas Patterson. (New York: Knopf, 1993). Copyright 1993 by Thomas E. Patterson. Reprinted by permission of Alfred A. Knopf, Inc.

Page 42: "First Parole Reform Hearing Elicits Strong Views," *Richmond Times-Dispatch* (Richmond, Va.: June 3, 1994) Copyright 1994 by *The Richmond Times-Dispatch*.

Page 43: "Crowd Echoes Allen's Cry against Parole," *The Virginian-Pilot* (Norfolk, Va.: August 27, 1994). Copyright 1994 by *The Virginian-Pilot* and *The Ledger Star*.

Pages 60–61: *The Battle over Abortion* (Dayton, Ohio: National Issues Forum Institute, 1990). Copyright 1990 by the National Issues Forum Institute.

Page 84: *Meaningful Chaos: How People Form Relationships with Public Concerns* by the Harwood Group. (Dayton, Ohio: Kettering Foundation, 1993). Copyright 1993 by the Kettering Foundation.

Pages 89–90: Compiled from several Center for Living Democracy writings. Reprinted with permission of Frances Moore Lappé and Paul Martin Du Bois, Ph.D., codirectors of the Center for Living Democracy and authors of *The Quickening of America: Rebuilding Our Nation, Remaking Our Lives* (San Francisco: Jossey-Bass, 1994).

Page 103: "A Comparison of Dialogue and Debate," *The Study Circle Handbook* (Pomfret, Conn.: Study Circles Resource Center, 1993). Copyright 1993 by the Topsfield Foundation, Inc. Originally adapted from *Comparison of Dialogue and Debate* by Sheldon Berman and the Boston Area Educators for Social Responsibility Dialogue Group. Copyright 1983 by Sheldon Berman. Reprinted with permission of both the Study Circles Resource Center and Sheldon Berman.

Pages 104–105: "Understanding Deliberation: A Guide for Journalists," by Michael Briand (New York: Project on Public Life and the

✦

Contents

✦

CHAPTER ONE

Overview

What Public Journalism Is

The grassroots reform movement that's known as "public journalism" was born out of widespread professional dissatisfaction. Starting around 1989, the reporters and editors whose work is described in this book began to find themselves increasingly restless with a style of journalism that just didn't seem to work. Many were veterans who had joined the newspaper business years or decades earlier, eager to serve the public interest and influence their towns, states, and nation for the better. Now they were faced with the fact that they hadn't accomplished much for their efforts.

In part, they were troubled by the low quality of much of their own work; in part, by evidence that the public they had intended to serve distrusted newspapers and increasingly didn't even read them. Most importantly, they saw that the very problems they had come to journalism to help solve still weren't being solved, or even being very intelligently addressed. Inner cities continued to decay, deficits to grow, schools to flounder; city hall and statehouse policies were as unfocused as ever. It was their business as journalists to push along the "national debate" on such issues, but by the 1990s any person could see that there was no national debate in the honorable, perhaps idealistic sense of a marketplace of ideas; rather, elections and administrations came and went, with mediocre half-measures winning out more often than sound full measures, and almost always with little or no public involvement.

The journalists who woke up to this situation had a choice to make. Like legions of editors and reporters before and around them, they could have written it off to the facts of life: rationalizing that newspapering is and always will be a for-profit, overnight business, which inevitably will force down its quality; that a distracted public doesn't appreciate the generally good service it's getting; that society's stagnation has all kinds of sources outside the newsroom, including mediocre public officials, porkbarreling, apathy, and the eternal game of politics; and that in any case the journalist's job is a limited one: "to cover the news, not make it." And there would have been an element of truth in each of those rationalizations. Instead, the first "public journalists" chose to take responsibility themselves. Newspapers, they argued, exist so that people can participate in an effective public life, and if the people aren't participating or politics isn't effective, then newspapers have somehow failed—in the same way, say, that an airplane safety system has failed if a pilot doesn't manage to use it properly and crashes. And so, just like the design engineers at Boeing or McDonnell Douglas would have done, they decided to go over the crash site of American democracy and ponder how they might do their jobs better.

Making Smart Decisions Easier

The answer, though it wasn't always conscious or complete early on, turned out to be straightforward: They decided that *journalism ought to make it as easy as possible for citizens to make intelligent decisions about public affairs, and to get them carried out*. This wasn't to trivialize the hard work that intelligent decision making requires, or to call for simplified reporting on world trade, AIDS, or the root causes of poverty. It was just to say that journalism ought to be ergonomically designed: efficient in what it's supposed to help people do. Journalists, just like human-factors engineers in the space-shuttle program or an automaking plant, should set out to learn everything they can about how their "clients" relate to their "work": namely, how citizens relate to democracy, how they get drawn into public affairs, what stands in the way of their participation, what information they need that they aren't getting now, what are the root causes of their alienation. At the end, editors need to ask themselves: "What would make it easier, given all this, for people to make responsible decisions about public affairs? What would make it easier for them to learn the facts they have to know? How could a national debate worthy of the name practically be constructed?"

Any journalist can see part of the answer by using common sense alone. Citizens make choices every day in their private lives. Why do they find it less alienating to choose a car than to choose a president, a welfare reform plan, or a national policy on health care? The basic problem isn't that public issues are so complex, because automobiles are also complex, and most Americans know as little about engine design as about workfare and HMOs. The difference lies in how the choices are made. When it comes to buying a car, the information Americans have available to them answers the questions they want to ask: automakers' brochures compare the salient facts (gas mileage, trunk room, price, etc.) of one car against another; magazines like *Consumer Reports* offer expert advice in plain, user-friendly language. As car shoppers they have ample opportunity to talk through their judgments with other people— friends and neighbors—who own the models they're looking at, and to test each one firsthand at a dealer's, if they see fit. And finally they know that their effort will pay off: If they *choose* a good car (and can afford it), they'll *have* a good car. None of this is true when the same people open their newspapers to make choices about public affairs. Regarding poverty and welfare, citizens may have to hunt through months of uncoordinated daily coverage to find the salient answers they are looking for. Concerning health care, reporters typically offer them experts who speak impenetrable jargon about this plan or that plan before they have even decided if they do or don't want universal coverage. Until the boom in talk radio and public forums, most Americans had no opportunity to talk out their opinions with welfare recipients or hospital bureaucrats, and of course, they still don't have any guarantee that putting time and effort into public affairs will lead to government action. Newspapers did not create all of these hardships, but the comparison makes it clear how little effort they've put into making decisions easy.

Still, common sense can take editors only so far. Just like Boeing's crash investigators, journalists have to identify what their common sense has self-evidently overlooked; they have to see the public with new eyes. Surely one of the reasons public journalism arose when it did was that by the late 1980s something new was in the air. In journalists' communities, forums, study circles, salons, town halls, and "listening projects" were multiplying at the grass roots. At the same time writers from several walks of life began to converge on the central question of what makes democracy work or fail. Political scientist Benjamin Barber in *Strong Democracy*; journalist E. J. Dionne in *Why Americans Hate Politics*; former federal cabinet officials John Gardner in *On Leadership* and David Mathews (now the Kettering Foundation's president) in *Politics for People*; researchers ranging from Richard Harwood, Michael Perry, and William Schmitt working with panels of typical Americans in *Meaningful Chaos: How People Form Relationships with Public Concerns*, to Robert Putnam investigating the success and failure of modern Italian governments in *Making Democracy Work*—these among many other thinkers not only started arguing that democracy was fixable, but set about investigating how to fix it with the pragmatism Americans habitually bring to the problems they truly mean to solve. In illuminating how democracy could work, they began to suggest how journalism might work within it. The public journalists were listening.

Of all the books that have appeared on this subject, probably the most influential among journalists has been Daniel Yankelovich's *Coming to Public Judgment: Making Democracy Work in a Complex World.* While it doesn't encompass the full scope of thought upon which public journalists are drawing, it provides a powerful example of how insights into the way people make decisions can be turned into concrete newsroom goals for making those decisions easier.

Yankelovich starts with his own profession, polling. He writes that he was long troubled by a certain schizophrenia in what we all call "public opinion": Sometimes this term described opinions that were shallow, easily swayed, inconsistent and thoroughly changeable from one poll to the next (the pejorative "public opinion" of political diatribes, which Yankelovich himself calls "mass opinion"). At other times it described views that were rock-solid, that people stood beside even if the pollster ticked off a dozen hidden costs or harmful consequences, because they had considered all these consequences beforehand and were willing to abide them (Yankelovich calls this firmer attitude "public judgment"). He saw that the first kind of opinion, which can't possibly support a democracy, sometimes evolves into the second, which can. And so he collaborated with researchers from an assortment of foundations, firms, and institutes to reason out what steps the public had to pass through to travel from one stage to the other: from mass opinion to public judgment. He fit the process into three parts—consciousness-raising, "working through," and resolution—each of which journalists would be better able to help along if they saw their job in a different light.

I. Consciousness-Raising

"Consciousness raising is the stage in which the public learns about an issue and becomes aware of its existence and meaning," Yankelovich writes. This phase, for example, with regard to the history of the AIDS crisis, was the period between the first incoherent references to the disease in the media and the date when most Americans finally knew what "AIDS" meant, could explain how HIV is transmitted, and told pollsters it was urgent to find some kind of cure.

Most of what journalism does very well, Yankelovich suggests, plays to this first phase of the process. Newspapers gather and filter information on a wide variety of issues and then insist on their importance. But journalists could reduce the chances that people will give up on these issues by also:

+ **Helping the public to set an agenda.** Societies, like individuals, can attend to only so many topics at once. Newspapers would do citizens a lot of good if they chose more judiciously where to focus public attention, weeded out excess information, and presented what was left in user-friendly forms (e.g., in focused supplements rather than in scattershot stories)—in other words, if they decided more aggressively than they do now what readers do and don't need to know. But it's essential not to misunderstand. Newspapers have to learn not to dominate the process; they must figure out how to follow the public's own lead. Apathy, Yankelovich argues, springs out of feeling ignored. Citizens are frustrated by the slates of "important issues" that editors and political leaders pass down to them by fiat; they're looking for an agenda that corresponds to the problems they themselves see. So while newspapers can go on trying to persuade people that this or that unpopular issue warrants attention, they'll engage citizens more if they learn to respect the priorities those citizens set for themselves, and focus news coverage tightly around them.

II. "Working Through"

Yankelovich writes, "For the second stage, I borrow a term from psychology, 'working through.' When the consciousness-raising stage has been completed, the individual must confront the need for change. . . . When people are caught in cross pressures [over different options for action], before they can resolve them it is necessary to struggle with the conflicts and ambivalences and defenses they arouse. Change requires hard work. . . . It is full of backsliding and procrastination and avoidance. . . . People must abandon the passive-receptive mode that works well enough for consciousness raising. They must be actively engaged and involved." They must, in short, get real with themselves. As an example, Americans worked through at least a few aspects of the health care crisis in 1992 and 1993, when, after trying persistently to convince themselves that they could pay for universal coverage just by eliminating waste, fraud, and abuse, they realized in growing numbers that they could not; and after toying with the idea of government-run insurance, they turned firmly against it.

Working through can be short-circuited by causes that vary from moving an issue too quickly off the front page to simple partisan wrangling. Journalists could improve the chances of keeping the process on track by:

+ **Reducing issues to choices.** Public debates are formless until they come down to choices. Clear alternatives are what make elections relatively easy for journalists to cover and citizens to focus in on—but alternatives exist even when there's no formal ballot to give them structure. (After all, there are only so many basic approaches to health care reform or poverty.) The press can help people enormously just by expressing each topic on the public agenda in terms of two, three, or more sharply etched alternatives. They should comprehend the broad range of options proposed by experts and leaders but also—like the agenda itself—embrace ideas the public values highly even if experts and leaders don't.

+ **Plumbing to core values.** Furthermore, Americans waste a lot of time arguing at the wrong level of abstraction. The real conflicts in most issues are over fundamental values rather than over technical answers; citizens really feel ambivalent, for example, over "tougher sentences or more rehabilitation?" rather than "more prisons or more boot camps?" The choices a paper articulates should be expressed in terms of such values—and journalists should recognize that people may be drawn to many or all viewpoints at once. The most difficult public choices involve conflicts not only *among* individuals but *within* them over things they believe in deeply (e.g., they want free speech, but no racism; they want universal health care, but no restrictions on choosing doctors and no escalations in cost). To the extent the press can bring these true conflicts into the open it can both make the conversation more honest and ease people's way to working through.

+ **Spelling out the costs and consequences of each choice.** Human beings by nature engage in wishful thinking, opting all at once, say, for lower taxes, increased spending, and a reduction in the deficit. The press should insist upon both realism and thoroughness, nudging people toward the greater maturity implied in the term "public judgment." They can start by simply listing and discussing the pros and cons of each choice in a systematic way.

+ **Bridging the expert–public gap.** If people can't make sense of expert opinion, they can't take part in policy debate—period.

Newspapers can certainly do more than they have done to translate technical language into everyday language and to weed out detail that's irrelevant to people's choices. But beyond this they must prod experts to speak directly to the values people are struggling to work through. This means promoting a much more two-way communication. It isn't only what experts want to tell the people that's necessary for good decision making; what ordinary people want to tell the experts is indispensable as well.

+ **Facilitating deliberation.** Before they can achieve resolution, citizens have a profound need to talk through issues with other human beings. This is something for which their daily lives provide few opportunities—especially when the people they need to talk with (say, when the issue is racism or welfare reform) belong to a different racial or socioeconomic group. The revolution in town halls and phone-in shows doesn't help here, for it isn't "Ask the Mayor" meetings or formal debates or expert panels that people need but constructive, focused, personal, consensus-seeking talk—talk among equals—what many writers are calling "deliberation" to distinguish it from debate. Because the press is one of the few institutions that regularly brings Americans together across social, racial, and economic lines, it is one of the few that can help them establish places for deliberation—perhaps within the pages of the newspaper itself.

+ **Promoting civility.** Deliberation does not flourish in the current social climate, where television pundits routinely shout over each other, presidential candidates sling mud, and opponents picture one another as foolish, venal, stupid, or propelled by ulterior motives. The press can help citizens make decisions just by setting standards of civility and open-mindedness more conducive to the marketplace of ideas and the concept of community.

III. Resolution

Yankelovich speaks of resolution as the successful end of working through—not just an intellectual coming-to-terms but an emotional and moral one, the actual making of a stable, responsible choice.

This is less a stage than a result, except that as many of the writers on democracy iterate and reiterate, people never feel satisfied about their choices until those choices have been acted upon. Their frustration follows directly from the broken link between their efforts to learn and deliberate and the actual public policy their officeholders set. Here, then, journalists can shore up people's motivation to come to judgment by:

> ✦ **Prodding action on the public's choice.** Once citizens have reached a judgment, the press ought to champion it as vigorously as it champions any other fundamental part of democracy, like free speech or the right to vote. To citizens, the certainty that their choice will be the basis for federal, state, and city actions is the practical expression of government by, of, and for the people. But the focus ought to extend beyond government as well. The public's choices may be achievable through the actions of foundations, schools, businesses, families, churches, voluntary associations, and individual citizens themselves. Journalists should invent ways to make this kind of action easier too.

This is what Yankelovich had to offer the public journalists; other writers and organizations, stressing different hurdles to citizens doing their job, led the editors who came across them to different (though complementary) ideas about the press's role. Virtually all the writers implied that the profoundest hurdle *journalists* have to overcome is a stunted picture of public life. As David Mathews puts it, over time our understanding of politics in America has become woefully professional and formalized, so much so that it has ceased to include either the problems people want on the public agenda or the actions that are truly sufficient to solve them. The "public arena" has become what governments and political "players" do; "issues" are the congressional bills and federal programs that experts argue over; "democracy" (between elections) is the business of getting bills passed and programs funded. Where is there room in this for family values or neighborhood watches, for all the things citizens have to do for one another and in cooperation with government to really improve their lives? To most Americans, a new crime bill isn't the issue, crime is; the public arena isn't there just to make law and policy, but to solve problems (one of the most urgent of which is the decline of community itself). Imagine what politics would look like if it started from this citizen's-eye-view. When, for instance, public housing tenants in cities such as Washington, D.C., call for community policing as just one step in an integrated plan including resident-run security patrols, tenant management, building neighborhood spirit, and providing after-hours recreation for teenagers, they are painting the "crime issue," "politics," "judgment," and "community action" in their true scope—and journalists will never be able to foster a national debate worthy of the name until they see these words from the same vantage point and understand them the same way.

There isn't always a straightforward way for journalists to apply the insights Daniel Yankelovich and his fellow writers are talking about here—but as editors starting with Davis Merritt, Jr., of the *Wichita Eagle* have recognized, they are an invitation to invention.* The first public journalists reasoned that if they could create ways of doing their work that buttress this process of "coming to public judgment," they could make the public happier with the news profession, make the newspaper more essential to citizens, help solve some of our perennial national and local problems, and get more job satisfaction in the process. The bulk of this book is a description of the experiments that have been tried at dailies from Bremerton, Wash., to Portland, Maine. These examples aren't "official" expressions of public journalism, because there is no such thing: Public journalism is nothing more than the conviction that journalism's business is about making citizenship work. In practice, there is only the pioneering, sometimes contradictory work of dozens of very loosely connected editors and reporters.

Heroes for a Post-Woodstein Age

Before proceeding to the nuts and bolts, it may be useful to look squarely at what public journalism is asking a reporter or editor to become. A different kind of journalism requires a different kind of journalist. For decades the press and the journalism schools, without always realizing it, have imagined in very narrow terms what a good reporter ought to be: The outlines look like some combination of Lincoln Steffens and Ida Tarbell, Edward R. Murrow, David Halberstam, Bob Woodward, and Carl Bernstein. Good journalists are the ones who root out the inside story, tell the brave truth, face down the Joseph McCarthys and Richard Nixons, expose corruption and go on crusades, "comfort the afflicted and afflict the comfortable." It's an extremely vivid image that colors everything journalists do—how they conceive of news quality, social worth, heroism and even happiness.

In facing the facts about citizen behavior raised by Yankelovich and other writers, the first public journalists realized that though this model still made sense for some parts of their work, it missed the main point. Public problems were going unsolved for reasons that crusades and heroism could do little or nothing to fix. (Making

---

*Merritt has in fact written a memoir—*Public Journalism and Public Life: Why Telling the News Is Not Enough*—that retraces how his dissatisfaction with conventional press practices led him to public journalism and recounts the questions and arguments that prompted the *Eagle's* creativity along the way. The book draws in business and reporting trends, political events, and personal experiences with which a great many journalists can probably identify.

PUBLIC JOURNALISM ATTITUDES

Public journalism as it's practiced differs from newspaper to newspaper, but the journalists who do the practicing seem to have strong similarities in temperament. Jay Rosen, the director of the Project on Public Life and the Press (a networking organization for public journalists), contrasts the attitudes of conventional and public journalists along the following lines. It's worthwhile noting that many of the best journalists profiled in this book started out in column 2 and found their way to column 1.

Public journalists believe	Conventional journalists believe
Something basic has to change, because journalism isn't working now.	The traditions of journalism are fine; if anything needs to improve, it's the practice.
In such a climate, experimentation and creativity are imperative; old habits, however "sacred," may have to go—though change must always be guided by ethical core values and an understanding of how democracy works.	Experimentation threatens to cross the line into unethical behavior, bias, and carelessness about standards. Besides, experimentation is usually a synonym for fad.
Citizens may well want to participate more intelligently in public life, but they find too many hurdles in their way.	The media and political life provide ample opportunity to participate; if people stay out or merely complain, it's their own choice.
Citizens deserve a bigger place in the newspaper itself. Papers should never "dumb down," but must reorient themselves around citizens' concerns.	News is a profession; journalists write newspapers, readers don't. Inviting citizens to judge what's news, making them the subject of coverage and the like are inherently dumbing down—a form of pandering.
Public life should work, and journalism has a role in making it work.	It would be nice if public life worked, but it's beyond our role to make it work and it's dangerous to think we can.

the newspaper into a snappier, jazzier, slicker "read" wasn't doing anything to fix them either.) So they groped around for other, more appropriate images of good journalism that would help focus their minds and sharpen their experiments. Here, then, are three interlocking metaphors for what public journalists, in the post-Woodstein age, can aspire to be.

Public Journalists as Experts in Public Life

Under the old model, a great police reporter had to be an insider at the stationhouse, the person who brought to light the truths that were printed and knew even the truths that weren't, the ultimate expert on crime, criminals, and police procedure. This gave police reporters much more in common with police officers themselves than with the citizenry they were supposed to inform. A "public" police reporter, on the other hand, aims to bring the police, their official overseers, the victims of crime, even the criminals, and the residents of various neighborhoods in a city into constructive dialogue with one another about crime. The center has shifted from the police blotter to the public agenda. This calls upon the reporter to be part diplomat, part interpreter, and to be an expert of a very different, subtler, and more creative sort: an expert in what each and every segment of the community wants, thinks, and worries about when it comes to crime. On the beat, a public journalist has to be equally intimate with ordinary citizens as with the professionals he or she covers, and is indispensable to each group as a way of communicating with the other.

Public Journalists as Civic Capitalists

Economists define capital—whether physical or "human"—as anything that improves the productivity of a worker: machines, education, job experience, managerial talent, or factory buildings. The writers on democracy have begun to talk about "civic capital" in a parallel way as anything that improves the productivity of a community—that is, its ability to meet crises, solve problems, live contentedly. Seen this way, a newspaper shouldn't just help along decisions; its role is much bigger. David Mathews writes in *Politics for People* that "problems divide people, so if they do not create solid working relationships before difficulties mount, there is little likelihood that they can create any sense of community in the midst of major conflict." In addition to giving readers what they need to work through the issues of the moment, public journalists have to look for ways to strengthen their community's goodwill, cooperative habits, insights into where other social groups are coming from, shorthand ways of talking, and so on—the groundwork factors of democracy.

Public Journalists as Full-Time Citizens

All the other ways of thinking about this movement come together in this one. Conventional journalists see the people who buy their newspapers as *readers*; public journalists see them as *citizens*. Both images are shorthand mental fictions; they don't quite capture people as they are, but like the "rational man" of economics and the "reasonable woman" of law, they identify precisely the aspect of people we professionally want to see. Citizens do not come in grades; they are equals. If the press's audience is made up of citizens, then journalists and politicians and experts are not exalted in any way. They are simply fellow citizens—with one key difference: They have the privilege of occupying themselves with public affairs fulltime, whereas all other people, having limited time, money, and access, are forced to do their work as citizens in spare hours.

At the most arrogant extreme, Woodstein-era journalists and officeholders identify themselves as the thinking class, and dismiss their fellow Americans as uninformed or apathetic. Public life is largely the story of the full-time citizens, the professionals who start off representing people and often end up replacing them. Such a worldview is both ungrateful and self-serving; but more to the point, it misses the proper relationship between full-time and part-time citizens: one of partnership. The people who buy newspapers can be compared to the man who has to work during the town meeting, and so asks his neighbor what went on; or the social club that sends a representative to the national convention, expecting her to report back. To the public journalist, people have their different roles, but the goal is for them to reason and work together as fellow citizens and equals.

It would be hard to dispute that today's newspapers rarely look or sound like citizens talking to one another. Horse-race polls do not sound like citizens talking to one another. Scandalmongering does not sound like citizens talking to one another. Sound bites do not, nor do puff pieces, "happy news," lightly edited wire copy, ex-cathedra editorials, haranguing op-ed pieces, expert jargon, trivial service articles. . . . The list goes disheartening on. Which only points up one respect in which public journalists are not (as they're sometimes portrayed) radicals departing from the canons of their profession, but traditionalists attempting a return to first principles.

Political newspapers began in order to serve—in a sense, to create—citizens; if they have failed to do this, it's similar to America's historic failure to live up to the words "all men are created equal": It's a temporary failure of practice, rather than one of intent. Lesser things came to seem important and got in the way. The Woodstein model is not the fundamental principle of journalism; treating readers as citizens is. And so to overcome the sense that journalism is doing something very wrong right now, many excellent journalists feel that the ideas outlined here are the natural place to start.

How to Use the Rest of This Book

The rest of this book is devoted to practice. Newspapers have tried wildly different experiments in recent years, all fitting under the name of public journalism. A few examples will hint at the variety:

- In North Carolina, the *Charlotte Observer* focuses its attention for six weeks at a stretch on a single high-crime neighborhood, reporting on the reasons for the area's problems and drawing help and suggestions from across the entire city. The paper's community liaison helps volunteers and local organizations coordinate efforts to bring the neighborhood back.
- Borrowing an idea pioneered in Charlotte, the Hyannis, Mass., *Cape Cod Times* consulted a panel of representative citizens to set priorities in covering the 1992 campaigns. After election day, the panel proposed setting a permanent agenda for Cape Cod. So the paper surveyed its readership, promised long-term coverage of their six areas of greatest concern, and drew 600 people to public meetings on these issues.
- Ohio's *Dayton Daily News* and Washington's *Spokane Spokesman-Review* offered free pizzas to any family or group who discussed the then-major topic on the paper's agenda and returned a questionnaire. The Daily News turned what it learned about juvenile violence into a yearlong project, "Kids in Chaos," that included expert panels, personal stories, and a citywide series of deliberative forums on how to respond to the violence.
- The *Wisconsin State Journal* in Madison created "grand juries" and "mock legislatures" composed entirely of citizens to deliberate over a property tax plan, the national budget, and health care reform, and then reported on the deliberations to spur wider public talk.
- In Norfolk, the *Virginian-Pilot* replaced its beat system with collaborative teams of reporters organized, not around institutions like local city halls or school boards, but around issues as

citizens see them, including "public safety" and "public life." It hired an innovative civic-affairs researcher to train "Public Life Team" members in how to report on these issues so as to engage people's civic interest as fully as possible.

+ In West Virginia, the *Huntington Herald-Dispatch* followed up a 12-page special section highlighting citizens' visions for economic renewal with a town hall meeting, cosponsored by a local university and a TV station. When the meeting recommended six task forces to push the issue forward, the *Herald* helped round up the necessary volunteers. By the end of 1994, without the paper's further involvement, the city had updated its strategic plan, applied for a federal grant, and put a development initiative on the ballot; the Chamber of Commerce and the task forces had become partners to keep the economic agenda underway.

These were big projects, but there have been small ones as well. In fact, experiments have ranged from the monumental extreme, at which a few midsize dailies have launched yearlong, newsroomwide, and very splashy let's-completely-fix-our-city projects; to the minuscule, at which other papers have, without fanfare, asked newsroom staff to chat with ordinary citizens about their concerns, or simply changed the tone of routine coverage from confrontational to deliberative.

Public journalism is (and virtually has to be) an invention of each newspaper that uses it. Just like every family invents its own way of talking, its own division of responsibilities, its own jargon, every community has to invent its own way of deliberating and taking action on its concerns. In some cities, politicians and grassroots organizations will embrace small steps at public journalism and take up the slack themselves; in others they won't. In some, community conversations will arise easily; in others, not at all. Journalism's proper role in support of democracy is a case-by-case question, determined by circumstances and taste.

This book's purpose, then, is to raise consciousness rather than to spell out a faith: to offer a panoramic view of how newspapers might be made more relevant to people as citizens, to explore what journalists are beginning to learn about citizen behavior, to lay out what editors and reporters have already done, and to speculate on where the profession might go from here. It consolidates the experiences of perhaps three dozen newspapers; the insights of Daniel Yankelovich, David Mathews, and other writers on citizen behavior and pragmatic democracy; and the work of a wide array of organizations outside of journalism, ranging from the Study Circles Resource Center to the MIT–Harvard Public Disputes Program. It's organized to follow roughly the sequential steps that a

A PHILOSOPHY, NOT A BEAT

Recently, an editor intrigued by the ideas of Dan Yankelovich and Jay Rosen suggested he might "conduct a few community forums" on urban sprawl in his town and then "do regular journalism" to report the relevant facts and figures. He was making a common mistake. Newspapers may, for all sorts of internal reasons, choose to test out public journalism on a very small scale; the changes it requires cause dissension in some newsrooms and go down fairly smoothly in others. But editors would be wrong to start small because they assume "treating readers as citizens" is—like an ombudsman's column or a special Sunday supplement—either an add-on to city hall coverage and investigative journalism, or else a competitor for scarce resources. Public journalism is an idea with applications for every page of the paper and every facet of the business. With few exceptions, newspapers that start into it, whether on a small scale or a large one, let the implications of treating readers as citizens seep into more and more of their work over time. Here, then, are a few examples of "regular journalism" subjects done in a public journalism fashion:

+ **Breaking news.** When Charlotte officials restricted access to a park in a white neighborhood that black youths liked to cruise through, the *Observer* ran interviews with all the predictable factions—but refused to focus on their grievances, instead pressing residents, cruisers, and officials to offer workable solutions. The solutions they offered were remarkably alike, as detailed in Chapter Four.
+ **In-depth reports.** The *New Orleans Times-Picayune* devoted a year, 23 staff members, and 163 full broadsheet pages to its series on race relations—but first it had to work through the newsroom's own racial divisions using concepts discussed in Chapter Three.
+ **Investigative journalism.** The *Detroit Free Press* exposed children's charities wasting money—as part of a project that has also featured public forums on children's issues and sent reporters out to volunteer in schools; see Chapter Four.
+ **Personal columns.** *Newsday*'s Dennis Duggan portrays the struggle for New York City's subways every Tuesday and Thursday—centering on the efforts of ordinary people who ride and work the trains rather than bureaucrats who run
the transit authority. This is one example of treating citizens as civic actors, as described in Chapter Three.

(cont.)

A PHILOSOPHY, NOT A BEAT (*cont.*)

+ **Campaigns for national office.** The *St. Petersburg Times*'s innovative Tampa bureau covered the 1994 elections in partnership with a CBS affiliate—insisting candidates address the agenda issues and questions posed by ordinary Florida citizens. During that year's U.S. Senate race, the *Boston Globe*, the *Boston Herald*, and several broadcast partners did the same thing. For still more examples, see Chapter Two.

+ **The city hall beat.** Both the Norfolk *Virginian-Pilot* and the Columbia, S.C., *State* continue to cover city halls and statehouses—but the reporters who cover them collaborate in teams devoted to issue-centered beats, an idea described in Chapter Three.

+ **Pulitzer Prize journalism.** Ohio's *Akron Beacon Journal* won the 1994 public-service prize for "A Question of Color"—in which the paper secured 22,000 citizen pledges to work for improved race relations and hired two facilitators to coordinate efforts in the community. For these techniques and others, see Chapter Five.

---

comprehensive attempt at public journalism would involve, but no single newspaper has tried all (or even most) of the techniques in this book. At the same time, some papers have been more successful than others for having incorporated a greater range of them—because at some level, the pieces of public journalism reinforce one another and add up to more than the sum of their parts.

Chapter Two deals with "public listening," the art of keeping the newspaper grounded in the concerns of ordinary people. Typically, an editor's first task in public journalism is to discover what's high enough on the public's agenda to warrant extensive coverage; this requires thinking afresh how to listen to people more subtly. Newspapers have used polls, focus groups, clip-out surveys, and many more creative, open-ended, and effective techniques first to identify agenda issues and then to reorient coverage around citizens' own questions. The end of the chapter compares an actual news story that was well grounded in public listening against a more traditional story that wasn't, and reflects on the role of just asking better questions in building civic capital.

News judgment is at the center of **Chapter Three**. A community (or nation) may take months or years to think through and act upon a single agenda issue, so a paper has to be canny if it's to keep the discussion moving over the long haul. According to Yankelovich, the press best helps its readers by reducing an issue to well-defined, value-based alternatives and by judging newsworthiness based on a particular story's helpfulness in choosing among them. But that's just the "intellectual" side of the story; there's an "emotional" side too. Several papers have learned that telling ordinary people's stories and dramatizing the community's struggle to solve its problems both roots people in an issue and helps them keep perspective on it over time. This chapter examines how newspapers have balanced the two sides.

Once citizens have their agenda, their choices, and the information they need, as a community they have to work through to judgment. **Chapter Four** distinguishes the deliberation required for working through from more familiar debates, town meetings, and press conferences, then discusses the ways in which newspapers have either created or formed partnerships with deliberative forums in their communities. The final sections show how editors and reporters have brought a deliberative attitude into the newspaper itself.

Chapter Five moves on to getting results. It draws on public listening techniques to map out how newspapers can recognize the evolving public judgment on an issue. Critics worry that public journalism encourages newspapers to become activists. This chapter describes how a handful of inventive newspapers have successfully acted as watchdogs in their communities, prodding both citizens and government officials to act on the public's judgment, without stepping "over the line." A straightforward discussion of public journalism ethics rounds the chapter out.

Finally, **Chapter Six** deals with public journalism as a profession and a business. Wichita's Davis Merritt, one of the first and foremost public journalists, likes to describe a successful newspaper as "a fair-minded participant in a community that works." This section laces together the entire book's themes to explore what that might mean. What is a "public" newspaper's place in its community? How does it relate to other media? How do you train public journalists? Can public journalism pay its own way? Finally, how does public journalism directly build community life?

This book has been designed both as a primer and as a desktop reference. Reading the chapter introductions one after the other should give readers a solid overview of public journalism "theory." Each subsection can then be read intensively for detail or skimmed for examples and sources. Interesting sidelights and noteworthy case studies are boxed within the text, and most sections end with a feature called "Pushing the Envelope" which proposes ideas for building on past work. A complete, annotated resource guide rounds out the book.

Although it's fair to guess that most of the people who read *Doing Public Journalism* will be working journalists, other people may come to it for many reasons. Everybody has a stake in the improvement of newspapering. To help those who are outside the newsroom, there is, first, a teachers' guide available under separate cover from The Guilford Press, and second, within the Index to this book there are short specialized guides for reporters, for experts who may have been (or may become) news sources, for scholars in fields whose work this book draws upon, and—of course—for citizens.

✦

CHAPTER TWO

Public Listening

Questions and Answers

Public journalism doesn't only aim to treat readers as citizens, it assumes that readers want to *be* citizens. By and large they're sufficiently serious about making their cities, states, and country work better that they would hammer out a smart agenda, ask experts and candidates smart questions, and strive for a smart set of solutions, *if* only they had the time, money, access, and professional expertise of journalists. The reporter's and editor's task, therefore, isn't to report facts in a vacuum (as in the *New York Times*'s front-page boast, "All the News That's Fit to Print") but to make up for the public's shortfall: to figure out (as only a good journalist can) how to round up a whole community's agenda and questions, and then to put out (as only a good journalist can) a readable newspaper with just the answers citizens are looking for. Public journalists aim to print "all the news that citizens want to know." Consequently the mortal sin for a public journalist is falling out of touch.

In theory, journalists act on the public's agenda in any conventional newsroom: They concentrate their time and effort on the most "newsworthy" stories, ask questions readers want or ought to want answers to, and push onward to new stories as the public interest moves on. In practice, the lines of communication between journalists and citizens are often random, fragmented, and full of static.

Typically, newspapers depend upon some combination of letters to the editor, phone-in lines, polls, overheard conversation, and brief interviews as forms of public listening, but—to be honest—rarely does the information gleaned from these snippets do more than get editors and reporters started. Such nitty-gritty details as making story assignments, designing interview questions, and allocating space have very little to do with the priorities of citizens and very much to do with those of journalists themselves. A great many newspeople would say this is how it has to be, because the assumption behind public journalism is wrong. When the public speaks to newspapers it rarely if ever sounds like it's taking the job of informed citizenship seriously.

In reply it has to be said that the ways in which journalists habitually listen to people do very little to encourage them to sound like good citizens. Polls rarely care about people's thoughtful nuances and doubts. Letters and phone-in lines (particularly when they're responding to editorials, columns, or op-ed pieces) invite narrow-mindedness at least as much as reflection. And reporters out for an interview typically shove people into cubbyholes before they even open their mouths. Crime reporters, seeing people as victims or criminals, ask, "How do you feel?" or "What led him (or her) to do it?" Election reporters, seeing people as voters, ask "Who will you vote for, and why?" Reporters on urban conflict, seeing people as blacks or whites, ask about nearly any problem "Was racism involved?" People duly respond as victims, criminals, voters, and members of a racial group—just as they would respond as consumers to "What's your favorite detergent?"

An idea to which this book will return many times, in many contexts, is that "the questions you ask determine the answers you get." So, if a newspaper wants to print stories about thoughtful citizens, it has to carefully reconsider how to encourage people to speak as citizens, and how to hear the citizenship in what they say. (Indeed, Jay Rosen defines public listening as "the struggle to hear citizens talk when residents speak.")

Techniques for Hearing Citizens

The straightforward approach is to ask people the kinds of policy and news-judgment questions you might ask an academic, a governor, or a city editor. Public journalists took to this idea early on. The *Charlotte Observer* asked area residents in 1992 what should drive the paper's election coverage; the *Oklahoman* surveyed 475 community leaders by mail to identify the problems facing Oklahoma City. Both these efforts were effective, but several newspapers have gone beyond them, and a number of organizations outside journalism have taken the idea of "hearing citizens talk when residents speak" to what is probably their practical extreme. While these latter examples may be beyond the scope of most newspaper work, a sample might be thought-provoking.

Rural Southern Voice for Peace (RSVP), based in Burnsville, N.C., works with activist groups in divided communities, helping them to design "listening projects" to learn about their political opponents, people they may have long dismissed as stupid, bigoted, callous or plain wrong. (Clients have ranged from antinuclear groups in military base towns to a peace movement inside Serbia.) The activists go out into the community armed with questionnaires, knock on doors, and hold half-hour- to hour-long conversations, the purpose of which is not to persuade but to listen. Since the ultimate aim is to build partnerships— or at least understanding—across old and stubborn divides, there's an obvious premium on coaxing out the fellow citizen in search of the common good beneath the opponent's exterior. The keys to this, RSVP argues, are patience, empathy, and a carefully structured set of questions. RSVP tells its clients:

+ In each interview, before you start asking the tough questions, try to connect with the man or woman you're interviewing on a personal level. Don't rush. You have to build the proper atmosphere to talk citizen to citizen.
+ Don't ask yes-or-no questions, or other types of questions that don't lead anywhere; instead, ask questions that "can lead to self-awareness and change . . . [that] evoke feelings and emotions."
+ Ask "clarifying questions" that challenge the person to examine and change ideas. If the person says, "Poor people don't want to work," ask if there are any personal experiences behind that opinion. Or present a few facts that challenge the person's idea, and ask for the person's further thoughts. Or ask a question that digs deeper into his or her feelings, such as "How do you think it affects a child to grow up in poverty?" or "What do you think can be done to help the poor?"
+ Don't just listen for the parts of the person's answer that immediately interest you. Let the person have his or her full say. Listen for the person's own agenda. Aim "to get full understanding of not just the words but of the person we're listening to."
+ Empathize. Treat the man or woman as someone who's also looking for the truth. If you can't empathize with the person's statements, find a way to empathize with the person.
+ Be truly interested. This is something you can't fake. Be open to changing your own opinions (even if you don't raise them in the conversation). In other words, go into the interview expecting to learn something of personal importance from this man or woman.

RSVP's *Listening Project Training Manual* (from which these tips have been adapted) includes eight sample questionnaires based on these principles. The excerpts in the box below are from the questionnaire used by a community group in Elkhart, Ind., to sound out neighborhood race relations.

"WHAT IDEAS DO YOU HAVE?"

Sample Questions from Elkhart, Ind.

1. How long have you or a family member lived in this neighborhood?
2. What is one of your best memories of this neighborhood?
3. What do you like most about living here? Why?
4. What is your earliest memory of being aware of your ethnic or racial background, and how do you feel about it?
5. Have you ever felt prejudice or disrespect because of your race or ethnic group, your gender or for other reasons?
6. What barriers do you feel relating to neighbors of a different race?
7. Are you able to talk openly about race relations with neighbors of a different race? If yes, what makes this possible? If no, why not?
8. If you had a chance, what question would you ask someone of another race?
9. What ideas do you have for how members of different races in this neighborhood could get to know each other better and build trust?
10. No neighborhood is perfect. What do you like least about this neighborhood?
11. What reputation do you think this neighborhood has among people who don't live here? Do you think this reputation is fair?
12. Do you feel safe living in this neighborhood?
13. How are the youth in our neighborhood being affected by drug dealing?
14. What would be some positive steps that could be taken to work at these problems?
15. Sometimes outsiders come into this neighborhood to deal drugs. Do you have any ideas about how to stop this?
16. How do you think police respond to calls from this neighborhood? What has been your experience?

(cont.)

"WHAT IDEAS DO YOU HAVE?" (cont.)

17. Would you welcome an increased police presence? Ideally, what should it look like?
18. From your experience, do the Elkhart Police and the criminal justice system treat people of different races differently?
19. What kinds of neighborhood programs and activities would you like to see?
20. You've talked about your hopes and concerns for this neighborhood. What are some things you have to offer to make this neighborhood more of the kind of place you want it to be?

From the *Listening Project Training Manual.* Reprinted with permission of Rural Southern Voice for Peace.

The finest newspaper work in public listening aims at something along these lines. The *Miami Herald* provides an excellent example. Since mid-1993 it has been conducting periodic open-format two-hour conversations with grassroots community groups. By rule the meetings involve more citizens than journalists and focus on the former's perceptions of issues in the community. The paper hired researcher Rich Harwood, whose surveys of citizen attitudes appear in *A View from Main Street America* and *Meaningful Chaos*, to train reporters in how to question and listen to best effect. By tape-recording, transcribing, and indexing each conversation, the paper has built up a hefty computer database, highlights of which it periodically circulates around the newsroom. The managing editor encourages everyone on the staff to browse from time to time. So far, *Herald* journalists have used material from the conversations to refocus coverage of ongoing news or to develop new stories entirely, such as a feature on urban fear, a six-part series on parental responsibility, and a guide to organizing at the grassroots level. The rest of this chapter will show how other newspapers have put public listening to work in more particularized ways.

Editors new to public journalism sometimes worry that this sort of thing uses up too much staff time for too little payoff. As to in-print payoff, it should be obvious by the end of Chapter Three that this doesn't have to be the case; papers including the Bergen County (N.J.) *Record* regularly turn community forums and open-ended interviews directly into newspaper copy. On one occasion, a somewhat skeptical *Record* editor printed a partial transcript of a forum only to receive about 75 responses to the page's normal one or two, and to find that skipping the obligatory staff-written article had freed his reporters to spend more time on other work. Some other journalists question how much—really—their news coverage can be improved by listening to ordinary people. Isn't it mostly a form of public relations? Experience has tended to cast away doubts. News coverage rooted tightly in the way citizens themselves see the issues can be powerful and effective, and very different from conventional stories, as this chapter's reprints and excerpts ought to show. The editors who worked on these particular stories now believe that they had been underestimating the public for many years. The more they listen intelligently to their readership, the more intelligence they hear.

How Do Journalists Hear the Public's Agenda?

It's easiest to see how listening can influence coverage by honing in on one concrete task. Take setting a "public agenda." To make it easy for citizens to make decisions on public affairs, newspapers first have to decipher which public affairs they'd like to make decisions about. Eric Utne, editor in chief of the bimonthly magazine *Utne Reader*, chooses topics for his magazine by inviting subscribers to periodic "editorial salons" and asking them point-blank, "What are you obsessing about lately?" Though the terminology used by newspaper journalists may differ, this is what listening for the public's agenda almost always comes down to. Expressed in the language of traditional journalism, it is simply listening carefully and intelligently to people in order to develop a better news judgment. The key lies in understanding what "care" and "intelligence" require.

Early public journalists sidestepped agenda setting altogether by experimenting on obviously important stories such as presidential elections or long-standing problems with race. More recently, the *Cape Cod Times* and the *Tallahassee Democrat* have hammered out explicit lists of long-term news priorities in close conjunction with local citizens (see boxes below). Unlike most newspapers that claim to identify "the public's agenda," they didn't just ask a random sample of people to say Yes or No to questions like, "Are you worried about crime?" or else to rank-order their priorities on a short laundry list of standard problems. Each invented some way of letting citizens identify issues for themselves, and (at the *Democrat* in particular) of defining these issues in a protracted give and take.

This "defining" doesn't come across vividly in brief sketches like those in the following boxes, but it's enormously important. Generally speaking, members of the press, politicians, and experts of all kinds are all far too quick at deciding what real issues consist of and at stuffing

THE CAPE COD TIMES

Like the Charlotte *Observer* and other papers, the 50,000-circulation *Cape Cod Times* sought advice on how to cover the 1992 campaign season from a panel of local residents. It was probably the smallest, least expensive panel on record: a dozen men and women chosen by the League of Women Voters from among a larger number who had volunteered for the job. After election day the *Times* asked its panelists what ought to drive coverage between campaigns, and together they, an editor, and a senior writer hit on the idea of the "Cape Cod Agenda," a short list of issues the paper could authoritatively "take to officials, and say this is what Cape Cod cares about."

The immediate question was how to secure that kind of authority. The *Times* decided to run a full-page ballot on a summer 1994 Sunday section front, explaining the agenda and asking readers which six issues belonged there. The citizens panel and *Times* staff had brainstormed 26 likely choices but encouraged people to write in others if they felt any were missing. The ballot also left room for comments on what the issues meant and what kinds of solutions warranted study. Seven hundred Cape Codders replied. On another Sunday front at the end of July, the paper explained how it had tabulated the ballots and fleshed out the six issues that had drawn the heavy votes: groundwater pollution, monitoring the activities of the new Cape Cod land-use commission, wetlands preservation, public transport, attracting new clean industry, and open space. (Managing editor Tim White says pithily, "Between 80 and 85 percent of the people on the Cape consider themselves environmentally conscious.")

White says that several more varied topics fell just short of making it onto the list, including what should be done about elevated cancer levels on the Cape. Editors dropped "crime prevention" though it slightly outpolled two other items, because the other two had sparked greater discussion over the years. The *Times* will devote serious coverage to the near-miss issues too. "The agenda is not the single, all-powerful force here of what we do as journalists. We did it in full recognition that there were several very, very important topics that were left out." Besides, it's still open to change through further public listening. The paper went on to sponsor four town meetings across the Cape, where 600 people discussed what policy makers ought to be doing and revealed their more nuanced views of the listed issues. In 1995 the *Times* intends to report on each agenda item in greater depth.

THE *TALLAHASSEE* DEMOCRAT

The *Democrat* launched into its own public agenda project on an entirely different scale. Funded by a Pew Charitable Trusts grant, in collaboration with two universities and local TV, advised by public-opinion researcher Rich Harwood, and working on a firm two-year horizon, it has been able to do with exhaustive preparation everything the *Cape Cod Times* did on a shoestring. As a result, it's handled a number of things quite differently.

The paper's actual public listening began in June 1994, not with a ballot or a poll but with a series of less representative, far more in-depth conversations. The Harwood Group spoke at length with 29 demographically representative area residents to get a preliminary feel for citizens' thinking: how they thought about Tallahassee and surrounding Leon County, about public life and citizen involvement, and what were the most pressing problems they ought collectively to solve. The findings aided in designing an unusually subtle major poll. That October, a Tallahassee research firm interviewed 828 randomly chosen citizens by phone, soliciting commentary as well as multiple-choice answers; it worked the results up into a statistical profile that was published the following month.

Where the *Democrat*'s project truly veered from the norm was in the way the results were presented. As with typical agenda polls, bar graphs were drawn to identify the most often cited issues: crime (55.7 percent), traffic (35.7 percent), juvenile crime (18.6 percent), growth (17.5 percent), and so forth—but the numbers and labels were ancillary to the four-part series's main push. The two lead reporters had phoned back participants in the survey for longer conversations. In their November 13 opening article they never referred explicitly to the statistics but instead described (relying heavily on the pronoun *we*) the community the surveys had revealed: "We remain many small communities within a community." "With all the growth going on around us, we're frustrated that we don't have more of a say." "We say we'd devote more time to helping solve community problems if someone would tell us how to get involved." "Most of us say we want planned growth. Translation: We want growth for the sake of convenience, jobs and a better quality of life. We don't necessarily want a fast-food joint or strip mall in our neighborhoods." The article wove particular issues together into a sort of biographical sketch of the city, with the question posed over it, What choices do we make from here?

(cont.)

THE *TALLAHASSEE* DEMOCRAT *(cont.)*

A sidebar described how the *Democrat* and its partners were prepared to take discussion farther: through phone-in shows on TV, a community dialogue at the state capitol, small-group discussions over the next few years, and in-depth newspaper coverage including a monthly agenda page.

---

them into stereotyped boxes. Typically the boxes are labeled either with short, well-worn catchphrases (e.g., "the environment," "crime," "abortion") or with the proper names of policy options now before the Congress, city hall, or the governor (e.g., "NAFTA," "the Cooper plan," "the Clinton plan"). Should citizens tell pollsters that they're worried about cutbacks at a particular factory, reporters will be telling officeholders at press conferences the next day that "the economy is number one on the American people's agenda."

In fact—even though this book will use such shorthand terms for the sake of convenience—they don't describe how ordinary people (or anyone else) truly experience the world. People have very specific troubles, concerns, and problems. They worry that their kids will be exposed to drugs or violence at the local public school. They hope conditions in the steel market won't lead to their plant's closing. They have medical bills and tax bills that put very individualized strains on their lives. They're angry at a bank policy that seems racially biased. They're losing the ability to juggle demands from bosses, kids, and friends. They're peeved at city council members and teachers who don't listen to what they have to say. They do not experience "issues," in short, but a grabbag of uncoordinated problems that they wish public and private action could solve. Turning those problems into issues that are coherent enough to discuss and resolve publicly is an art, and what evidence there is frankly shows that ordinary people practice this art quite differently than most journalists do.

One of the most insightful books to take up this process is the 51-page Kettering Foundation report *Meaningful Chaos*, already referred to several times, which studied "how people form relationships with public concerns" through intensive focus-group research.* Its conclusions suggest

---

*Another good source is Chapter Seven of *Common Knowledge: News and the Construction of Political Meaning*, a more academic book and one that explicitly contrasts the way journalists and citizens see particular issues.

that left to themselves people do not discuss issues in terms of specific policies or plans; these are too narrow and shorn of context. Nor do they separate, say, "crime" and "poverty" into two discrete problems; they see them as so intimately interrelated that they must be discussed in tandem. Chapter Three deals with *Meaningful Chaos* and the way people describe public issues in more detail; one of its sidebars includes an exercise in "naming and framing" issues for the newspaper. The essential thing to realize here is that standardized categories won't do. But a truly open-minded approach to public listening (something akin to the *Democrat*'s in-depth conversations, the *Times*'s town meetings, or Eric Utne's editorial salons) ought to reveal both how people cluster together their problems, and which clusters of problems seem the most urgent to resolve. These clusters are the real issues on "the public's agenda."

Once the *Times* and the *Democrat* had fleshed out the half-dozen clusters of problems most troubling to the residents of their communities, they pledged to cover each one in depth and over time. To a public journalist, the only point in identifying the public's agenda is to use it. Many editors would regard such a move as dangerous; that's why they run their own agenda polls as occasional boxed features and refer back to them maybe once a year. Their rationales fall into two groups: What if the public doesn't know which issues are really important? Or what if they do, but the newspaper in its arrogance does a bad job of public listening and gets the list of issues wrong? To be flexible and safe, day-to-day coverage ought to center on whatever professional journalists regard as newsworthy.

People who raise the first objection are often thinking back to those great press folk heroes, the courageous reporters and editors who "told the unwelcome truth" when majorities didn't want to face, for example, race problems in the 1950s or the AIDS epidemic in the 1980s. They're implying that Americans need brave men and women (principally journalists) to choose the right agenda when the public itself won't. But it's not precisely true to say that "the public at large" wasn't aware of civil rights and AIDS or didn't think them important. Majorities weren't and didn't, but significant *minorities* in each era thought these to be the most overwhelming problems of their day, for reasons both personal and compelling. Newspapers shouldn't have needed courageous editors to discover these issues; all they needed was some good public listening, and a belief that reporting on what the community is thinking means the community as a whole. Public journalism believes this; a journalism based on respect for all citizens can't help but be pluralistic. The public agenda shouldn't be made up of the top five or six vote getters on a list of issues (which is why untempered polls are a poor way to engage in public listening); rather, it should consist of whatever problems are so critical to majorities or minorities that they have to be resolved if the community is to work well. There are few if any truly urgent problems (apart from comets hurtling toward Earth or shoddy regulation of savings-and-loans) that so few people are experiencing they can't be picked up by public listening.

Which brings us back to the second question: What if the newspaper purports to hear the public, but in reality hears only itself, or the most vocal members of the community, or the bad statistics that came out of an ill-designed poll? What if it gets the list of issues wrong? The managing editor of the *Cape Cod Times* still worries that the Cape's elevated cancer rate (not on his agenda) might be more important in the end than some of the environmental issues that are. The next chapter will talk a great deal about the roles of tentativeness and patience in public journalism. Major issues unfold slowly and are resolved slowly; reporters don't need to cap articles with conclusions or judgments if neither are yet warranted. It's probably wise for a public newspaper to settle on its agenda slowly: perhaps propose it in the paper, then invite feedback, and then add to it and then subtract. If cancer sufferers on Cape Cod think the depth of their concern outweighs the breadth of feeling about groundwater pollution, they should have a place in the newspaper to persuade the editors and the majority if they can. If others think the public transport issue has been put on the list wrongly, they should be able to challenge the process in a letter to the editor. On those rare occasions when comets are hurtling toward Earth, journalists can propose bumping another issue off the list to make room for astrophysics. The public at large should be invited to respond and (when enough talking has taken place) it should then be deferred to.

This going back and forth, as in a perpetual conversation with the community, is an important quality check whenever public journalists take what their more traditional peers regard as dangerous steps, such as choosing in citizens' name what choices to deliberate over, or identifying and championing the "citizens' judgment" on an issue. It's what makes public journalism defensible, and what gives public journalists authority. And it works. Community response has been strongly positive toward both the Tallahassee and Cape Cod projects; the gratitude that people feel because they are finally being consulted in an intelligent way has overwhelmed any sense that they may have been consulted wrongly. And that gratitude is the ticket to most other things the paper wants to do.

Not long ago, Jay Rosen ran into Hodding Carter III and asked him what he thought of letting citizens set the newspaper's agenda. Carter, of course, had been one of those courageous editor-folk heroes of the civil rights era himself, running the *Delta Democrat-Times* of Greenville, Miss., from 1962 to 1977. His father had won a Pulitzer Prize in the 1940s for editorializing in favor of racial tolerance. Was it true, Rosen asked, that without iconoclastic journalists rushing to tell unwelcome truths, the 1960s reforms would have been hopelessly set back? Carter replied that even the question was wrong. He and his father weren't iconoclasts. Those famous crusading editors all had great fellowship with their communities, the result of mutual trust that had been built up over many years. It was only *because* of that trust that white readers were willing to listen to the harangues on race. Had it been courageous outsiders writing the editorials, or true iconoclasts who had never spoken for the collective sense of the community, they would have been entirely ignored. When Rosen tells journalists this story he now caps it by saying, "Remember, your aim isn't to *print* tough, challenging stories your readers don't read, but to get those stories absorbed into the life of the community."

✦ PUSHING THE ENVELOPE

1. The agenda projects cited above asked people to identify the community's most pressing issues directly. The Bergen County *Record* tried a different way of getting at the public agenda. It asked county residents to identify what factors made Bergen's quality of life good or bad. What trends threatened the good factors' future? What trends promised to make the bad factors worse? Reversing these threatening trends became the regional agenda. Such quality-of-life projects may prove a good way to prod fresher thinking on what a city's real challenges are.

2. Creatively naming an agenda project can also help citizens think more freshly. A paper could, for example, ask people to think not about "Our Agenda," but about "Our Children's Agenda" or "An Agenda for the Next Generation." This might promote a longer term view of the problems to consider. It's wise on the same grounds to define ahead of time whether the paper is interested in, for example, Tallahassee's agenda, or Florida's agenda, or a national agenda.

3. Americans rarely dig down as far as their actual troubles, problems, and concerns when answering agenda surveys. The habit of thinking about public issues as a narrow range of familiar suspects including crime, poverty, and the environment is very hard to break. That's why Eric Utne's question—which never uses the word "issue"—turns up so many more varied topics for discussion than the typical newspaper poll. Jay Rosen suggests that newspapers should survey readers to find out not only the top five *issues* on their agenda, but also the top five *troubles* or *problems* in their own lives. One colleague who did just that found that for many of his friends "time" was the most formidable problem. His friends said they didn't have time for their kids, for themselves, for getting their minds and

spirits out of the overworked rut they'd dug themselves into. At first glance "time" doesn't seem like a public issue at all, but in fact job sharing, shorter work weeks, flextime, "parent pools" who share childcare, and the like are all possible facets of a public solution to the "time" issue. It's not outrageous to guess that, had readers of the *Tallahassee Democrat* or the *Cape Cod Times* considered "time" as an issue, it might have outpolled many of the traditional issues on both papers' agendas.

4. So far public journalists have focused on hearing the *content* of issues people want on the paper's agenda, but as *Meaningful Chaos* makes clear, readers have insights to offer on the presentation of these issues too: how they ought to be reported on, what kinds of comparisons or graphics would make them clearest, what voices would be most authoritative, and so on. To tap these insights the Washington State *Olympian* runs special reports every Sunday in which stories, graphics, and art must all have citizen involvement.

✦

An editor could design weekly or monthly features to remind readers about the views of minorities (or journalists) whose issues didn't make it onto the paper's agenda; this would help to keep the agenda-setting process fair in everybody's eyes. Two ideas:

5. A periodic personal profile drawing out "One Person's Agenda." The subject might be chosen because her viewpoint is unfamiliar (say, a peace scientist or a lay minister), or her opinion is respected (say, a retired community leader), or a group she belongs to is underrepresented on the agenda (say, a cancer sufferer on Cape Cod). This column would be her chance to wax angrily or touchingly or whimsically on her priorities for the public debate. In the hands of a good writer, it could be fun as well as informative.

6. An editorial box modeled on the *New York Times Book Review*'s "And Bear in Mind." To supplement its weekly bestseller list, the *Review* prints precis of perhaps a dozen less popular books that its editors think especially noteworthy. An ed board concerned about the public's lack of interest in specific issues (say, immigration or a foreign crisis) could keep those issues before the public in a similar way—gently insisting upon them without upsetting the agenda to do it.

Listening for the Long Haul

"Public" newspapers have been stunningly creative about their listening over the past several years. Community conversations, clip-out ballots, citizens' panels, and (of course) new variations on polls and focus groups are only a few of several dozen techniques they've invented to keep their fingers on the citizenry's pulse. Almost always the methods work best in combination: a few in-depth conversations alongside broader based ballots; relatively cheap and frequent editorial meetings together with relatively rare and expensive formal polls; time-intensive "listening projects" supplemented by daily or weekly brown-bag lunches at malls or community forums. This is because the mandate for public listening, when it's spelled out in detail, is ambitious in the extreme: not just breadth of understanding or depth but both at the same time; not just to get a nuanced sense of where the community stands once (as in the agenda projects as they've been described up to this point) but to keep hold of the nuances at every point as the public debate evolves; most unconventional of all, not just to understand citizens in some descriptive sense but to draw out of them usable questions and solutions—to make the newspaper, in Chapter One's words, continuously the best expert on the community's public life. That so many public journalists have hammered together ways of doing this, without either bankrupting their employers or disrupting their ability to put out a daily product, is truly a remarkable thing.

It seems odd to some people that public journalists look to citizens themselves for questions and solutions. It really shouldn't be. If a newspaper's intention is to make it easy for people to make decisions about their problems, then it ought to be people's own questions the newspaper seeks answers to, not its reporters'. (The book will address solutions in Chapters Three and Four.) It's essential to recognize that reporters are not clairvoyant, and the questions they invent when left to themselves are definitely not just more polished, professional renderings of questions citizens would ask. Thomas Patterson showed that during the 1992 campaign ordinary Americans wanted information reporters never thought to ask for (see box below). PBS news anchor Jim Lehrer discovered the same thing while he was moderating that year's presidential debates. When laypeople were given the chance to question candidates in the second debate, in Richmond, Va., they demanded things like personal insight (George Bush's experience with economic hardship) and greater civility (a pledge to stop mudslinging)—the kinds of things they might insist upon in serious personal or community-level conversations. Instead of writing this off as naive, Lehrer recognized it as an opportunity, and during the third and final debate pressed the candidates to give fuller answers to the questions they had sidestepped in Richmond. He thus established a working model for public journalists' questions: ordinary people supply the content, professional journalists make sure they're answered.

HOW CITIZENS AND REPORTERS ASK QUESTIONS

In his 1993 attack on press-driven presidential elections, *Out of Order*, Thomas Patterson compared the questions callers asked then-presidential candidate Bill Clinton during an appearance on *Larry King Live* with those asked by professional journalists at a George Bush press conference. Against stereotype, ordinary Americans, he concluded, tended to ask the real "problem-oriented" questions, while reporters asked about political strategy. Here are paraphrases of the first seven questions from each encounter:

Citizens asked Clinton	Reporters asked Bush
1. What is your view on trade between the United States and Mexico?	1. Ross Perot claims you're hiding something from him. Will you commit yourself to debating him and Bill Clinton?
2. Why didn't you attend a meeting of black newspaper publishers, and why do you not speak about black nations?	2. Is it proper for Perot, with vast wealth and no spending limits, to use that to attain the presidency?
3. Would you give money to Russia?	3. You say you haven't been good at getting your message across, but don't the polls indicate a rejection of the message itself?
4. Would you refuse loans to Israel?	4. Hasn't the pattern of the primaries been such that the American people are looking for an alternative to you?
5. How would you make the economy more competitive?	5. You've put Pat Buchanan behind you, isn't Perot the inheritor of the anti-Bush vote?
6. Have you changed your campaign approach by going on talk shows?	6. Do you share the view of Ross Perot as a man who if he doesn't get his way stomps off and goes home?
7. What would you look for in a Supreme Court nominee?	7. It looks like you'll get a hostile reception at the Rio environmental conference. If that's so, why go?

By now a number of newspapers have made this into policy, starting with the *Charlotte Observer* during its own 1992 election project. It initially seemed strange—maybe amateurish, maybe even demeaning—to professional reporters on these papers to find themselves passing on the questions of hairdressers and college students. But over time, many have said, they came to feel newly empowered, since they are now able to tell candidates, officials, and experts to answer questions because "the people" are asking them. It's a kind of authority they'd never felt when the words were all their own. And yet just as in Lehrer's case it still requires tenacious and disciplined journalists to bring it off well.

Here are some of the ways public newspapers keep in touch with their communities, gather questions from citizens, and get them answered. They:

Put Listening in the Job Description

Miami's community conversations are the preeminent example, but there are others. The *Des Moines Register* launched its public listening in 1993 by requiring all full-time news personnel to conduct at least four face-to-face interviews with residents of the metropolitan area, just to find out what was on their minds. It pooled ideas from the 600 conversations to create questions for a subsequent telephone poll, which led in turn to a five-article series identifying key issues for the region. (Now in Des Moines, as in other public journalism towns, newsroom staff regularly canvass the city, sharing brown-bag lunches with residents from every part of town.)

Ask People to Send in Thoughts and Questions

Scores of papers have encouraged readers to mail, fax, phone, E-mail, or simply drop questions and comments by the editorial offices in response to promotional ads, clip-out ballots, "We'll Answer Your Question" features, and the like. Context often makes the difference between a stimulating response and a dull one. Agenda projects draw well. In 1990, the Boulder, Colo., *Daily Camera* pegged its request for reader input to an upcoming meeting where community leaders would plan the region's future; 2,000 residents mailed in the ballot. Two years later *Oklahoman* reporters targeted surveys to 475 key community leaders, asking each to elaborate his or her personal vision for central Oklahoma; it published a hundred responses and built a regional plan around them. In Fort Wayne, Ind., the *News-Sentinel* had the temerity to take public journalism to its logical extreme. It asked representatives of city neighborhoods simply to tell the paper what it could do to make their local efforts more effective: no prior guidelines, no constraints (except on requesting financial assistance), a complete tabula rasa. It promised to commit itself for a year to any neighborhood whose proposal it approved. The interest was immediate and widespread. The *News-Sentinel* has chosen a new target area each year since 1993, organized neighborhood-wide forums in each as well as monthly meetings with local representatives, and then has done what it promised: provided coverage and support in journalistically appropriate ways tailored to fit each place's needs—helped citizens at large do their own work.

Put Together a Panel

The *Charlotte Observer* pioneered the idea during its project "Your Vote in '92." After conducting a random-sample poll of 1,003 area residents to find out what issues national and state candidates ought to discuss, it convinced 500 of them to stay on as regular advisers through November. With the panelists to rely upon, the paper had a good sense of what to cover, when to cover it, and when to move on to new styles of coverage as the season progressed. Polls and strategy stories were consistently downplayed; in a U.S. Senate race, environmental issues were moved to the front burner while topics previously dominating the news were shoved back. Editors even issued ultimatums to candidates to answer "the people's" questions. Perhaps a dozen daily newspapers have copied Charlotte's idea and taken it beyond its election context, from the aforementioned *Cape Cod Times* with its small general-purpose panel to the Columbus, Ga., *Ledger-Enquirer*, whose news staff meet each month with community leaders, educators, and ordinary citizens to review recent articles on education topics and help plan upcoming coverage.

Organize Conversations among Citizens

Maine's Portland Newspapers, the Minneapolis–St. Paul *Star Tribune*, the Dayton, Ohio, *Daily News*, the *Tallahassee Democrat*—all these public newspapers and many, many more have organized conversations out in their communities, mostly to encourage the deliberation over public choices that will be discussed in Chapter Four. Forums have become a sort of mascot or leading indicator of public journalism. Each one is, of course, also an excellent opportunity for listening to citizens talk as citizens. During small-group forums that Florida's *St. Petersburg Times* helped organize across Hillsborough County for the 1994 election cycle, reporters went around gathering questions in one-on-one conversation and also handed out forms so that every participant could mail some in. After each forum the paper posed the questions to competing candidates and printed answers in a grid format, so that "no comments" were very conspicuous. But conversations do not have to be so goal-oriented. In 1993, the *Spokane Spokesman-Review* offered a free pizza to any group of friends or neighbors who met to talk about the region's problems, successes, and hopes, and who then mailed in written summaries of their conversations. Fifteen hundred took up the offer, and since then the charming idea has spread to other cities.

Let Citizens Ask Questions Directly

The *Wisconsin State Journal* invited citizens to participate in a 1992 presidential candidates forum as part of its "We the People" initiative. Subsequently, as noted in the last chapter, citizens have served as panelists in mock legislatures and grand juries, grilling members of Congress and state officials on topics ranging from health care to the national deficit. Facilitators helped participants hone their questions before the forums and organized voting to select which were the most important questions for the "witnesses" to answer. In 1994, Boston's two great competitors, the *Herald* and the *Globe*, actually joined forces to sponsor a senatorial debate in which members of their two citizen panels asked the questions.

Go Out into the Community

Papers such as the *News-Sentinel*, having targeted particular neighborhoods for coverage, ordinarily make a habit of meeting local leaders and citizens in situ. A few papers have either proposed or actually started to go out and about in a more free-wheeling, open-ended way. For a 1993 project on Oklahoma City's visual image, the *Oklahoman* surveyed everyone who visited its booth at the Oklahoma State Fair. The *Spokesman-Review* invented, and then postponed, plans for a "newsroom on wheels," which would travel from neighborhood to neighborhood attending events and eavesdropping on local talk—effectively standing in line at banks and laundromats all across Spokane. The *Olympian* has organized field trips during which reporters go around an area just knocking on doors and asking questions, much as RSVP's listening project volunteers do.

Find Out Where Citizens Talk

A cannier means to the same end is to target just those places where, in the words of the Bradenton, Fla., *Herald*'s executive editor Wayne Poston, "public opinion bubbles up." To deepen its understanding of what local residents wanted in a new schools superintendent, the *Herald* set up booths at what it identified as key places (including a flea market and a black church on seniors' night) "where people go and talk about community events." Each booth carried a big sign saying "Talk to us about education." In Kansas at the same time, the *Wichita Eagle*'s Davis Merritt, the Pew Charitable Trusts, and focus-group researcher Rich Harwood were turning this same idea into a form of social science by setting out to discover exactly *how* public opinion arises in Wichita. Right now, Merritt says, "We start our coverage at the agenda level of city halls and governments, but by then the issues are already pretty developed. The thought was, "Can we map the places where issues initially arise?" Harwood's team first pumped the *Eagle*'s reporters for everything they knew about a few given neighborhoods, then went out into Wichita periodically to walk the streets, hold focus groups, and just hang out. It found the first-sources it was looking for. In November 1994 when Harwood associate David Mermin came to Wichita for a periodic visit, the *Eagle* was headlining the impending close of a Dillon's market, the only big grocery store in impoverished near-northeast Wichita. Mermin had heard about it two months earlier. At first draft, Harwood's "map" suggests that public discussion bubbles up through four different "levels" of places, only the top two of which are nowadays tapped by reporters at the *Eagle*. "In one sense," Merritt says, "we're trying to recapture what really good local reporters did 30 years ago. If you wanted to find out what was really going on, they knew what bars or barber shops to hang out in. We've lost that in journalism, and now we're trying to rediscover it in this organized sort of way"—one of the many senses in which public journalism is an extremely traditional form.

✦ PUSHING THE ENVELOPE

Reporters are said to be the eyes and ears of the newsroom; in public journalism that has to be made literally true. Editors need to think through not just how an individual reporter listens out in the field, but how that listening works its way back to all the other beat reporters and the writers, editors, and other staff who have to stay put during the day. The *Miami Herald*'s database and newsletter represent one approach. A paper could alternatively stage 15-minute end-of-the-day bull sessions, during which reporters would talk about what they'd seen "in the field" much like scouts on an explorer's team, and the entire staff might toss out questions or ideas for improving coverage.

✦ SIDEBAR: USING POLLS AND FOCUS GROUPS

So far this chapter has played down both polls and conventional focus groups—for good reason. Public listening aims to understand a community like Jimmy Breslin understands New York City or Bob Woodward understands the D.C. Beltway: with insight, subtlety, and nuance. Rather than flagging which labels (e.g., "crime," "schools") people most respond to, it looks for the web of idiosyncratic problems they actually experience. Rather than pigeonholing them with multiple choices, it looks for the questions and concerns that spring up from them without prompting. It is inherently a *deep* approach, and so not easily susceptible to broad and impersonal approaches like polling. As the previous section made evident, public listening both broad and deep can be performed at sustainable cost by reporters alone, without recourse to polling firms at all.

Still, nearly all public journalists have used formal polls and focus groups to shore up their listening, typically either (as with the poll from which the *Charlotte Observer's* citizens' panel was drawn) as a reference point before more intensive reportorial methods, or else (as on the *Tallahassee Democrat's* public agenda, following in-depth conversations) as a check on what the intensive methods seem to have revealed. They're like the lab tests a good doctor sends out to ratify a diagnosis: Sometimes they lead the diagnosis, sometimes they follow it, but they're never a substitute for personal knowledge and examination. The Wichita *Eagle* studied years of past polling to prepare for 192 open-ended interviews with Wichitans that launched its 1992 "People Project"; from there on out, to explore feelings on things like health care and government gridlock, it met citizens through call-in shows, letters, town meetings, and "idea exchange" booths. After an initial where-we-stand poll to get things underway, most of the *Indianapolis Star's* 1993 race relations project relied on standard factual reporting and insights into citizen thinking drawn from monthly public forums. A year later the paper conducted a second poll to flag possible shifts in public attitudes. The *Akron Beacon Journal* used focus groups more creatively for its Pulitzer-Prize-winning "A Question of Color" coverage, impaneling blacks-only, whites-only, and mixed groups to illuminate shared and race-divergent perspectives. These were carefully designed groups—well aimed to bring out the aspects of citizenship they were looking for—but still their implications were given more subtle shape and nuance by less formal sorts of listening (among them, surveys of blacks and whites in the newsroom).

Good public journalism polls must also be consciously designed (like all public listening) to encourage respondents to think

✦ and answer as citizens. This is hard in a mass, multiple-choice survey but not impossible. A few tips:

Ask Deliberative Questions

Chapter Four lists types of questions that may encourage sources to "deliberate"; the beginning of this chapter explained how Rural Southern Voice for Peace uses a staged series of questions to get people to speak as citizens. These questions are mostly open-ended and thus unsuitable for polls, but they have characteristics that can be adapted into yes/no or multiple-choice questions, such as asking what motivates a person's opponents on an issue, or what might make for common ground. One particularly useful style of question is the "Would you support X even if it meant Y?" form. For example, "Would you support building prisons even if it meant less money for schools?" or "Would you support censorship of TV violence even if it gave power over what you watch to an unelected board?" To Daniel Yankelovich in *Coming to Public Judgment*, deliberation is all about facing people with the consequences of their options and getting them to choose. In any event, anyone designing a public journalism poll should post a reminder on the wall that "the questions you ask determine the answers you get."

Design Polls That Are More than Polls

Polls can be conducted in ways that incorporate deliberation directly, usually by making the questionnaire only one part in a longer process. Public Agenda, a New York–based research group founded by Yankelovich and Cyrus Vance, conducted an experiment with Brown University years ago in which cross sections of the American populace—focus groups, more or less—were invited to intensive three-hour discussion workshops on relations with the Soviet Union. They were presented with four mutually exclusive choices for the future of U.S. policy, and trained facilitators led them through a choice-by-choice discussion of arguments pro and con; on a compressed scale, this parallels the news coverage and public discussion advocated in Chapters Three and Four. By the end, most participants no longer tried to embrace two or three options at once. Their opinions were far less likely to be shaken by changing the wording of a polling question or bringing up a possible bad consequence of their choice. In short, the exit poll showed only a remnant of the fickleness for which the polled public is so regularly disdained. In 1994, Britain's *Independent* newspaper raised the same technique to the level of a statistically significant poll.

✦ With its television partner Channel Four, it brought 302 representative Britons together for a weekend in Manchester to deliberate with party leaders, experts, and one another about ways to reduce crime in the United Kingdom. The meeting resulted in both a set of statistics and a popular piece of television.

Know When Results Are Meaningless

As the next chapter will argue at much greater length, every issue has a life cycle, and at some points within it people's opinions reveal nothing. Particularly at the point when they first see that their choices all have costs, opinion becomes erratic in the extreme, careening back and forth between what seem like rocks and what seem like hard places. Personal conversations pick this up; often people will freely admit that they don't know enough to form a judgment. Polls on the other hand typically miss it; as Dan Yankelovich says, mass opinion and public judgment look like the same thing in percentage terms. Somehow a paper has to be wise enough to see worthless poll results for what they are and to tell its readers to ignore them. Public Agenda uses three warning flags to do this: *First*, it scans poll results for logically inconsistent answers. In the Brown University experiment, many participants started off saying that the United States should struggle aggressively for military dominance, but should also cooperate with the Soviets on resolving our differences; obviously the respondents hadn't thought through the dynamics of this love–hate relationship. *Second*, Public Agenda tests whether people alter their opinions when questions are asked in a different order or using slightly different words. Americans tend to be in favor of school vouchers, for example, when the question includes the word "choice" but to oppose them when the question refers to "religious schools" (that is, one of the specific choices parents might elect to use their vouchers for.) *Third*, Public Agenda looks for variance in results when consequences are added to the questions. Poll numbers varied dramatically on a cause Americans seemed to be solidly behind in 1994: universal health care coverage. Poll after poll had shown stratospheric majorities of 70 and 80 percent in favor of making coverage available to everybody—but as soon as "even ifs" were added such as higher taxes and restricted choice of doctors, the numbers plummeted. Maybe it doesn't need to be said, but on issues that people have truly worked through polling shows little or no inconsistency and volatility. Americans remain solidly for or against the death penalty, for example, no matter how pollsters ask them about it.

✦ PUSHING THE ENVELOPE

Political scientist James Fishkin invented the idea for the *Independent's* Manchester crime forum in his short book *Democracy and Deliberation*. Initially, though, the "deliberative opinion poll" was supposed to be a bookend to U.S. presidential campaigns. Before the New Hampshire primary, a representative sample of Americans would gather in one place for several days to meet all the aspiring candidates, to judge them face to face, and to deliberate over issues with the candidates and with each other. As in Britain, the event itself and its entrance and exit polling would be widely broadcast and reported. Fishkin argued that this way, instead of campaign issues and candidates arising and disappearing haphazardly, or because they are or aren't of interest to early primary states, Americans would get a push to think about issues and candidates in a broader, more rational way right from the beginning. PBS and MacNeil/Lehrer Productions intend to televise such a poll in the runup to the 1996 presidential election. Newspapers could, either alone or in collaboration, stage such a poll in the leadup to local, state, or national election campaigns.

Sentencing Reform from Two Perspectives

The brass ring here is producing journalism that's unmistakably written from the citizen's point of view. This chapter has insisted that ordinary Americans see issues in a subtler, more sophisticated light than the press and other political "players" do (at least publicly), that they see problems as more interconnected, and that listening to them with greater care and intelligence—greater attentiveness to the whole thing they're trying to say as citizens—has the power to bend and shape good journalism into something significantly different from what it is at most newspapers today. Cumulatively, the work described in this book is the proof of that. Here though is a small piece of evidence: two short articles written after town meetings held in Virginia during the summer of 1994. Governor George Allen had been holding hearings, then traveling around the state to promote his plan to abolish parole. The *Richmond Times-Dispatch* went to one such meeting and saw a story about the plan; the *Virginian-Pilot*—whose "Public Life Team" has been trained by the ubiquitous Rich Harwood, and which has internally worked over public journalism probably like no other paper—went to a later town meeting and saw things a different way.

From the *Richmond Times-Dispatch*, June 3, 1994:

First parole reform hearing elicits strong views
Victims of crime, and an ex-inmate, speak up
by Frank Green

ALEXANDRIA—It was not until the end of the standing-room-only "town meeting" last night that someone finally stood up to the juggernaut that has become Gov. George Allen's bid to abolish parole and reform sentencing.

Law enforcement officers, crime victims, the loved ones of murder victims and others all spoke at length, sometimes compellingly, about the need to fix what they see as a broken system of justice and to better protect the public from violent criminals.

Jerome Jordan listened sympathetically to the horror and pain. But he grew impatient.

"I'm sitting here and my stomach was turning. We've heard from everybody, but we ain't heard from nobody that's been in the penitentiary. I been in the penitentiary," said Jordan, a former addict and convict now clean, off parole and about to become a counselor.

Jordan was among the last to speak in the Alexandria City Council chambers at the first of four hearings scheduled by the Commission to Abolish Parole and Reform Sentencing. He asked that the chance for those who can be reformed not be eliminated.

"People get killed in the penitentiary, too. It ain't no playground down there. . . . I just got tired of taking the whipping," said Jordan. "I'd just like to say the system does work."

The commission's "Proposal X," disclosed in April, called for the impo-sition of mandatory sentencing guidelines. However, last night the commission indicated that it now favors a narrow range of sentences for judges to consider.

Under the new proposal, the maximum sentences would be cut for various crimes, bringing them down to levels closer to the sentences now actually served by inmates. Judges, with cause, could deviate below and above the guideline range.

Sentences for violent and repeat offenders may be stiffened, however. The proposed guideline ranges are still being developed.

Other states have ended parole and imposed guidelines, some with dismal results requiring the reimposition of parole in order to relieve overcrowded prisons, and massive prison construction.

However, if enacted, Virginia's guidelines will be the first in the country based on historical data about the length of time actually served by Virginia inmates.

Under Proposal X, offenders would serve a minimum of 85 per cent of their sentences. Between parole and good-time sentence reductions, Virginia inmates now serve an average of 30 per cent, with a low of 21 per cent.

The plan will be refined further before being presented to Allen and then considered by the General Assembly in a special session in Septem-

---

Reprinted with permission of the Richmond Times-Dispatch.   *(cont.)*

ber. Allen wants the changes to be effective in January.

"The time for debate is over," said Allen. "What we need to do is abolish parole, keep murderers and rapists and armed robbers in prison longer. We need to build the prison space necessary to make sure that they are put away."

"And those who say that we cannot do this, [that] you cannot bring truth and honesty to the sentencing system of Virginia, are, as far as I'm concerned, defeatists who accept fear and violent crime as a way of life," Allen said.

He said he recognizes there are economic and social reasons behind some crime.

But, the governor continued, "The vast majority of less-advantaged people, the vast majority of unemployed people and the vast majority of children who come from single-parent homes never kill, never rape, never maim anyone."

First to speak last night was Stanley Rosenbluth whose son and daughter-in-law were murdered in Chesterfield County last Thanksgiving weekend.

"My family will always suffer, and if something isn't changed to protect us, the victims, then we are in big trouble," he said.

Elsie Taylor-Jordan, an Alexandria anti-drug activist, said she is angry about the drugs that are destroying part of the black community.

"Those people who have done the killings are on drugs," she said. And it is the people who are getting rich supplying the drugs who must be punished, not the addict, she said.

"Build treatment centers," not jail cells, she urged.

The commission's next town meeting has been set for 7 P.M. Wednesday in Roanoke at the Virginia Western Community College. Those wishing to participate should call 786-5351.

From the Virginian-Pilot, August 27, 1994:

Crowd echoes Allen's cry against parole
On courthouse steps at Beach,
women tell of brutal crimes and penalties cut short
by Tony Wharton

VIRGINIA BEACH—One by one, the four respectable, middle-aged women told their hair-raising tales of brutal crimes committed and punishment cut short.

In front of Gov. George F. Allen and an enthusiastic crowd of his supporters on the steps of the courthouse Friday afternoon, the four went on to

---

   (cont.)

firmly endorse his plan to abolish parole.

"We have a system that kills hope of justice," said Dorothy Soule, whose son Paul was stabbed to death in Suffolk in 1979. His killer served less than half of his sentence before being paroled, she said.

Dale Pennell of Newport News told how her sister was raped and murdered in her Ghent apartment. "I represent the growing ranks of homicide survivors who want more protection," she said.

Moments later, Allen said, "It would be great if they were the only ones in the commonwealth. Unfortunately, they are not."

The four were part of a well-orchestrated string of appearances by Allen, Attorney General James Gilmore and a host of political allies across the state in an effort to persuade the General Assembly to approve Allen's plan. The crowd carried placards that read: "Abolish Parole Now!"

What some of the women said afterward—but Allen did not hear—is that they consider his proposal a good beginning, rather than the entire answer, to solving the crime problem.

First, Soule said, she wanted to make one thing clear: "I am for the governor's recommendations, very much so. Something has got to be done."

However, she also said, "We have got to reach these kids in the home. We can't wait. We have to see to it that these single parents take parenting classes."

"It's not anything that starts with big spending. It takes people investing in people."

Allen hasn't heard that side of

Soule's passion on the issue because they haven't talked. She has appeared repeatedly in public to back his plan, but she has never had an opportunity to personally tell him her entire vision for combating and preventing crime.

Allen's proposal, which goes to the General Assembly in a special session opening Sept. 19, is about punishment. Pennell, a high school principal, said that is one-third of the package that needs to be crafted to deal with crime.

"This is the beginning," Pennell said. "It's one of three things. You have to have punishment, but you also need prevention and rehabilitation. I'm still very interested in seeing all those things happen. I don't see them as opposing each other."

On Friday, Allen focused on punishment and attacked rehabilitation.

"Don't let them start talking about all kinds of social programs and tinkering," he said. "We are long past soft tinkering with this liberal parole system. People want action."

"Instead of blame and excuses, it's time to use incarceration, because we know that works. Incarceration is prevention."

Pennell said, "You can't really say this program focuses on prevention, except in the important area of incarcerating people who would otherwise be committing crimes."

She said she was pleased to see that Allen's plan includes work camps and drug treatment facilities, and she hopes he is serious about those parts. "Those are little baby steps toward rehabilitation," she said.

The distinction between these two articles goes much, much deeper than who does most of the speaking. The Richmond piece accepts without question that sentencing reform is the issue; although packaged as a town meeting story, it is really a follow-up report on the governor's reform plan. Its three quotations from ordinary Virginians (each sounding a single familiar note, just loudly enough to pigeonhole one "for" and two "against") have no effect on the direction the story ultimately takes. The writer reserves all his nuance for minor variations on the two-month-old Proposal X. (This official-minded take on crime led the *Times-Dispatch*, six days later, to set readers up for the next town meeting by detailing—in a longer story, with two large charts and no citizen input—a new study on the single narrow problem of sentencing repeat offenders.) All of this might have been fine, important journalism *if* this was the information Virginians really needed to decide upon their collective response to crime. But was it? The *Virginian-Pilot's* public listening led it to think not. Its article not only starts with citizens (specifically, those who have come out to support Governor Allen's call), it gradually finds its benchmarks and comparison points in the way they see the issue: as more complex and shaded than the governor or the Richmond paper apparently do. These citizens indeed favor abolishing parole—they have been victims themselves—but they see it as part of a larger strategy, one also involving prevention and rehabilitation. Not only do they reject the idea that "incarceration is prevention," they don't see the usual alternatives like work camps and drug treatment as any more than "baby steps" at the comprehensive goal they're looking for. Governor Allen may believe that the merest talk about prevention threatens to steal the thunder away from taking action on parole ("Don't let them start talking about all kinds of social program and tinkering"), but the two ordinary Virginians, Soule and Pennell, do not. They can fight to "Abolish Parole Now" at the same time that they advocate parenting classes and other social programs, and they would prefer it if officials and experts discussed solutions in these terms. If this is indeed what the staunchest supporters of sentencing reform believe, then the technical and narrow focus of the *Times-Dispatch's* coverage commits the mortal sin of journalism: It simply misses the point.

✦ PUSHING THE ENVELOPE

As this comparison shows, a paper doesn't necessarily do public journalism by adding bells and whistles like community forums. The first and foremost way of making a story more "public" is by adjusting the reporter's own attitude and style. To bring this off both reporters and editors have to be so thoroughly familiar with the different styles of public and traditional journalism that they can go back and forth between them with ease. The *Virginian-Pilot* teaches this lesson by assigning its reporters (when time permits) to write two versions of the same story: first the "public" version, to actually go into print, and second, a traditional version. A few other exercises to the same end:

1. At news-budget and story-assignment meetings, journalists can ask each other, "How can we ratchet up the public journalism in this story?" For example, a former *Charlotte Observer* editor reflected not long ago that, while the citizen-panel approach to the 1992 election was on the money in many ways, he feared that citizens would have been better served if the *Observer* had looked more closely into Bill Clinton's character. *His* remedy was traditional: if he had it to do over again, he'd investigate Gennifer Flowers and events in Clinton's past even if citizens *weren't* interested. The *Oregonian* took a different and more "public" approach to the same problem. It kicked off its 1994 election coverage by reporting what scholars had to say about the qualities of good leadership; this got readers thinking. To go a step farther, the paper could then have run a clip-out survey asking readers what aspects of character (if any) they would like the paper to investigate, and what aspects they think are either private or irrelevant. A good public newspaper can always invent ways to nudge people toward issues it considers important, without abandoning its basic commitment to coverage based on public listening.

2. At postmortems, instead of discussing how the headlines and story-play might have been better on yesterday's page one, editors could discuss the public journalism. Did the stories on page one start from citizen viewpoints? If not, why not? What are we assuming about citizens, to have given that story such prominent play? Drawing on ideas to be discussed in Chapter Three, did the front section set up a strong narrative? Did it make choices clear enough, soon enough? And so on.

3. The publisher could appoint an internal ombudsman. The ombudsman would read through the whole paper each day just to look for the public journalism quotient and the assumptions being made about citizens: Where are we treating them as intelligent, or as dumb? Where are we talking to them, versus above or below them? Where do we start with their perspective, or subtly ignore it? He or she could then circulate memos to make staff aware of successes and failures—particularly the subtle ones that stand a good chance of escaping notice.

Building Civic Capital

Before moving on, it's worth looking at some of the inadvertent effects of public listening—not those on the newspaper but those on citizens themselves. Newspapers and broadcast journalists get a consistent reaction from the public whether they're staging forums or call-in shows, running clip-out ballots, or consulting citizen panels: "How can we do more?" "What do we do next?" Men and women have come up to *Miami Herald* editors after a community conversation to ask how they can get involved permanently in community discussion groups. At the close of the *Independent*'s deliberative weekend on crime in Manchester, England, many of the participants wanted to take their closing ballots home to give them more thought and work. Citizens have thanked the *Dayton Daily News* and the *Spokane Spokesman-Review* for their forums and asked them to continue. An abbreviated list of responses like these appears in Chapter Six under the heading "Some Evidence of Success," but it's more than just evidence that the newspaper is on track, it's a sign that ordinary people are becoming involved with each other, giving up what the press usually calls their apathy, building up the goodwill and energy to participate more as citizens—in Chapter One's abstract way of putting it, they are building civic capital. This is a mere by-product of public journalism as it's practiced so far, but it might as well be a conscious by-product, so that journalists can maximize it in everything they do.

To quote Kettering Foundation president David Mathews on civic capital at greater length than in Chapter One: "If there is no sense of community, it stands to reason that it will be difficult to solve common problems. A purely instrumental, problem-solving politics isn't adequate by itself. People in a community have to have public spirit and a sense of relationship. They have to be positively engaged, not just entangled with one another. Problems divide people, so if they do not create solid working relationships before difficulties mount, there is little likelihood that they can create any sense of community in the midst of major conflict." What, then, is the best way for a newspaper to build that "public spirit and sense of relationship"? The community-connectedness movement has tried on one level but not always the right one; we Americans need to socialize through our newspapers not just as we'd socialize at a bake sale, but as we'd socialize in the Athenian agora, as fellow citizens sharing ideas. Looking back, the newspapers discussed in this chapter have built a spirit of fellow citizenship in a number of different ways:

+ **By committing to the long term.** Cape Codders clip out their ballots in full expectation that the *Times* will continue to carry the ball. The *Tallahassee Democrat* and the *Fort Wayne News-Sentinel* promised readers that they would follow through on the public agenda and neighborhood projects for at least two years and one year, respectively. Citizens are willing to do their part of public listening wholeheartedly as long as they believe it's a route toward, and not a mere substitute for, the part of democracy that solves problems.

✦ **By setting up a process people regard as fair.** People in Akron saw that the opinions of whites and blacks each got a full hearing in the *Beacon Journal's* focus groups. Community leaders in Fort Wayne accepted the process of selecting the *News-Sentinel's* target neighborhoods as basically sound. Despite the small number of citizens who actually took part in setting the Cape Cod and Tallahassee agendas, few readers of the *Times* and the *Democrat* object to them as good starting points for further discussion.

✦ **By doing easy things first.** Truly hot-button issues such as race relations or abortion become easier to grapple with if people have heard each other's voices, deliberated, and found common ground on less divisive things already—if they have, for example, settled on a public agenda (as in Cape Cod and Tallahassee), asked questions together at a senatorial debate (as in Boston), voted on what to ask witnesses at a mock grand jury (as in Madison, Wis.), or contributed ideas to a citizens' panel (as in Charlotte).

✦ **By showing respect for ordinary people.** The *Democrat* and the *Virginian-Pilot* took pains to write about citizens' whole thinking on public issues; papers such as the *Herald* and the *Charlotte Observer* listened to them at unprecedented length; the *Eagle* was committed enough to hearing what citizens have to say to go on a truly quixotic search for the ultimate sources of opinion in Wichita—and by a kind of Hawthorne effect,* the evidence of serious interest just by itself makes citizens more productive.

✦ **By demonstrating that good people aren't alone.** People see murder, scandal, competition, and utter vacuity easily enough on their streets and in their newspapers; they can't always pick out the qualities needed to make the community work. Frances Moore Lappé and Paul Martin Du Bois of the Vermont-based Center for Living Democracy, an organization that searches out democratic innovations, say that from what they see in their travel, much of the time "people feel that they're the last sane

---

*Hawthorne effect: sociology term for the fact that people increase their effort when they know they're being paid attention. In the late 1920s, industrial psychologists set out to study the productivity effects of changing hours, wages, work space, lighting, and the like on workers at Western Electric's Hawthorne factory in Cicero, Ill. Over the course of a year, each time they tinkered with conditions—even for the worse—productivity went up. Amazingly, productivity continued to go up even when they brought conditions back to what they'd been at the beginning.

person on Earth—and if you feel like that, you feel pretty lonely.
. . . [People don't see that] they are in fact linked to thousands
of other people who share the same concerns." The *News-Sentinel* showed the links simply by inviting other parts of Fort
Wayne to help solve the problems of troubled neighborhoods;
the*Virginian-Pilot* showed the links by revealing that even
staunch advocates of tougher sentencing want active programs
for rehabilitation and crime prevention.

✦ **By making meaningful participation fun.** Perhaps the greatest
enemy of citizenship is the deadly dull city council session, the
tedious PTA meeting, the perfunctory reporter asking for quotable half-sentences from the audience. The *Wisconsin State
Journal's* mock legislature, meanwhile, was an intriguing challenge for everyone who participated. The *Spokesman-Review*
pizza parties were neighborly get-togethers at heart. Almost
everywhere invitations to public listening get a large response,
often outstripping the maximum number (if any) that the paper
can accommodate.

In cities including Akron, Dayton, Columbus (Ga.), Wilmington
(Del.), Bradenton (Fla.), and Spokane, this kind of citizenship-building
has produced real results, from more thoughtful contributions in the
newspaper; to the creation of new civic groups; to reforms in government plans, programs, and budgets; to actual riverfront redevelopment;
to a palpable optimism about the future of the community itself. Over
the next four chapters, this book will comment on additional ways of
building civic capital as they arise.

✦

CHAPTER THREE

News Coverage

Working for Results

Ordinarily, what gets printed in a daily paper may be "newsworthy" for all sorts of reasons. Public journalism, however—despite the many forms it takes—inevitably comes to center on two tests of news value: Does this piece of writing or reporting help build civic capital? And does it help move the public toward meaningful judgment and action? Which means the final word on a public journalist's news choices can never come from the publisher, colleagues, or the Pulitzer Prize committee, but only from what happens or doesn't happen in the community as a whole.

This sets a benchmark of realism almost foreign to the American news business. Reporters and editors tend to *think* of themselves as realists because they see through so much of the outside world's cant— they "call things as they see them" and "print uncomfortable truths"— but seldom do they turn their critical eye on the ineffectiveness of their own work. Judged on what common news decisions actually accomplish, most are probably more quixotic than hard-nosed. Editorial pages will run scathing pieces exhorting their communities to wake up, get rid of bigotry, unite against demagogues, take action, help the homeless; very often nothing will come of it, and yet the next week they'll go right back and run still more scathing exhortations on the new topics of the day. National editors will print long, familiar arguments between Republicans and Democrats over which party can best "fix the economy" when they know full well that (realistically speaking) no party can fix the economy in a globalizing market, and the jobless rate on election day will have more to do with the business cycle than with policy set in Washington; they see their job as presenting even phony arguments in tough, comprehensive, well-thought-out packages rather than as insisting that the pols discuss more realistic goals to begin with. Collectively (and strangely) journalists take enormous pride in "putting out a good paper" even when it ends up wrapping the proverbial fish the next day. Like those Southerners who romanticize the Lost Cause of the Confederacy, they honor each other for merely fighting without actually fighting to win.

This makes no sense to public journalists. Realistically speaking, there's no point in publishing information people can't (or won't) use; consequently the newspapers in this book expend unprecedented effort on helping citizens buy in to the decision-making process. A community can't make progress on its problems if the public dialogue is polluted; so they refuse to let anyone's grandiose claims, wishful thinking, or sheer laziness pull their discourse off track—even if it's the public's own laziness or grandiosity. Far from pandering to readers, public journalists challenge them (and all other citizens) to do what really has to be done if public life is to succeed. They work from a conviction that citizens will come to see this kind of newspapering as a more essential part of their lives, will continue to read it (and pay for it) even if they balk now and then when their own complacency, bigotry, or wishful thinking is put on the spot. Public journalists, in short, are the clear-eyed pragmatists that conventional journalists only pretend to be.

How Issues Unfold over Time

As an example and a convenient starting point, look at the question of pacing—of how newspapers expect the public to react to their coverage over time. Very often editors try to deal with a huge issue within the scope of one article; if not a single article, then a package; if not a package, then a series. The *Philadelphia Inquirer's* brilliant 1991 series "America: What Went Wrong?" compressed the causes and effects of Carter- and Reagan-era economic trends into 25 pages. Probably all the purely factual information a layman would need to make wise policy choices was contained in those pages—an achievement sufficient to win the *Inquirer* a floodtide of praise and imitation. But apart from a temporary national revulsion at a decade of greed, no choices *were* made. A "great read" on the page was a dud in real life. Why?

It would have been obvious if the *Inquirer* had put itself in an ordinary citizen's shoes: The series was too much to digest in a short time, and Americans had no idea where to begin or what to do with it. Newspapers almost never take into account the reality that decision making is a process, a story that unfolds in real stages as the months and maybe even years go by. Big decisions on general direction are succeeded by smaller decisions on plans, and then by decisions on details. People have to know what's going to be decided when, where, and how, if they're to stay interested and involved. In conventional thinking, pace and staging aren't even issues in putting out a paper. Information has no expiration date. On breaking news, reporters take their cue from the mayor or the city council, the foundation issuing a new report or the lobbyist rebutting an old one; it lets them decide what aspect of, say, crime or deficit spending will be discussed today. On enterprise assignments like the *Inquirer's*, editors schedule series in terms of how they'll fit within the production demands of the newspaper rather than how they'll fit within readers' lives. Facts are expected to pile up until they reach some kind of critical mass, and then people are expected to use them somehow to make their decisions. (The "somehow" is never examined too closely.) In practice this just doesn't work. People forget. They lose focus or interest. They end up talking about too many different things all at once. They just get overwhelmed.

Daniel Yankelovich argues that there's a definite, if slow, rhythm to the public's working through a difficult issue, one that is often obscured by the faster cycles of congressional sessions and the newspaper business, and the press's indifference to pacing continually grates up against it. Until journalists look at the public's rhythm concretely this will probably sound like mumbo-jumbo—but fortunately, that's easy enough to do. Yankelovich cites health care reform. From the press's point of view, health care was without doubt the nation's number-one issue from 1992 through 1994. Newspapers gave it fantastic attention, lavish both in detail and in scarce news space, beginning with campaign coverage of people like Bill Clinton and Harris Wofford and culminating, throughout 1994, in a fine-point comparison of White House, centrist, and Republican health care plans. Everyone talked in terms of passing one bill or another before midterm elections. When that didn't happen, journalists and politicians moved with characteristic restlessness on to new business, and health care dropped right off the public agenda radar. Yankelovich's polling meanwhile showed that by mid-1994 ordinary Americans had only just gotten a handle on the true dimensions of the issue. People had been restlessly opting for one solution after another, hoping to pay for reform entirely through the elimination of waste and abuse. Gradually they had rejected a government-run insurance system. Now large numbers had begun to turn their eyes elsewhere, convinced that universal coverage would require more money, or rationing medical procedures, or restricting choice of doctors, or all three. They were primed to face that difficult set of choices next—but suddenly there was no longer an organized national conversation within which to face it. Congress and the media had rushed out so far in front that they had run out of steam; to mask their practical failure they had convinced themselves, implausible as this might sound, that Americans had simply ceased to care in 1994 about the issue that had obsessed them in 1992. And so, though the public had made some solid progress in its thinking, it was ultimately left with nothing to show for its effort.

Public journalists try to use the same techniques of public listening that help *ground* news in the public's concerns to *pace* it at the public's rhythm; this is one of the many ways in which they attempt to be experts in public life—the one corps of professionals in society to have their hands firmly on the social pulse. What this typically means is that their coverage is more patient than the majority of American journalism. The *Cape Cod Times* and the *Tallahassee Democrat* spend months simply hammering out a public agenda; the *Huntington Herald-Dispatch* builds citizen involvement in planning the county's economic future steadily for a year. The coverage doesn't accumulate randomly; it fits into a larger, long-term plan. The *Dayton Daily News* works gradually from encouraging people to talk informally about teen violence in May 1994; to printing personal stories and expert information in June, July, and August; to helping organize formal public forums in September; to reporting on what judgments citizens have worked through for the remainder of the year. They plan to take the public pulse again in 1995 and see how to go further. The point isn't to let a single issue overwhelm all the other news in the paper; public journalists aren't sprinters, putting all their energy into a single burst (as the *Inquirer* did in "America: What Went Wrong?") but marathon runners, making their progress with small, well-paced spurts of effort linked by long-term concentration on the goal.

Practically, this is probably smart; many of Chapter One's writers on democracy insist that the United States finds itself returning to tediously familiar debates on health care, poverty, race, and the like every couple of decades largely because it doesn't take time to address them right the first time. Professionally, this kind of patience can be enormously liberating. Stories no longer have to be compressed; reporters don't have to leap so far to conclusions. Papers like the Bergen County *Record* can print transcripts from public meetings, send their staff off to cover other aspects of the story, and get an unprecedented response from the readership, all at once (as described in Chapter Two). Public journalists would argue that—in grappling toward the solution of a public problem—people care far more whether they're making *solid* progress than whether they're making *fast* progress. Simply setting the public agenda in a responsible way, describing an issue for the first time the way people in the community see it, identifying the real alternatives they have to choose among: Readers respond to petty progress like this with remarkable enthusiasm. Americans are no longer congratulating the media for its onslaught on health care, but they are still congratulating the *Cape Cod Times* for its agenda project, the *Dayton Daily News* for its work on teen violence, and the *Wichita Eagle* and *Charlotte Observer* for work they began in 1992.

The key to good practice is to see public issues literally in terms of a *story*, and then to tell it with the canniness of a practiced storyteller. Journalists do this already when they cover national campaigns or long trials, because the major turning points in the plot are laid out explicitly: candidate announcements-to-primaries-to-conventions-to-debates-to-election day, or else crime-to-investigation-to-arrest-to-arraignment-to-trial-to-verdict. Reporters know how to stage their coverage, because they have a good idea what will be decided today, versus next week, next month, or next year. They know when to go deep and when to go spare. Although every public issue potentially has a plot of this sort, journalists typically don't see it because it hasn't been written out for them.

At one Project on Public Life and the Press workshop, two reporters from the Norfolk *Virginian-Pilot* were arguing over an article one had written on a declining neighborhood scheduled to receive city aid. The article had straightforwardly described Hall Place's look and feel as well as the ambivalent things residents had to say about whether it could be saved from growing crime, poverty, and vacancy rates, and whether they would stay around to help save it. One of the writer's colleagues felt that he ought to have added—as a public service—that this was in fact *not* the kind of "neighborhood ready to help itself" that the city had said it intended to help: It was poorly organized, divided, and there was a very good chance it would end up as a waste of public money. The writer suspected all this to be true, but as the two of them talked more they both came to realize that the simplest truth was that they didn't know yet if Hall Place would succeed. Neither did the city, nor the residents who lived there. The article as it stood was the perfect setup for a story that would take place over the next year or two: the story of whether this neighborhood could save itself, a story to be punctuated by as yet unforeseeable local efforts and crises, gains and losses. If the writer had said, "The evidence on the street indicates Hall Place will fail"—a common enough conclusion for an in-depth article of this sort—he would have been cutting the story short. It would be exactly like saying "The butler did it" in the first scene of an Agatha Christie mystery: Not only would it steal away most of the intrinsic interest in the story, but in fact, if things were left to unfold without comment, it might simply turn out not to be true.

Conventional news coverage cuts stories short not only in forcing conclusions but in a number of other ways. As a broad generalization, breaking news tends to center around bringing out a story's emotional impact: establishing human interest and importance—something newspapers do very well. But they stick to the formula too long. What more do we really need to know about the emotional impact of the latest Bosnian atrocity, AIDS death, or race riot in south-central Los Angeles? Issues mature quite rapidly past the point where pathos, horror, and anger are the most helpful things—the things that will move the story forward, and help Americans to make decisions—but the press often sticks to this one corner of the story. Less often, newspapers immerse themselves in the niggling technical details of a story (like the comparison of still-tentative health care plans), losing sight of both the emotional questions Americans are still wrestling with and the broader policy questions. The surest cure is to try to recognize how a story will unfold right from the beginning, and plan out how to pace the story in a similar (though necessarily more tentative) way as editors already plan out election and trial coverage.

A good mental aid is to think of a public issue in terms of two parallel stories, both of which need to be told, side by side, as the public works to make its choices and get them carried out. Once again let's take health care as an example. On the one hand, the story of health care reform is about "the facts": the problems with the current system, the various proposals for reform, arguments for and against each one. Over time citizens have to wrestle with the facts in order to choose a realistic set of policies; if newspapers don't provide them with the relevant facts at each stage, then help set up opportunities to deliberate over them and make reasonable choices, people either won't decide what to do at all, or will decide badly or divisively. Getting real about democracy, people have to face the facts. On the other hand, the story of health care reform is also about "the narrative": the emotional story behind the problem that drives people to solve it. Citizens have to feel a national debate is important, coherent, and hopeful enough to keep them involved; otherwise they will drop out. A newspaper has to tap the relevant sources of interest and enthusiasm at each stage in the story. In other words, to be realistic, people have somehow to be drawn in by an issue and held, maybe for months or years, not just as passive readers but as active citizens. Although it's somewhat artificial to separate "the facts" from "the narrative," a paper that asks itself two distinct questions—"What are we doing this week to move forward the *facts?*" and "What are we doing this week to move forward the *narrative?*"—will probably find it much easier to keep a story on track than a paper that confuses the two, or doesn't ask that kind of question at all.

THE FACTS AND THE NARRATIVE

The facts	The narrative
The intellectual work of citizens coming to grips with an issue. To take action at all, citizens have to decide rationally which actions stand the best chance of really ameliorating the problem.	The emotional story of citizens coming to grips with an issue. To stay with an issue over the long haul to resolution, citizens have to find practical ways to keep their eyes on the prize and to stay motivated, involved, confident, and active.
A newspaper can help by hard-headedly spelling out the nature of the problem and the basic options available—not just the pros but also the real cons of each. It can go on to promote public discussion, either at forums or on the news pages themselves, and to act as a sort of bulletin board for concrete solutions and the public's evolving sense of common ground (if any). Finally, it can play the watchdog, making sure that officials, organizations, and citizens themselves act according to the public's consensus.	A newspaper can help by presenting the issue in ways that resonate for people, among them: making the problem personal, showing how it affects people's lives, and keeping it coherent. They can continually report on the community's progress toward "solving its own problems." They can foster a sense of drama and possibility, for example by involving citizens in forums that cross formerly unbridgeable racial, class, or ethnic lines; or by allowing citizens to coordinate their efforts through the newspaper; or by profiling other communities or individuals who have solved this particular problem.
Questions for journalists: "What do people have to decide *right now?*" "What facts do we need to give them to make their decision?" "Are our sources, and the citizens we see in public forums, being realistic?" "What do people have to decide *next?*" "Do people seem to be coming to any common ground?" "What does that common ground mean, in nuts-and-bolts terms?"	**Questions for journalists:** "Are people getting more involved in this issue, or more indifferent to it?" "What's tuning them out?" "Do they see us making progress?" "Is the tone of our coverage helping them to cooperate, or making them more adversarial?" "Can readers see the long-term story behind what we're running today?" "Do readers feel it's easy to get involved and, if they don't, what can we do about it?"

(cont.)

THE FACTS AND THE NARRATIVE *(cont.)*

The facts	The narrative
Useful concepts:	**Useful concepts:**
✦ Issue framing	✦ Civic capital (see Chapters One and Two)
✦ Choices based on core values	✦ *Meaningful Chaos* report on what factors get people involved and interested in public affairs
✦ Strategic facts	
✦ Putting expert information in public terms	
✦ Going back and forth from deliberation to reporting	✦ The master narrative
	✦ The "ten arts of democracy"
✦ Deliberation: tapping citizens for ideas (see Chapter Four)	✦ Deliberation: setting a deliberative rather than an adversarial tone (see Chapter Four)
✦ Spotlighting a public consensus (see Chapter Five)	✦ Acting as a facilitator and bulletin board for community action (see Chapter Five)
✦ Comlementary action (see Chapter Five)	

✦ PUSHING THE ENVELOPE

Citizens get a better sense that they're moving forward if they can see where they stand on a timeline (as they can during a presidential campaign, which always gathers momentum in the spring and ends in November). A paper could invent some kind of "You Are Here" feature for each public issue, showing readers what they've achieved so far and where they're going. This might be a simple box explaining "where we were five years ago on this issue." Or it might be a visual timeline running across the top or bottom of the page, with a red line moving gradually toward the goal, as in a fundraising drive. Daniel Yankelovich and John Immerwahr's sequential, seven-stage model of coming to public judgment in "The Rules of Public Engagement" (in the 1994 collection *Beyond the Beltway*) would make a workable template for the first half of such a timeline, leading up to the point of public action; it gives fairly objective criteria for where the public "is" on an issue over what may be years of deliberation. It's especially important for people to see progress during these talking phases, when there aren't big initiatives, new laws, or new government programs to point to; otherwise, they may press for any immediate solution (even a bad one), or else lose interest altogether.

✦

Part I: Telling the Facts

Pacing the actual choice-making side of a story is easy *if* a paper does its public listening well. At any point in time, people will see the top issues on their agenda in a certain collective light: In the last chapter, for example, the *Tallahassee Democrat's* poll respondents told it that "the growth problem" was fundamentally not about stopping or accelerating economic growth, but about giving citizens more control over which developments to approve and which to reject. The choice to be made was just how to do this. At the outset too officials, experts, and ordinary citizens will have a range of answers to an issue's central question: To look at Virginia's crime problem as profiled also in Chapter Two, getting tougher on criminals, putting more effort into rehabilitation, and catching youngsters before they turned to crime were all avenues the *Virginian-Pilot's* public wanted to explore (even if Governor George Allen did not). If a newspaper pays careful and open-minded attention, it can pick out the community's current "framing" of an issue just as those two papers did. The task then is to set the issue up in a way that allows the public to deal with it fruitfully. Perhaps the best way is to divide the problem into definite, distinct choices.

Clear alternatives, as in election campaigns and trials, make stories

---

IS CRACK COCAINE A MORAL ISSUE?

Chapter Two talked about grounding news coverage in the public's point of view. What's not so obvious is that every point of view is really an outgrowth of particular core values. Journalistic clichés such as "telling the story as it is" show, in Jay Rosen's eyes, that the press hasn't come to terms with this. Not recognizing how intimately their basic way of looking at a story—their "framing"—depends upon their own values, journalists often fail to notice when the public sees the issue through an entirely different lens. The "crack cocaine issue," for instance, is about reducing the flow of crack cocaine—what else *could*

(cont.)

IS CRACK COCAINE A MORAL ISSUE? *(cont.)*

it be about? In his lecture on "the power of framing" Rosen likes to provoke reporters by asking if it would make any less sense to treat crack as a business story:

On the city desk: The crack evil	On the business desk: The crack trade
"The most common way [to cover the crack story is to view it] from a police or crime perspective. Here you focus [your reporting] on the complaints of neighbors, the attempts by cops to shut the dealers down, the drug murders, the arrests and convictions, and so on. . . . The values of lawfulness and public safety create the story. Social values are being violated, and that's what makes the crack trade 'news.' "	"A very different way of telling the story would be to view [it] as a neighborhood business. Here you would describe how the business is run, the way decisions are made, the various interests involved, the relationship between this business and the rest of the neighborhood. . . . The people who sell crack are upholding certain social values even as they violate others. For example, they start at the bottom and rise through hard work. They have to be on time; they have to be organized. Most of all they learn about money."

Which is the "right" way to report about crack? Rosen argues that the facts themselves don't tell reporters which frame to use. Either the police frame or the business frame (or each of half a dozen more) has the power to produce good, solid journalism. Each presents the reader with a different set of truths. But each also grows out of a very different hierarchy of values. The first question a reporter ought to ask himself or herself when writing a story isn't "What goes in the lead?" but "What are the values that ought to guide this story?" Does this way of telling the story promote democratic talk, or work against it? Is this what's really at stake to John and Jane Doe, or not? A good reporter should be as intimately conversant with the public's values on crack (or any other issue) as with the crime and medical statistics, the police, or the leaders of the community. Any reporter who fails to see this isn't "telling the story as it is"; he or she is allowing the values for which the story is speaking to be chosen by default.

easier both to explain and to grapple with—a good thing. But as reporter E. J. Dionne argued in his popular book *Why Americans Hate Politics*, people are put off when public issues are reduced to alternatives that strike them as false: no abortion versus casual abortion, hate speech versus political correctness, or the president's confusing plan versus the Congress's foggy plan. The trick to marrying clear, vivid news coverage to multifaceted questions like abortion, questionable speech (or, say, City X's redevelopment) is to express them in terms of choices that strike people as authentic.

The Kettering Foundation suggests that ordinary Americans are drawn into public issues when they're discussed in terms of deeply held, if often conflicting "core values." (At least that's where to begin until some common ground on core values emerges.) Thus everyone, whether nominally pro-life or pro-choice, believes to varying degrees in the sanctity of fetal life, the individual rights of women, and a societal interest in how children are born and raised; each must work out a balancing act between these in his or her own heart, and work out another, more political balancing act together with others as a society (see box, below). When we recognize we have this in common, we can empathize with one another's struggle in ways that people on opposite sites of a picket line

---

THE CORE VALUES OF ABORTION

When participants in the National Issues Forums discussed abortion in 1990, they avoided the familiar either/or of "pro-choice" versus "pro-life," dividing the issue instead into the following three points of view. (The NIF network calls the points of view "choices"—as does this book—in order to stress the hard work people must do in weighing them against one another and accepting trade-offs among them; the Study Circles Resource Center, on the other hand, prefers the term "perspectives," to avoid the implication that people must choose one point of view in its totality and reject all the others. Unlike the choices in an election, the choices in discussions of core values are not mutually exclusive; they are analogous instead to primary colors—building blocks from which all other colors can be made. People are struggling to find some concrete set of laws, policies, and actions that combine the choices in a proportion with which they are morally, intellectually, and emotionally comfortable, not necessarily at one of the poles.)

(cont.)

THE CORE VALUES OF ABORTION *(cont.)*

Choice 1—Affirming Life: Moral Claims, Legal Sanctions

The unborn child, who is no less human than its mother, has an inalienable right to life. As important as other values are, they must give way to our obligation to protect human life.

From the issue book:

> "This does not mean that abortion is never permissible," writes psychologist Sidney Callahan. "But it does make clear how heavy a burden the argument for abortion must carry. It will have to justify killing one who is equal in dignity to each of us."

Choice 2—Abortion Rights: Personal Choices, Private Decisions

The central question is "Who decides?" Since a woman's freedom depends on her ability to control her reproductive process, women must have the right to legal abortion.

From the issue book:

> Stating the majority view, Justice Brennan declared, "If the right of privacy means anything, it is the right of the individual, married or not, to be free from government intrusions into matters so fundamentally affecting a person as the decision whether to bear or beget a child."

Choice 3—Respecting Differences: Private Lives and the Public Interest

When there is a compelling reason, women should be permitted to choose early abortion. At the same time, the community's interest in potential life must be given the attention it deserves.

From the issue book:

> "This is not," says John Silber, "the same as the pro-choice position. It is possible to believe that abortion ought to be legal without believing that it is an unconditional right, or even that it is morally justified in more than a limited number of cases." . . .
> "A political community in which abortion becomes common-place and a matter of ethical indifference, like appendectomy," Ronald Dworkin continues, "would certainly be a more callous and insensitive community."

Adapted with permission from *The Battle over Abortion*, an NIF issue book.

simply can't. Discussing abortion in terms of "murder" or "trying to dominate women" only polarizes and obscures what's really at stake. Grappling with core values *exposes* what's at stake—and makes eventual compromise look not like a wishy-washy act of expediency but a rational accommodation to the ambivalence within all of us.

In choices framed this way—as competing goods and deeply held beliefs—facts, figures, and the commentary of experts all belong in the background because they serve mostly as constraints to the debate. When it comes to health care, for example, Americans ought properly to spend their time weighing "core values" against each other, including universal access to care, cost constraint, and the preservation of medical excellence; health experts and econometricians can figuratively stand behind the people's chairs, telling them how much of one they must trade to get a little bit more of another. When the experts disagree, the people must take a considered gamble (just like CEOs and U.S. presidents take gambles) on which of their advisers is right. But even here, the debate over facts is important only insofar as it helps move along the debate over values. To the extent citizens hold to this rule, when they eventually speak they will be able to set clear guidelines within which the experts and technicians, officeholders and community leaders can do their work.

This concept of choice, once you "get" it, is entirely straightforward. At least two national networks of discussion groups use it already: the study circles movement, on which the Pomfret, Conn., Study Circles Resource Center (SCRC) offers a wide range of material; and the more organized National Issues Forums (NIF), with an information office in Dayton, Ohio. The best way to learn may be to browse through a few NIF issue booklets on questions like criminal violence, poverty, debt, or immigration (the Kettering and Public Agenda foundations release three new booklets every year) or to participate in forums and study circles directly. Or, for an exploration of the theory behind the practice, you can read Daniel Yankelovich's *Coming to Public Judgment.* The actual shepherding of an issue from the ill-defined state in which it first appears in popular talk ("crime," "drugs," "schools") to a set of useful choices is a hard process the NIF network has managed to hone, from a dozen years' experience, into an easily learnable skill; it now teaches the skill at yearly regional public policy institutes and explains it in a step-by-step guide for community groups, called (appropriately enough) *Framing Issues.*[*] The sidebar at the end of this section recounts how a panel of Kettering associates—about the same size as a typical newspaper editorial board—managed in two hours to turn "the schools

---

[*]The Study Circles Resource Center covers some of the same material in its booklet *Guidelines for Creating Effective Study Circle Material.*

issue" into four citizen-oriented choices among values. There's no reason a newspaper staff can't do the same thing in similar time.

Although plenty of newspapers continue to base public journalism projects on the obvious, conventional alternatives (e.g., Candidate X vs. Candidate Y; yes/no for a referendum; white residents near a city park vs. black cruisers playing their radios) or have dispensed with alternatives altogether (e.g., What should we do with our city?), a growing number are using value-based alternatives to good result. The *Dayton Daily News* (see box, below) and the Pottsville (Pa.) *Republican* have reprinted NIF issue books either in whole or in part and sponsored city-wide series of forums based on their choices. The Minneapolis–St. Paul *Star Tribune* made both NIF and SCRC discussion guides available to participants in its "Minnesota's Talking" roundtables. Although no paper so far has framed a major issue on the NIF model from scratch, the *Wichita Eagle* took a few giant steps in that direction during its 1992 "People Project." As part of eight-plus full pages of step-by-step discussion on (once again) the health care issue, the *Eagle* devoted two-thirds of a page to a box entitled "Where Are You Coming From?" in which the core values idea was explained and divisive areas like access to care, cost control, prolonging life, and the role of government in health care were broken down into the personal values that lay behind them. Readers were encouraged to think through their own feelings on the various viewpoints. This fell short of the Kettering approach only in not going on to cluster the values into three or four coherent policy choices, and then to concentrate future news coverage on the pros and cons of each choice. (The *Eagle* also drew out core values in "People Project" coverage of crime and education.)

Newspapers that purport to tell the public how it views a particular issue and what its choices should be, of course, face the same credibility problem as papers like the *Cape Cod Times* and the Tallahassee *Democrat* that purport to name the public's agenda, and they have an opportunity to solve it the same way: They can make their framing of a public issue tentative and invite the public to comment upon and improve it.

✦ PUSHING THE ENVELOPE

1. The Norfolk *Virginian-Pilot* identified the core values and choices in a race-charged land rezoning controversy simply by asking four proponents and four opponents of the rezoning "What brought each of you to take such a personal interest in this issue?" The answers quickly showed that neighborhood overload and city council high-handedness played at least as important a role in the fight as racism. Newspapers could make the *Virginian-Pilot*'s question a standard starting point for coverage.

THE *DAYTON DAILY NEWS*

The Kettering Foundation sits a few minutes' drive from downtown Dayton. Early in 1994 its issue-framing experts were completing a new National Issues Forum discussion guide, *What Should Be Done about Juvenile Violence?* while editors at the *Daily News* were looking for a model public journalism project on some problem of abiding local interest. A collaboration seemed only natural. So, then-metro editor Martha Steffens and her team started meeting with Keith Melville of NIF to hammer out a year long project eventually called "Kids in Chaos."

At first the journalists had intended to frame the issue independently—"journalistically"—but their own rough draft was so close to the NIF guide's that for simplicity's sake they adopted the NIF framing as it stood. Melville and his colleagues had turned up three clusters of "core values" in Americans' thinking about teen crime: (1) society should punish it more toughly; (2) family, schools, and media should teach less confused standards of right and wrong; and (3) juvenile crime is almost inevitable if social and economic root causes aren't better addressed. The series—at least initially—would focus on these.

On April 17, the *Daily News* announced in a front-page editorial that it would give a free pizza to any group that would talk about teen violence and send its comments back to the paper. (This idea was frankly stolen from the *Spokane Spokesman-Review*.) It would send participants both a coupon and a packet of thought-provoking questions based on the three NIF choices. More than 300 groups comprising 2,000 citizens responded.

The kickoff editorial also laid out the timetable for all that was going to follow: Ideas from the roundtables would be published in mid-May. Soon afterwards 130 experts on juvenile violence would convene to look them over and talk about ways to approach the problem. Stories would follow reporting on kids who had been either victims or perpetrators of violence, and on civic groups that had rescued teens from drugs or crime. The left and right page margins would be filled with statistics, pledges from citizens, laundry lists of suggested actions, and substantial ideas for reducing teen violence by everyone from parents and police to third-graders. Such food-for-thought coverage would remain high through September, when the paper would publish the NIF discussion guide in full and cosponsor community forums (eventually 34 of them) at which large, mixed

(cont.)

2. Papers like the *Daily News* and the *Eagle* are moving gradually toward framing issues right in the newsroom, but a newspaper could just as well set up a community-wide forum explicitly for framing a public agenda issue. Or, a television partner could broadcast a model issue-framing session while the paper provided kits to guide smaller, local or backyard discussion groups through the process. Given the popularity of agenda-setting forums, pizza parties, and community roundtables, there's no reason to think a framing forum wouldn't be popular too.

3. Often a creative presentation of a problem can prime the pump for framing it as an issue. The *Charlotte Observer* kicked off its neighborhoods project (see box in Chapter Five) with a unique crime poll. Instead of surveying a representative sample of Charlotte as a whole about the causes and cures for crime, it surveyed 401 residents of the hardest hit neighborhoods. These were the people most affected by crime, and so the most expert about it as well. The news package included features on each of the separate courses of action the respondents suggested to combat the problem ("Add police, improve courts," "Curb drug abuse," "Get neigh-

---

THE *DAYTON DAILY NEWS* (cont.)

groups of people could discuss the three choices systematically. Kettering would train volunteers to moderate the forums. AT&T, the Crime Prevention Association, and Wright State University would sponsor the experts' meeting. TV and radio would cover the roundtables. The United Way would help organize the forums. From the start, Steffens and editor Max Jennings cannily ensured that the project was going to be an effort of the entire city and not just of the *Daily News*.

Two thousand people eventually participated in the September and October forums, while many more contacted the paper to offer tips and stories or else joined one of the dozen-or-so new antiviolence projects that arose in the city. While all the dialogue didn't produce a specific policy on teen crime, it did narrow the problem in definite ways. Men and women at several forums insisted that the effect of TV and music violence was overblown; one forum flatly refused to waste time on it. People were almost always willing to pay higher taxes if it would help their kids, but overwhelmingly they talked about private responsibility rather than public policy. The paper quoted a junior high principal saying the problem wasn't kids in chaos but families in chaos. "Boy, did that resonate with people," Steffens says. "'Man, was he right!' people told me." Hence when the *Daily News* resumed the project in 1995 it had a new title and emphasis: "Fixing Our Families."

bors involved," and so on), incorporating ideas, direct quotes, detailed poll statistics, and other facts and figures of interest. Although the *Observer* didn't go on to frame the crime issue—the project went straight to action instead—the poll got readers thinking about crime in a comprehensive, focused way.

✦

The sidebar below insists that "the most useful framing for an issue is the one that takes the views of every segment of the community into account," but that's a mandate journalists are bound to misinterpret. "Segments of the community" does not mean liberals and conservatives, nor blacks and whites and Asians, nor rich and poor, nor men and women; there are no usual suspects when it comes to a community's constituent parts, because diversity is entirely particular to the issue at hand. There is no "black" viewpoint on affirmative action (just ask Shelby Steele), no "women's" viewpoint on pornography (just ask Camille Paglia), no "conservative" viewpoint on gays in the military (just ask Barry Goldwater). A public newspaper seeking to canvass its community's views has to ask itself at the outset: "What are the segments of the community *when it comes to this issue?*" "How many different takes on this issue do we get when we go out on the street, or read through the letters to the editor?" "Who are the stakeholders here?" "Who's most affected by the issue, and who does most of the affecting?" Here are a few practices that may make this easier:

4. Stage conversations among the paper's staff, as the *New Orleans Times-Picayune* did in the leadup to its race relations project (see "Civic capital in the newsroom," below). When journalists see how divided their peers can be concerning an issue, it gives them a small inkling of how divided the public may be and where the divisions may lie. This will leave reporters better prepared (i.e., more open-minded) when they listen to the public.

5. To build on the *Wichita Eagle's* idea, run a "Where Are We Coming From?" box at the outset of issue framing, in which the paper enumerates the whole gamut of basic viewpoints or interests known to *it* on the issue. At the end it asks readers, "Are you here? If you don't see yourself in this box, phone or write to let us know."

✦ SIDEBAR: A SHORT COURSE IN ISSUE FRAMING

Kettering Foundation president David Mathews writes in *Politics for People* that "in a rush to solutions, it is easy to overlook the way an issue is framed. But the way a problem is framed almost predetermines the kind of solution we will find and whether there will

✦ be any shared sense of purpose. It also affects who will be drawn to solving the problem and the amount of public will that will be generated." His point extends not just to the choices people are asked to grapple with (the "issue framing"), but right down to what the problem is called (the "problem naming"). Does the United States have a *welfare* problem or a *poverty* problem? The first name is not only narrower, but seems to many people to imply that the poor are at fault. Does the country need to improve its *schools* (in which case, only parents and teachers need be concerned) or its whole way of *raising children* (in which case even childless couples and employers may have a role)? This seems like semantics only until you come up against some of the thornier issues. Were the Los Angeles riots a matter of law and order, or of social injustice? And how do you set up the discussion if you want people on both sides of that divide to take part?

Kettering freely admits that framing and naming is an art, but it has worked very hard to practice the art systematically. Its guiding principle is that the most useful framing for an issue is the one that takes the views of every segment of the community into account: The name must be agreeable to all, and the choices must encompass everybody's favored solutions. Coming up with such a framing in everyday practice requires a small, diverse group of citizens and community leaders (though no more diverse than an editorial board with community members invited) and information culled from broader public listening to keep the panel honest. What follows are the minutes of one issue-framing exercise that took place in Dayton, Ohio, in May 1994. Eight men and women—teachers, journalists, and foundation officers— were trying to name and frame how Americans wanted to talk about "schools":

Step One: The Panel Studied Its Public Listening.

In preparation for a proposed National Issues Forum book on "the schools issue," Kettering had commissioned the Harwood Group to conduct focus group research into "How citizens view education"; since March 1993 Harwood had held lengthy discussions with six panels, pausing intermittently to rethink its approach. Its principal conclusion was that people are worried about declining schools but see them as part of a much larger problem. Before trying to define that problem, the framers read through Harwood's preliminary report, which included extensive quotations from ordinary Americans.

✦ Step Two: It Asked Itself, "What Do People Say Is Causing the Problem?"

Drawing partly on the report, but also on their wider experience and personal feelings, the panelists rattled off 22 diverse ways in which Americans describe the roots of "the education problem." (On this occasion, they described the causes behind the problem, but in other issue-framing sessions they usually describe the problem itself.) A designated moderator—one of the eight—prodded the others to clarify and distinguish the descriptions. Toward the end, he also asked them to consider what viewpoints, if any, weren't yet represented on the list. Here then was a first list of possible takes on the "education problem":

1. People don't value children.
2. Too much pressure on everyone prevents education from succeeding.
3. The kids themselves have bad attitudes.
4. No one accepts responsibility; everyone blames someone else.
5. There isn't enough communal (person-to-person) support.
6. There isn't enough societal (national) support.
7. Funding is inadequate.
8. Nobody acts, because they don't trust others to fulfill their responsibilities.
9. People worry they'll get in trouble if they help or discipline other people's children.
10. Adults fear kids.
11. There's a breakdown in morals, discipline, and so on.
12. Most people feel responsible only for themselves.
13. Educators aren't leading.
14. People don't see a way to help.
15. School employees put themselves first and kids second.
16. People want the best for their own kids, but don't care about other people's kids.
17. Education experts won't listen to nonexperts.
18. People have left everything to professionals.
19. Rigid teacher contracts have resulted in a decline in professionalism.
20. People rely more and more on formal rules (for settling issues at school, etc.), which makes it harder and more time-consuming to do what's right for kids.
21. A general lack of social trust leads to more formal rules.
22. Violence and conflict are inevitable because schools and

✦ other institutions are designed to reinforce class and race
differences.

Step Three: It Made a Second List of the Emotions, Values, and First Causes "Behind" Those Descriptions.

The panel members were asked next to work through their first
list item by item and come up with motivating factors (presented
here in no particular order). The assignment was intentionally
vague in order to elicit as diverse a set of moral and practical
"core values" as possible. What ultimately prompts Americans
to see the education problem as they do—to consider it important, troubling, or worth their attention; or to suggest the causes
they do—includes:

1. Respect for children.
2. Valuing the future (both the children's own and society's).
3. The desire for personal security.
4. A conviction that kids should be happy and joyful.
5. Fear of the consequences of acting.
6. Sadness coming out of pessimism.
7. The desire to be connected, to be involved.
8. The desire to do good.
9. Anger at a lack of respect for ordinary people.
10. Lack of trust; the conviction that others are selfish.
11. A belief that, historically, informal rules (in schools, in society)
    have been unfair.
12. A need for certainty and order.
13. Democratic ideals.
14. A sense of fairness.
15. Valuing a "balanced life."

Step Four: It Made a Third List of Pragmatic Steps.

Here the panel looked for actions that would work to rectify one
or more of the causes or allow people to act upon one or more of
the core values. Drawing once again on both the Harwood Group
interviews and personal experience, it settled on 13 ideas. Ordinary
citizens, social groups or governments could:

1. Provide safe opportunities for adults to interact with kids, for
   example, at churches, in schools, and in neighborhoods. En-

✦   courage mixed-age groups. These groups shouldn't isolate teenagers and shouldn't let them isolate themselves.

2. Innovate in daycare. Work out ways for neighbors to watch each other's kids. Encourage parents to help at school, for example, with security.

3. Create institutional incentives for parents to take time with kids (e.g., paid or unpaid parental leave).

4. Create new community programs (e.g., neighborhood kid watches).

5. Offer parenting classes. Found a Parents Anonymous.

6. Provide more after-school activities.

7. Build visible community coalitions.

8. Enlist the media in presenting a more balanced view of the state of schools and education (to counter exaggerated fears).

9. Start a structured public dialogue about education.

10. Get parents, teachers, and administrators together to discuss how to make school rules more flexible.

11. Rebuild civic trust in small chunks (i.e., school by school, or in face-to-face collaborations on specific issues).

12. Train education professionals to show greater respect for public input.

13. Create opportunities for mutual responsibility between experts and laypeople.

Step Five: First Working Individually, Then Together in Pairs or Threesomes, and Finally as a Group, the Panelists Consolidated the Three Lists into a Comprehensive Vision of the Problem.

Hopefully, there are enough general patterns to people's description of the problem, beliefs about its causes, or favored solutions that the myriad views of rich and poor, childless and childrearing, old and young, teachers and laypeople, majority and minority can be reduced somehow to three or four coherent, distinct, yet comprehensive points of view: the "choices" on the "schools" issue. (If this can't be done, then citizens don't even agree enough to hold a sensible conversation.) This part of the exercise is purely intuitive. One group identified three historic trends behind the problem, while a second saw half a dozen abstract connections between the solutions. In the full-panel discussion, however, the members agreed that the third group had come closest to a way of looking at the problem that was at once coherent, expressive of people's

✦ "conflicts and ambivalences," and all-inclusive. It had seen that four different types of actors were held responsible for education problems, and the same four were named as part of distinct attempts at a solution. This group's alternative orientations to the education problem were:

Choice 1: American institutions need to value kids more than they do.

Choice 2: Neighbors and communities need to collaborate more in raising kids.

Choice 3: Parents, teachers, and students need to take more personal responsibility.

Choice 4: I (whoever I might be) need to take more personal responsibility.

Step Six: The Panelists Named the Problem.

In the end, the group at Dayton couldn't agree on a name for the "education problem," though it noted some things an appropriate name would have to convey, for instance, that the problem Americans really worry about is bigger than schools, yet not as big as "children's issues" in their entirety. (Citizens in the Harwood study still saw such things as child abuse and teaching values in the home as separate issues from education.) The name that came closest to winning the group's approval (but was still judged to be too broad) was "Raising kids in America: What are we doing wrong?"

What's Newsworthy?

Once an issue from the public agenda is framed as a set of choices, the main task of the public journalist is to help people decide which choice (or set of trade-offs among choices) they want. In this, it doesn't matter if the choices are framed according to the Kettering Foundation's "core values" model, or whether they are different electoral candidates, or pro- and anti- sides in an old, divisive debate like abortion or free speech. The information newspapers ought to provide is that set of facts, arguments, statistics, interpretations, personal anecdotes, and comparisons that will enable readers to form their opinions and—according to Daniel Yankelovich's definition of high-quality public judgment—accept responsibility for the consequences of those opinions. Kettering calls this type of information "strategic facts": the facts that can sway judgment. Everything else is background, trivia, or irrelevant.

To distinguish strategic facts from just plain old, traditionally newsworthy facts, take a look at the *Charlotte Observer*'s coverage of the 1992 presidential and senatorial election campaigns. This was the year of Gennifer Flowers; Ross Perot's conspiracy story about his daughter's wedding; celebrity tacticians like James Carville, Mary Matalin, and Ed Rollins; and almost certainly more opinion polls than had ever been conducted in any previous election. These were all over most newspapers' front sections—yet they were practically invisible in the *Observer*.

That year, the editors relied on ordinary North Carolinians themselves (through the paper's precampaign agenda survey and 500-member citizens' panel) to tell them what they needed to know. People told them to stick to a specific list of issues, to candidate profiles, and to reader questions, which the *Observer* did. In one senatorial race, it actually forced a candidate who did not wish to discuss the environment until late in the campaign to discuss it immediately—because this was an area voters felt might swing them in the election.

The question "What will help the community come to public judgment?" doesn't exclusively mean letting readers direct a paper's coverage; it has led to other sorts of answers in other cases. In the *Observer*'s coverage of the dispute over closing Charlotte's Freedom Park (told in more detail in Chapter Four) the issue was a conflict between white residents living near the park and black youths cruising through it in their cars. The paper printed (as many papers would) about a dozen long verbatim statements from the interested parties—white residents, black cruisers, and community leaders—but atypically it accepted only statements that suggested areas of common ground. "We choose not to focus our coverage on conflict, but on possible solutions," wrote editor Richard Oppel in his introductory note. "We sought to draw out the best ideas. What are the problems? What should be done?" Accusations weren't strategic facts; they wouldn't help the *Observer*'s readers figure out what to do. Ideas for concrete action would.

In the Portland *Oregonian*'s lead-up to a referendum on an education sales tax, the strategic facts were boxed answers, often on the front page, to reader questions about what the tax proposal meant and how the referendum worked. For the *Detroit Free Press*'s "Children First" campaign—as much oriented to individual citizens' responses as to government action—strategic facts have included lists of resource agencies and direct-action alternatives parents can choose to better protect their children. Choosing which facts to tell readers means knowing intimately what a particular community is trying to decide, when, and how.

Just how important it is to separate the strategic facts from the chaff—to print only those things that will help citizens make the decisions they face *right now*—becomes immediately apparent when you consider information overload. A newspaper can get its facts right and yet present them in a way that's not coherent or sensitive enough to help readers through their months or years of learning about, deliberating over, and coming to judgment on a public agenda issue. It can swamp *today's* discussion of health care priorities with *tomorrow's* strategic facts on the Clinton plan versus the Cooper plan. In fact, this is what usually happens.

An insightful (though jargon-laden) book in this regard is political scientist Doris Graber's *Processing the News: How People Tame the Information Tide*. Intensively studying a score of Evanston, Ill., residents through much of 1976, and checking what she learned against a larger sample from several states, Graber concluded that Americans—realistically aware that they can't absorb *all* the news information they're exposed to—blithely ignore about two-thirds of it. Of the remainder, they forget half the news stories partially and a quarter of them entirely within a matter of days, retaining only a rough impression of what the stories meant. ("In such cases," Graber writes, "media facts apparently have been converted into politically significant feelings and attitudes, and the facts themselves forgotten.") What's most disturbing is that the *way* people cut through the mass of information is largely random. Boring headlines, a busy day, a confusing presentation, the fact that friends are talking about a different event—any of these things can make people skip past a story (and once they have skipped it, they will rarely go back). They try to be rational, but considering the sheer volume of information their busy lives force them to ignore, they find it very hard. As a consequence they have trouble keeping track of and deliberating about complex issues over time. In fact, they tend to be intensely conservative, selectively forgetting facts that contradict the way they tend to think about (say) the Congress, immigration, or Candidate X because of the hard work involved in changing the existing "pictures in their heads."

What they need is some sort of framework for presenting the news that takes both the information tide and the long haul into account. Pacing is the real secret; knowing how a story will play itself out in the long haul paradoxically frees a paper to concentrate just on what's important today. Much more will be said about this below, under "Telling the Narrative," but papers can also ease the information problem just by thinking differently about reporting facts. Graber found, for example, that people remember stories much better than facts or statistics; the Columbia, S.C., *State*, has therefore centered its "To Raise a

Child" series on the life stories of child "heroes" who escaped from poor or violent backgrounds and the adult "heroes" who helped them. She also found that repeating facts was essential for people to catch those they had missed and to become confident about their judgments; an increasing number of papers offer reprints, on-line backgrounders, monthly summary pages, or periodic reexaminations of major stories. And as to combating the sheer number of strategic facts, the *Philadelphia Inquirer* in "America: What Went Wrong?" and Maine's Portland Newspapers in several "expert reporting" series have given reporters unusually long deadlines to master the complexities of a huge issue, judge between conflicting expert opinions, and then boil them down into relatively simple, coherent pieces. From public journalism's viewpoint, the *Inquirer* failed in not keeping a closer eye on what decisions Americans at that moment had to make; but the idea itself was magnificent. Where busy people can't possibly sort through all the twists and turns and contradictions of a story, less truly *is* more.

✦ PUSHING THE ENVELOPE

1. According to writers such as Doris Graber, people often miss essential parts of a story as it develops and thus lose the ability (and interest) to follow it over time. One of the simplest ideas public newspapers are talking about now is to run a month-end box summarizing everything that's appeared that month on each public agenda issue.

2. Another way to chip at information overload would be to publish boxes of "key facts" and "key questions" about an issue as often as possible, and explicitly tie news stories (through a logo or some other device) to the particular facts or questions they do the most to illuminate. (Key questions and facts—to keep the paper neutral—should probably be those most prominently heard in the paper's public listening.) Assignment editors could seek out stories that show the key facts and questions in a new light, or solicit reactions to them, or reinforce them in some other way. In pedagogy, this is sometimes called a "basic skills" approach. You can't expect people to retain all the details on an issue, but you can keep the most important ones before them through creative repetition.

3. Yankelovich and Immerwahr's "Rules of Public Engagement" (see "Pushing the Envelope," p. 57) has something to say about choosing strategic facts too. At each of the seven stages through which Americans come to public judgment, they are trying to make different *classes* of decisions, and so they need different *kinds* of facts in order to succeed. For example, once Americans have decided that a problem is urgent (in response, perhaps, to horror stories or dire warnings in the media), they respond with warmth and attention to broad alternative views of how it should be solved. Thus the strange popular interest in talking about "managed care," "the Canadian plan," and "malpractice reform" when they were first brought into 1992's health care debate. Citizens may embrace one or another alternative with ready enthusiasm. Only then— as they come to see the potholes and shopwear in each proposal—do they admit that core values are in conflict and respond to information that brings the conflicts into high relief.

The Twin Roles of Experts and Ordinary People

So how does a journalist decide what strategic facts to report today? Sooner or later it becomes apparent that there's a regular back-and-forth rhythm to talking well about public problems. Practically speaking, democracy is rarely if ever a matter of making one choice, and almost always a matter of narrowing in on a decision one step at a time. At first people work through the conflicting core values Kettering talks about; then they move on to more specific questions of detail, and then to still more specific questions (if the issue is important enough to give them the patience). Eventually the public gets tired of talking, by which time (one hopes) governments, businesses, schools, churches, and ordinary people have received enough guidance that they can tailor their actions to what "the community" wants them to do. To take up health care reform again, from 1992 to 1994 newspapers bombarded citizens with information on the broadest "costs and options" for health care, until people gradually came to the conclusion that they'd love to make coverage universal if they could only swallow the price, but that letting government manage the insurance system was a risk they didn't want to take. Had things gone as they should have, newspapers ought then to have bombarded citizens with information on the "costs and options" of reining in premiums and extending coverage by more palatable means, until people made some choices among those trade-offs and thus reframed the problem more narrowly. Then the press would have told them the new "costs and options," and they would have chipped away at the problem still more, and so on, back and forth. Eventually citizens would have made enough choices to declare victory and let the actors in Washington and elsewhere go out and take action.

This cycle—from costs and options to reframing the question, costs and options to reframing (or put differently: from listening to talking it over, listening to talking it over)—is the natural cycle of "telling the facts." Generalizing grossly, costs and options are the province of economists, doctors, academics, and other experts; framing is the province of citizens, so a public newspaper will find the day's story sometimes in the voices of experts, sometimes in those of citizens, depending on where a public issue stands at any particular time. Has the paper answered all the basic questions citizens are asking about the problem as they see it right now? Then it's probably time to start holding forums where they can make choices, and stitching the conversation together through the news pages. Does public listening show that people have found new common ground? Then it's probably time to get the experts talking about the issues on which they're still apart.

Speaking more carefully, a good reporter ought to clearly understand what you need to know from the public that you can't know from anybody else, and what you need to know from experts that you can't know from anybody else. Reporting should grow directly out of this knowledge.

Often, for example, "costs and options" can come from ordinary people. Many newspapers treat the printing of citizen voices as a kind of welfare system for the news-space-impoverished—a service aimed much more at good community relations than at forwarding the debate on public issues—but public journalists think differently. They're perfectly comfortable drawing on citizens for ideas. The *Charlotte Observer* was drawing on citizens for "costs and options" when it asked residents and cruisers to suggest solutions to the Freedom Park standoff. On its "Kids in Chaos" pages the *Dayton Daily News* treated ideas on reducing violence from parents, teachers, and students to as much space and respect as ideas from experts. Most dramatic of all, the Bergen County *Record* brought the New Jersey state treasurer together with ordinary citizens who had agreed to study the state budget for a week, and in five hours they found $570 million in substantive cuts, without (in the editor's eyes) being insensitive to any unrepresented constituents (see box, below). Conversely, experts can often provide important input on the framing of a question: In the example used already, economists would tell a newspaper's readers right off the bat that "how Washington can fix the economy" is the wrong question to talk about in a global marketplace. The test of anyone's contribution is "Does it keep the conversation honest? Will it help us get to a solution that will work?"

The hardest task may be to set up a newspaper conversation in which experts and citizens really talk with each other in a constructive way—contribute each according to their abilities, in a lingua franca all of them can understand. That this doesn't happen today is primarily the fault of experts and journalists who think that speaking to ordinary people's questions, in common language, is synonymous with dumbing-down. The suspicion that citizens can't evaluate technical ideas, let alone be a source of them, runs very deep.

THE BERGEN COUNTY *RECORD*

"Could you do a better job of cutting the fat out of state government than the bureaucrats in Trenton? You might be one of a dozen *Record* readers to meet with state treasurer Samuel Crane and come up with $600 million in suggested cuts in the $15 billion state budget."

The *Record* threw its readers this challenge on May 12, 1992, and overnight nearly 100 phoned the paper's hotline to leave their names, hometowns, ages, occupations, and best budget-cutting ideas. From those, reporter Mary Amoroso and colleagues quickly selected eight whose ideas seemed interesting and who roughly represented the demographic variety of Bergen and Passaic counties: a union shop steward, a productivity consultant, a retired bookkeeper, a sales representative for New Jersey Bell, a college junior, a cable TV ad manager, a surveyor, and a factory manager. The treasurer met with them for an initial two hours to explain the basic mechanics of the budget, then each took a copy of the whole document home and studied it for a week. On May 26, they met for two and a half hours more to negotiate their common program.

Amoroso says that, though there was "a requisite period of venting because people felt misunderstood," the citizens were excited by the opportunity and moved on quickly to an intelligent weighing of their options. They would suggest a specific cut or innovation, and treasurer Crane would tell them why this would or wouldn't save money and estimate how much. Although many of their proposals came straight out of the day's news (particularly from Republican critics of Governor Florio), a few were entirely original: For example, changing homeowner rebates into tax credits would save $2 million in check-writing costs, and cutting back on state-rented office space would save $20 million. What's more, the citizens showed a decidedly independent streak, refusing to make cuts affecting seniors and education that Republicans were touting quite loudly.

By the end, the eight panelists had identified $567.5 million in cuts. Crane (who had agreed to participate, Amoroso feels, out of a sense of adventure and public relations) went away impressed. He was surprised that the group hadn't cut funding for the arts, higher education, or New Jersey public TV. "I didn't hear a lot about 'Let's cut drug treatment and AIDS funding.' "

Amoroso says, "State governors and treasurers are worked on by a whole lot of other groups than citizens. But because we printed [what the citizens had to say], I think that gave [them] impact."

Daniel Yankelovich devotes two chapters in the middle of *Coming to Public Judgment* to the ways in which working through the issues can be stopped in its tracks by the elitism, technical jargon, abstruse arguments, and sheer turf-consciousness of experts. The citizens interviewed for the Kettering report *Meaningful Chaos* and for *Processing the News* amply confirm this, saying that they lose interest the moment politicians, economists, arms control experts, lawyers, doctors, and professors begin to fog up an issue. And Yankelovich argues that fogging is indeed what these experts often do:

> The economists who define the [competitiveness] problem in terms of yen/dollar exchange ratios are doing two things simultaneously: They are making both an intellectual and a turf-related claim. . . . "Hands off," they are saying, "this is our game." . . . It would never occur to them to regard average Americans as intellectual equals who approach the problem from a different perspective, just as their fellow experts [in other fields] do.

What makes things worse is that it wouldn't occur to many journalists either. Editors who have tried to make expert information reader-friendly say they often find themselves fighting their own staffs, who enjoy the prestige of being able to speak the same language as their sources. For decades, arms control reporters, as much as arms control experts, liked the power that came with saying, "This is our game." They shared the assumption that arms control questions couldn't be discussed responsibly except in terms of "throw weights" and "MiRVs"—that anything else would be pandering, oversimplification, or demagoguery.

Of course this isn't true now and never was. The truly strategic facts about an issue can usually be explained in short order so that any thoughtful person can understand them; in experiments with citizen panels, Public Agenda found that just two hours of education and discussion could do the trick when it came to complex issues like solid waste disposal and global warming. Besides this, technical issues are often irrelevant. What Public Agenda's global-warming panelists haggled over in the end weren't the details of chemical equations, but three questions of common sense: Does a consensus of scientists think global warming is a threat? If there isn't a consensus, do we want to take a chance on being wrong? And how much will the corrective actions harm our economy or cramp our life style? Any president, senator, or *Washington Post* columnist would have arrived sooner or later at exactly the same point. It's clear now thanks to 20/20 hindsight that even on arms control, the deciding question was always "Can we trust the Russians?," not anything like "How does their throw weight compare to ours?"

In some public debates citizens, precisely *because* they have no expertise, can even identify the *technical issues* more acutely than many experts. Yankelovich recalls that when global competition became a major issue a few years ago, economists and trade officials invariably talked about exchange rates, retraining, labor market skills, and other clearly "economic" variables; Americans at large talked about drug use in the schools, Wall Streeters out for a quick buck, the short-term outlook of business, and workers doing less than their best on the job. Both types of factors were important, but in any fair analysis—looking back—the public's value-based factors were probably more important than the technical, parochial factors favored by the experts. It isn't simply a Pollyannaish assumption on the part of public journalism that the public has intellectual weight to contribute to discussions of complex issues. It's a fact.

Journalists somehow need to shift discussion of public issues from expert-speak into everyday language, from the economist's or lawyer's turf onto the home turf shared by all citizens. Public newspapers have come up with at least a few tips for making this so:

Find the Public's Starting Point

Citizens usually have a preliminary idea of where an issue (like competitiveness) stands and how it ought to be discussed. Once again, it often centers on an ambivalence over values rather than around technical issues. Make that the basis for coverage; have experts explain their reasoning whenever they ask people to take other factors into account. The *Dayton Daily News* found the public's starting point on teen violence through its pizza party meetings, then made it the lens for talking with experts from then on. The *Charlotte Observer's* excellent 1992 election coverage is also a good model (although any example of carefully tuned public listening would serve as well). The *Observer* respected what its readership felt they had to know about the candidates, and started everything from there. (On issues for which editors feel they need some prelistening guidance, Project Vote Smart's periodically updated *Reporter's Source Book* contains a cheat-sheet of the national public's starting points on a number of issues.)

Refuse to Accept Jargon

Steve Smith, then managing editor of the *Wichita Eagle*, encouraged reporters during the 1990 and 1992 election campaigns to be more aggressive with their expert sources by refusing to leave a question behind until it was answered in ordinary language and addressed the specific concerns citizens had raised.

Make a List of Good Questions

Asking things in a slightly different way may help reduce jargon or move a discussion toward the public's point of view: "Can you put that in everyday language?" "How would someone in (another field) make that point?" "What moral (or value) issues are at stake in this problem?" "What would you say to someone who was most concerned about (something your public listening has shown the public to be concerned about)?" "What does the public have to make up its mind about here?" A list of archetypal questions such as these could be circulated among reporters as food for thought.

Don't Waste Much Space on Nonstrategic Facts

Often it's an overabundance of facts and figures that alienates readers most: Experts swamp them with petty details just like a corporation's legal team would swamp a class-action lawyer with files and records. Sometimes papers go at excruciating length into the conflicting views of experts ("X says North American free trade will produce jobs," "Y says it will cost jobs") when the sentence "Respected experts disagree" would give people all the information they can use. Sometimes sidelines of overriding interest to experts get plenty of coverage despite being irrelevant to the decision readers face; call this the Quemoy–Matsu syndrome, after the ultimately meaningless issue that dominated the Kennedy–Nixon debates. Filter.

Use a Physical Format that Puts Citizens in Charge

Sometimes just changing the way experts and citizens are linked up makes changes in reporting either obvious or moot. Once the *Virginian-Pilot* hit on the idea of treating political candidates as job candidates, the rest was clear: It printed resumés and track records, and judged the politicians' performance in the same sorts of ways citizens are evaluated on the job. The most fertile idea in the *Wisconsin State Journal's* mock grand juries and legislative panels turned out to be having citizens and lawmakers switch places, figuratively and literally. In on-camera sessions broadcast by local PBS and CBS affiliates, demographically selected citizens on the "grand jury" interrogated members of Congress and state officials about costs and options for issues at hand. Citizens sat above;

officials and experts sat below, at the witness table. By putting citizens in the driver's seat, the *State Journal* made sure that the issues would be discussed entirely in the public's terms.

✦ PUSHING THE ENVELOPE

1. Yankelovich argues that very often experts don't think the public has an intellectually respectable starting point on public issues. They don't know how to address an issue in the public's terms. Perhaps reporters could begin their expert interviews, before asking a single question, by explaining the public's take on the issue. Thus the reporter functions as a new kind of expert—an expert in representing the public's starting point—rather than imitating the technical expertise of a knowledgeable specialist.

2. In everyday conversation, people ask for explanations the moment they misunderstand one another. A newspaper could make the same habit public through a daily or weekly "I Just Don't Get It" page. Readers could send letters to the page spelling out which arguments, facts, or viewpoints on an issue they simply don't understand, despite the reporting that's been done in the paper. Citizens writing in might flag jargon or conclusions that don't make sense, or raise what seem to them like obvious questions no news story has addressed. Or reader A might insist that, in spite of real effort, he simply can't understand how letter writer B or the source quoted in yesterday's lead story could hold that viewpoint in good conscience. Equally important, experts and public officials might be invited to explain what *they* don't get about the *public's* take on an issue. The page editor could select those letters that either ask the most thoughtful questions or demonstrate the best-faith effort to understand the thing the writer just doesn't get; he or she would then seek out the response that seemed most constructive in each case—alert the news division, print a clearer explanation of the point at issue, or just leave a letter open for other letter writers to respond to. The editor might at some point publish a short guide on how to write a good, thoughtful "I Just Don't Get It" letter.

3. Conventional journalists underrate life experience as a source of expertise. At times the best sources about the deterrent effects of imprisonment may not be statisticians, but prisoners; the best sources about welfare may not be sociologists, but welfare recipients. (This isn't only because they may *know* facts the professionals don't, but because their attitudes, demeanor, and character are important facts in themselves: citizens make a lot of their judgments just by reading human beings.) Reporters can ask themselves when searching out expertise, "Whose behavior is at issue here?" and "Who is in a position to know

the answer to my question *directly?*" Isabel Wilkerson of the *New York Times* interviewed a support group of "welfare alumni" in Chicago to elicit their thoughts on welfare reform. They were not self-serving. The alumni, just like sociologists, politicians, and society at large, were divided on how much aid to give and what conditions to place on it, but they analyzed many lesser questions (such as the effect of prosecuting deadbeat dads) with a nuts-and-bolts authenticity that nobody before them had brought to the discussion. (They said prosecution simply wouldn't work; the men have no money, and they'd only take out their anger on the mothers and children. Much better to insist that the men *spend time* with their kids.)

4. While the *Wisconsin State Journal* invented a clever way to put citizens in charge of a story at the reporting end, it's equally important to put them in charge at the writing end—in other words, to make them the story's actors rather than its acted-upon. Institutional journalism tends to make Senators, police officers, and social workers the actors. Look even at journalism that relies heavily on quotations from "ordinary people" and you'll usually see that the quotations just set up a problem for experts and officials to solve. This isn't the way it has to be. *New York Newsday's* twice-weekly column "In the Subways" almost always begins either with New York commuters or with the busy, often overtaxed subway trains and subway stations they use every day. It chronicles their struggle to make the subway system work for them—which sometimes involves civil servants and politicians, but sometimes does not.

◆

Part II: Telling the Narrative

Maybe the biggest challenge in pursuing a story that unfolds over many years is keeping people's interest. Newspaper readers will inevitably let important stories go unread, miss information, skip public forums, be distracted by other things; it's unrealistic to assume that, just because in part of their life they wish to be good citizens, they'll take a few hours every day from work and family, say, to follow the dry evolution a congressional crime bill or to crib up on the mechanics of managed care. (Even journalists will do this kind of thing only if they're paid.) To be a burden citizens actually assume, democracy has to be either a fairly light or a very willing burden. So a public journalist has to learn how to tap the motivation people *do* have for as long as it takes to work through the more intellectual task of sorting alternatives, setting policy, and acting.

The focus group study *Meaningful Chaos: How People Form*

Relationships with Public Concerns makes the bold attempt to portray this civic motivation head-on. It identifies nine factors whose presence draws people to become more fully engaged in an issue, and whose absence drives them away (see box, below). Most of the truly successful public journalism efforts so far, even when unaware of the report, can be seen in retrospect to have directly tapped into one or more of the nine factors. People say, for instance, that they long for a greater sense that their own actions can make a difference (to which the *Detroit Free Press*'s "Children First" project responded by listing direct actions people could take to aid children, and the *Wichita Eagle*'s "People Project" by providing the names, phone numbers, and addresses of official agencies, volunteer groups, and the like for every issue on its agenda). People say they learn best from voices that ring true to them, even if these aren't the voices of officials or experts (following which papers such as the *Dayton Daily News* and the *Oklahoman*—see Chapter Two—cast an unusually wide net looking for "community leaders" to brainstorm approaches to teen crime and regional development). People say they can't address a public issue in fragments; they need history, breadth, completeness, and coherence (which accounts for the success of the *Philadelphia Inquirer*'s "America: What Went Wrong?" as a series *and* a book, and for the great response to, say, the breathtakingly comprehensive reporting on New Orleans race relations done by the *Times-Picayune*).

At least one paper, the Norfolk *Virginian-Pilot*, has tried systematically to embed all nine factors from *Meaningful Chaos* into its daily reporting—a fact already visible in its article on sentencing reform from Chapter Two. Reporter Tony Wharton went to Governor George Allen's town meeting consciously looking for the "connections" people drew among issues (such as sentencing, prevention, and rehabilitation) and the "room for ambivalence" they insisted upon (refusing to accept the governor's either-or statements about toughness and social programs). At one point his focus on the nine factors actually brought him up short. Tempted to stress that the citizens he'd spoken with disagreed with the governor, favoring the social programs he opposed, he realized this wouldn't sound "authentic" even to his own sources. They wanted tougher sentencing as much as the governor did; their agreements were at least as profound as their disagreements. So he included a paragraph saying this in just so many words. (For more on the *Virginian-Pilot*, see the box later in this chapter.) If they serve no other purpose, then, the nine points in *Meaningful Chaos* are good strings to tie around a reporter's finger—like "who, what, when, where, and why"—to keep him or her on track.

HOW PEOPLE GET DRAWN INTO PUBLIC LIFE

Meaningful Chaos highlights nine actors, institutions, or qualities of public discourse that help people to become active and impassioned about an issue:

Connections: People tend to enlarge, rather than narrow, their views of public concerns, making connections among ideas and topics that society tends to fragment.

Personal Context: People relate to concerns that "fit" with their personal context—not only their own self-interest, but that which is meaningful or imaginable to them in their lives.

Coherence: People want public discourse to tell the "whole story" on public concerns—with explanation, memory, and a sense of overview. They are seeking a deeper sense of understanding and meaning.

Room for Ambivalence: People resist polarization on public concerns, seeking instead room for ambivalence—a gray area in the public debate in which to question, discuss, test ideas, and gain confidence about their views.

Emotion: In attempting to make public life more "rational," we may often strip away emotions from public discourse, thereby draining the energy that is vital to people in forming and sustaining relationships with public concerns.

Authenticity: Information and individuals must "ring true" to people.

Sense of Possibilities: People are seeking a sense that action might occur on a public concern, and that they might play a personal role in it.

Catalysts: Everyday Americans, not just experts and elites, are key catalysts in helping people form relationships with public concerns.

Mediating Institutions: People need places to come together to talk and act on public concerns.

Adapted with permission from *Meaningful Chaos*.

The Story behind the Story

An even more powerful tool for public journalists draws on people's love of the dramatic. Why, for example, do so many people read campaign stories? In part for all the honorable civics book reasons, but beyond that, largely because the race for office is a great unfolding drama—the story of who will win—full of what ABC Sports used to call "the thrill of victory and the agony of defeat." Even the smallest page-12 short draws its interest and (what's more crucial for keeping a huge story coherent) its assigned place in people's thinking from this underlying plot. So, Bill Clinton smoked marijuana? Should I change my vote? How will his opponents react? What will the press do with the story? *Now* who will win? Americans have no trouble stripping campaign stories to their essential points because they understand what Jay Rosen calls the "master narrative" so well.

All stories that capture the public's abiding attention have a dramatic premise—a "story of . . ." or "master narrative"—inside them. During the final weeks of 1963, people could tune in and out of any news broadcast without confusion because everybody understood the context: What will we do now that John Kennedy is dead? How is Jackie holding up? What will Lyndon do differently? From mid-1994 onward, it was O. J. Simpson: Did he kill his ex-wife? Would a jury be willing to convict him? The Bible itself has a simple master narrative: humanity's creation, fall, and redemption. You do not have to read Leviticus to understand what's going on in Job, or to put it in its proper place. Once you know the premise, you can join the story at any time.

On the flip side, based on the evidence in Doris Graber's *Processing the News*, it's the news stories that don't tie obviously into a comprehensible and compelling drama that people skip, forget, or end up being confused by. They can't be absorbed as easily and so they're typically not absorbed at all.

Public journalism—always, in every case—has an extremely powerful built-in narrative to draw upon. As Rosen describes it: "The struggle to come to public judgment is a drama. It is an excellent drama. This is what all other public journalism stories are about. Will the community succeed or fail? Can Dayton, Ohio, come to grips with juvenile violence? We do not know. That's the drama." *Wichita Eagle* editor Davis Merritt took full advantage of this when he launched his paper's 1992 "People Project" with a front-page essay that read, "We have it within our reach to powerfully affect our surroundings and to rejuvenate the idea of collective problem-solving. That, in turn, can rebuild communities at all levels. But we must solve it ourselves.

Government can't do it. . . . At the end of [this project], we'll know an important thing about ourselves: whether we have the will, given the opportunity, to take responsibility for our lives and our community."

Such an introduction is not only a compelling hook, it also instantly organizes all the news coverage that's going to follow it: This week we'll listen to opponents of (say) capital punishment, next week to its proponents, so that the week after that we can deliberate, and the week after that we can see if we're able to struggle through to some common ground. *Why is yesterday's Supreme Court ruling important?* Because of the points it makes about bias in capital cases. *Why should this murder victim's story compel me?* Because (besides its intrinsic interest) it raises an issue we must all take account of in our decision on the death penalty. To the extent that a newspaper can tie its stories into deep narratives like this one, people will know exactly how to read it, what to retain, and what to forget.

Here are a few tips for establishing a master narrative:

+ Set it up loudly, clearly, and with dramatic flourish, as Davis Merritt did. ("People Project" reprints are available from the *Eagle*.) Make the process by which the community will come to public judgment explicit, and give it a timeline if it's at all appropriate (e.g., when there's an ongoing legislative review of the death penalty or a UN deadline for war in the Persian Gulf).
+ Always leave the story open, as the *Virginian-Pilot's* reporters learned to do in covering the Hall Place neighborhood. Never imply that the outcome of a community's working through is a sure thing—not only because this adds to the story's drama, but also because, in fact, the outcome never *is* sure.
+ Use logos to tie stories in. The logo can be as simple as a generic shield saying "Coming to Judgment on [Issue X]." The stories don't even have to be principally about Issue X. One group of reporters has suggested a new type of analysis sidebar nicknamed "What's the Real Story Here?" in which a breaking news story would be milked for its links to a master narrative. (A Tallahassee reporter wanted to do this when civic groups tried to pull *Heather Has Two Mommies*, a book about children with gay parents, from a public library. The story warranted its own coverage; but the *real* story, she suggested, was a more fundamental conflict over homosexuality and the extent or limits of tolerance.)
+ Flag progress. Let people know when the community has achieved something or moved on to a new stage in the master narrative. The *Akron Beacon Journal*, for example, in its Pulitzer-Prize–winning racism project, moved step by step from an

examination of the issue in early 1993 to its "Coming Together" initiative later in the year. It then solicited citizen pledges to "do all I can in 1994 to improve race relations," printing 22,000 of them that January, and can in future follow up on what citizens have actually done.

✦ Always let people know what's going to happen next, as the *Tallahassee Democrat* has done in its agenda project and the *Dayton Daily News* in its work on teen violence. Not only will the anticipation make readers more attentive, but the paper's commitment to the story will help convince them that participation is worth their time.

✦ PUSHING THE ENVELOPE

1. So far editors have mostly relied either on intuition or on studies like *Meaningful Chaos* to tell them how to draw readers into the narrative. It would be possible, however, to survey readers explicitly for what would help them come to judgment, on everything from story content to graphics and format. As this book stresses throughout, there's no reason to guess what readers' needs are when it's possible to simply ask them.

2. Good retrospective reporting ("Twenty Years Ago in Tucson") might give citizens a sense that coming to public judgment is a tradition to which they already belong; the idea is to create a canon of "Great Moments in Public Judgment." Perhaps the editor could invite local historians or community leaders to write about crises that the city has struggled with in the past. Reporters could interview participants to find out why the effort worked or failed *then*. (The mid-1990s has seen handfuls of documentaries that review the civil rights movement in this way.) Alternatively, the paper could chronicle how other towns, cities, or nations worked through a major problem. Beyond their inspirational value, such reports could help people get a feel for the shape, the pace, the setbacks, and the victories of a community solving its own problems.

How Do You Report on Civic Capital?

Chapters One and Two have already talked about building civic capital as a means to foster smoother decision making, but it's more than just that; it's something that exerts a pull on most Americans in and of itself. Newspaper agenda polls—when they're subtle enough to include it on a list of choices—almost always turn up "the lack of community" as a major problem, right alongside crime, environment, traffic, and taxes.

People feel keenly that there's not enough goodwill or communication in places where they live; that there's far too much stridency; that governments don't listen to them, bosses lord it over them, clerks and social workers disregard them, and strangers won't help them. The citizens who asked "How can we do more?" and "What do we do next?" in Chapter Two's section on civic capital were aiming at this problem, as much as any other. So, for instance, was Rodney King when he asked during the Los Angeles riots, "Can we all get along?"

Put another way, in back of the drama of making individual choices or solving particular public problems, there is always a still deeper and more compelling master narrative: "Will this community work?" "Is this community succeeding?" "Can we make a good life with one another?" If a newspaper needs as a practical matter to tap its readers' deepest motivations, there is no greater political motivation than this. Journalists who have recognized the fact are looking for ways to report on civic capital directly, as a beat or subject in its own right.

The time has come, then, to look at civic capital a bit more systematically. Frances Moore Lappé and Paul Martin Du Bois of Vermont's Center for Living Democracy have done this in a particularly intriguing way. In their book *The Quickening of America: Rebuilding Our Nation, Remaking Our Lives* they make the case that it isn't just newspapers, politicians, or writers like Yankelovich and Mathews who are rethinking democracy right now but people in all roles and walks of life. Corporate managers are breaking up hierarchies in favor of more fluid, cooperative teams. Public schools are teaching students mediation skills as a way of lessening racial and gang tension. Public activists in the Communitarian movement and the Industrial Areas Foundation (among many other groups) are trying to foster community-mindedness and grassroots cooperation as a route to solving neighborhood problems. Because they're all working independently of one another and in wildly different spheres, they may not see themselves as actors taking part in a common cause. But in fact they are all trying to deal with the same set of basic problems—the upshot of social isolation, bad communication, top-down decision making, and the like—and they are, entirely without coordination, hitting upon the same set of basic solutions. Lappé and Du Bois boil these down to 10 generic skills that they call the "arts of democracy" (see box, below). The more people practice these 10 skills in different areas of life, the more likely public life will succeed and the "lack of community" problem diminish.

The idea is a wonderful one even if the list itself is not complete. A newspaper can give its readers a benchmark of the community's health by taking any hard-news beat it already covers—politics, city hall, crime, or business—and asking when, where, and how much

TEN ARTS OF DEMOCRACY

The Quickening of America looks panoramically at how 10 generic democratic skills are being applied in factories, economic policymaking, governance, neighborhood renewal, broadcast and print media, social work, and schools. Here is a thumbnail sketch of each, drawn from a number of Center for Living Democracy writings:

Active listening: The active listener makes an effort to empathize, asking probing and constructive questions. This allows people to develop public relationships based on honest recognition of each other's legitimate interests.

Creative conflict: People agree to disagree while searching for common ground, in order to create an environment that's safe for difference. Honest, creative confrontation deepens understanding, generates new options, and prevents commitment to premature solutions.

Mediation: Having a neutral party facilitate interaction among parties can help people in conflict hear each other. A mediator asks questions to discover common interests and works to enhance mutual respect and reduce the likelihood of unproductive conflict in the future.

Negotiation: In negotiation, people keep focused on key interests, rather than getting sidetracked over differences about the means to achieve them. Searching for common ground or a solution that meets some interests of each party makes it more likely that all parties will uphold whatever agreement is reached.

Political imagination: People gain from an ability to suspend the givens of today's social and political arrangements. By imagining the world as we wish it to be, we set goals and spur creativity toward positive problem solving. Martin Luther King's "I Have a Dream" speech is a fine example of political imagination.

Public dialogue: There are few but growing opportunities for Americans to come together to talk as citizens. Different from grandstanding or from casual conversation, public dialogue requires diverse people to commit themselves consciously to exploration, asking new questions, and listening to points of view not shared by all.

(cont.)

TEN ARTS OF DEMOCRACY *(cont.)*

Public judgment: People examine the values that underlie alternatives and the trade-offs that result from making tough choices among them. By doing this publicly, they end up making choices they are then willing to help implement.

Celebration and appreciation: Taking the time to express joy and appreciation for what one learns as well as [for] what one achieves sustains involvement in public endeavors. While it's easier to show appreciation for allies, recognizing the hard work and goodwill of adversaries is also essential.

Evaluation and reflection: By discussing what worked or didn't work after every meeting, event, or public action, a group becomes stronger and reinforces the lessons it has learned.

Mentoring: People in a democracy share a responsibility for guiding one another in learning these arts of public life. Individual mentors, unlike institutions, can tailor lessons to novices' needs.

Compiled with the help of the Center for Living Democracy.

citizens are practicing certain basic skills. A newspaper can *foster* the community's health by creatively trying to embed those skills in its reporting, the same way the *Virginian-Pilot* tries to embed the nine factors of *Meaningful Chaos.* By public listening plain and simple a paper does useful work in this direction. But business deskers, for example, could also investigate malaise on the factory shopfloor, using the "arts of democracy" as a framework. Editorial writers could hold public figures accountable for failing to "actively listen" or "negotiate." The op-ed page could solicit think pieces on how to improve "public dialogue" or "evaluation and reflection" at PTA meetings and political conventions. Editors could put together a special report on what mediation is and how mediators do it. A standard year-end page could celebrate "Progress We've Made This Year" on each of the newspaper's list of democratic skills.

Among the papers currently trying things along these lines, the *Tallahassee Democrat* is conducting periodic polls to track citizens' attitudes toward democracy and participation over the course of its public agenda project. (For more examples, look ahead to Chapter Four.)

✦ PUSHING THE ENVELOPE

Social commentators and public journalists have proposed a number of less systematic, but still interesting, ways of reporting on civic capital. Among them:

1. The National Civic League proposes paying more attention to ad hoc coalitions. Frequently these days the bodies that move public issues forward are not permanent institutions but temporary ones, involving shifting alliances of business leaders, labor unions, advocacy groups, government agencies, and the like, often making brethren of traditional adversaries, such as liberal women's groups and conservative Christians in the fight against pornography, or vocal supporters and detractors of affirmative action in a common attempt to delink race from adoption rules. The coalitions are created to push forward a solution to a particular problem, then they break apart and vanish when the problem is solved. A newspaper could assign one of its reporters to an "adhocracy beat" either to report on coalition building from a traditional news perspective or as an example of civic capital being born.

2. Harvard professor Robert Putnam stresses the civic capital formed by long-term, first-person socializing. To him, bowling leagues and Boy Scouts are more important than bureaucratic watchdogs and million-member lobbies because they establish the trust, shared norms, models of behavior, and support networks that—like grease in an engine—make the economy and society run not just well but without undue drag. His book *Making Democracy Work* and his article "The Prosperous Community" inadvertently suggest dozens of reporting projects for a journalist subtle enough to see them, for example, (a) analyzing whether new antipoverty programs actually build social capital (like national service) or destroy it (like 1960s-style urban renewal); (b) portraying the closing of a town's factories as the dissipation of an economic resource—the social capital of the people who lived and worked there, who must now disperse to towns where they will once again be strangers; (c) investigating the differences in social capital between a wealthy area and a poor one, or a crime-free and a crime-ridden neighborhood; (d) reporting, half-seriously and tongue-half-in-cheek, how the reporter's city spends its leisure time—bowling together, or bowling alone? In front of the TV set, or singing in church choirs? To get right to the nub: building social capital or letting it wither?

3. Starting close to home, a newspaper could run a section on "how you can best use this paper." This (or a truly citizen-friendly "On the Media" column) might, for instance, teach people how to write for a newspaper in a deliberative manner, or report on efforts that have been made in other cities and countries to bend the media to citizens' needs.

The *Spokane Spokesman-Review* already trains citizens to express their opinions through its "interactive editor" program.

4. Alternatively, the paper could prepare a hard-hitting series on "the media's effect on public life," reported in typical investigative journalism style. Reporters would interview the "victims" of media coverage, those who've been misrepresented or whose viewpoints have been ignored. Pollsters could ask citizens to rate the service they get from the media, and to identify what the media ought to be doing that it isn't doing now.

5. In the past, Minnesota's *St. Paul Pioneer Press* and a few other dailies have asked citizens point blank, "What should our city look like?" in order to develop agendas for physical redevelopment. A newspaper could do an analogous thing regarding the redevelopment of civic capital. It could think out loud with its readers about "What would our city look like if politics and community life were working as they should? Who would be meeting with whom? What would they be talking about? What would the newspaper be doing?"

6. Applying the same idea to projects on specific agenda issues, it's often obvious early on who will have to cooperate on a solution. For example, even before citizens have enumerated their options for reducing teen violence, they know that schools, parents, police, various city and state agencies, and teens themselves will have to act together in the end. At the project's launch, therefore, the paper can report on how well these actors are interconnected. It can place them on a map with lines running among them. A bold line might show that as things stand now teens have regular dialogue with the parks and recreation department. A dotted line might show that parents rarely talk with police. An absent line might show that family services workers and prosecutors don't talk with one another at all. The editorial page could encourage all these people, over the course of the project, to meet with one another more often and to strengthen their lines of communication; it could report on their progress now and again, or print an updated map at the end. By then, if everyone's talking, common action is that much more likely to succeed.

7. Journalists could do a project on the notion of practical democracy itself. They could explore the ideas of public journalism, how National Issues Forums operate, the work of writers like Lappé and Du Bois, Putnam, Benjamin Barber (*Strong Democracy*), Robert Bellah (*The Good Society*), Daniel Yankelovich (*Coming to Public Judgment*), Amitai Etzioni (*The Spirit of Community*), and David Mathews (*Politics for People*). As Mathews argues, much of the work people do in their own communities is truly "political"—solving problems in common—but they don't think of it that way. By pairing local activities and institutions with the ideas in these books, journalists could place the life of the community in the larger context of fellow citizenship and practical democracy.

✦ SIDEBAR: CIVIC CAPITAL IN THE NEWSROOM

Working on the same premise as Lappé and Du Bois, a few newspapers have asked themselves what public journalism's insights into politics would look like if they were applied in the newsroom itself.

The *New Orleans Times-Picayune* and the Columbia, S.C., *State* hypothesized during their race-relations and "To Raise a Child" projects that if gloves-off deliberation was a good idea outside the paper, it would be a good one within the paper too. So, rather than assigning a reporting approach to their teams or letting reporters work individually on separate assignments, editors encouraged reporters to sit down as a group and negotiate an approach agreeable to everyone. They discovered that working through the strongly held and divergent perspectives in a single newsroom was a prickly and often painful process, but that it produced a more deeply felt product in the end. Comprehending for the first time the vastness of their own differences, reporters became more sympathetic to differences among citizens at large.

The *State*'s daily grind has integrated other public journalism tenets too. With his eyes on both *Meaningful Chaos* and management theory, for example, editor Gil Thelen broke up the old beat system. Traditional beats like "the statehouse" and "city hall" simply aren't organized the way ordinary Americans think about public affairs; they follow institutions rather than issues. So he regrouped his reporters into new beats and teams clustered around interdisciplinary ideas like "governance," "leisure," "quality of life," and "community roots." Public journalism's egalitarianism suggested tinkering with the hierarchical, wheel-and-spokes, editor-tells-the-reporter structure of assignments too. As this chapter has argued, experts and citizens, leaders and led, are both sources of good judgment; ideas and decisions ought to be able to flow *up* as well as *down*. Democracy works best through deliberation among equals. So at the *State* each reporting team has reorganized its coverage from the bottom up, asking itself why it's covering this subject or that, and trying to develop a collective sense of what information citizens might really want from it. Guessing is supplemented by meetings with community activists and advisory groups; for example, the governance team meets with the government employees it covers to discuss how future coverage could better clarify the news and help citizens make their judgments. A box later in this chapter describes similar innovations at the *Virginian-Pilot*.

✦ PUSHING THE ENVELOPE

1. Journalists could consciously reconsider every aspect of newsroom routine—from story meetings, to work with copyeditors, to waiting for an interview, to how they spend lunch—and ask themselves, "Is there a more public journalism way of doing this?" Brainstorm. Look for little opportunities to ratchet up the social capital of the newsroom, or to reorient old habits a few degrees closer to citizens' concerns.

2. Just to provoke thought within the newspaper, a staff member could be assigned to read through Robert Putnam's book on social capital or Lappé and Du Bois's book on the arts of democracy, and then take an inventory of the civic capital in the news organization. Do editors show much political imagination? How well do reporters use creative conflict? How much do women and men throughout the staff trust and support one another? Who isn't talking to whom, and who ought to be? Posted on a prominent noticeboard, this inventory might spark some lively exchanges.

✦

Postscript: Facts and Narrative Together

Public journalists have sometimes gotten lost trying to balance "telling the facts" with "telling the narrative." The *Dayton Daily News* (see box, p. 64) did a nice job by alternating stories on, for example, expert forums and roundtables, where ideas were discussed, with stories featuring people talking about how juvenile crime has affected them. When it ran highly personal pieces such as life stories of violent kids, it made sure to stuff the page margins with statistics, samples of rap lyrics, citizens' ideas, suggestions from volunteer agencies—whatever facts seemed most "strategic" to the issues the main articles were raising. Individual stories often contained a good mix in and of themselves; a piece on third-graders' fear of violence contained a box in which they talked about where they were learning values and what the community could do about youth crime. Always people were shown *thinking*, and the ideas themselves were part of the story. Finally, the "Kids in Chaos" project had an amazing narrative drive. Everyone knew where it was heading; everyone knew the upcoming fall forums were about working through hard choices. And when people ultimately changed their minds about the nature of the issue—when they reframed "the facts" to focus on families rather than funded programs—the *Daily News* was sensitive enough to change the direction of "the narrative" too.

Working on earlier, more limited projects, the Minneapolis–St. Paul *Star Tribune* and the *Wichita Eagle* balanced "facts" and "narrative" in much simpler ways. Jeremy Iggers of the *Star Tribune* just wanted to give citizens a place to talk with one another about general social problems. In 1992, he organized an open-ended series of roundtables (collectively called "Minnesota's Talking") to take place once a month at scores of sites throughout the Twin Cities, open to all comers. In a typical month, 700 to 1,000 citizens showed up. Each forum was keyed to a published study guide from either the National Issues Forums or the Study Circles Resource Center, but since participants would move on to a new topic each month, the conversation had to be exploratory rather than conclusive. Inside the newspaper, he blended "facts" and "narrative" by running side-by-side reports a few days after each month's discussions: One piece cobbled together quotations from roundtables across the state, with one argument answering the previous one and leading on to the next—a sort of collective transcript of the public's ideas. The companion feature provided "you are there" sketches of a few randomly selected meetings (a rural one with hugs and baking; an earnest suburban one that stuck tight to business), offering a picture of the human face of deliberation.

The *Eagle*'s "People Project" was more ambitious, but still fundamentally short term. Editor Davis Merritt introduced it with the dramatic essay quoted already, then at regular intervals the paper would publish two successive four- or five-page packages addressed to a selected issue, including crime, schools, and government gridlock. To help people think together, each package contained a clip-out questionnaire; the dates and times of community meetings or "idea exchanges" where citizens could go to talk with reporters, experts and one another; in-depth reports on people's answers to strategic questions (e.g., "Do we need higher, measurable standards in our schools?" and "Do we need more emphasis on discipline and values?"); and the aforementioned "core value" boxes. (The *Eagle*'s radio and TV partners held on-air forums to continue the discussion.) But the editors knew that people needed inspiration too. So among the idea-oriented pieces they interspersed "success stories," for example, about a mother who had turned a local school around, or a tutoring program that worked. Full pages went to listing volunteer and advocacy organizations under the title "Places to Start." Photos and on-scene reports tracked how Wichitans were reacting to the experience of exchanging ideas and coordinating action. Regarding one issue, the paper printed the names of every citizen who had participated.

Doing It Daily versus Doing a Project

An entirely different question of balance has caused a lot of internal debate among public journalists: Is it best to do big, news-space-intensive projects (as in Dayton) that go at a public agenda issue until it's completely exhausted, or simply to apply ideas about strategic facts and democratic arts to ordinary, unspectacular news coverage, day in and day out? Many of this book's experimental newspapers started with single-issue projects and grew restless either with the demands of that level of coverage or with seeing public journalism ghettoized in just one part of the paper. They have led the argument to make public journalism mundane. (The *Virginian-Pilot* is an unusual example of a paper that started from the opposite end of the spectrum; see box, below.) On reflection the whole idea of all-big versus all-small is wrong-headed. There are occasions when each sort of coverage is called for. The test of realism resolves the dilemma very well.

To begin with, the half-dozen issues that top a city's or state's public agenda are almost always so large that they will take months or years to deliberate over and act upon. Clearly there will be times during those months and years when coverage has to be intensive if citizens are honestly to hold a common conversation and come to a decision. Just as clearly, there will be other, fallow times when people may be deliberating outside the paper in community forums, or else gradually learning more about an issue, or else putting it aside for a rest or to turn to other things. Any presidential election campaign would make a fine example. At times coverage is all-encompassing and intense (e.g., during the New Hampshire primary, Super Tuesday, the party conventions, and then from the typical early autumn debates right up to election day); in between those times, coverage falls back to the ordinary and mundane. Although newspapers typically assign one logo to all campaign coverage ("Your Vote in 1996"), practically speaking it's really a series of small projects spaced out over a one-year period. All the big, encompassing projects in this book—from the *Tallahassee Democrat*'s two-year agenda project to the *Dayton Daily News*'s ongoing teen violence project—follow the same pattern. Editors put together major coverage at certain turning points in the plot, then simply track the issue(s) or look for simple tie-ins from the news budgets over the weeks or even months in-between. They do it as a project and do it daily both, at different times.

Meanwhile, there are all the ongoing issues that *don't* top the city's agenda. Of necessity, to keep the paper's resources and attention focused on the issues citizens are most concerned about, these problems have to be given shorter shrift. But it's still possible to treat them with full public journalism regalia. The *Wichita Eagle* did just that when the Kansas legislature took up the question of capital punishment in 1994. (This is a perennial issue for the state: Legislators and governors had considered and eventually nixed the death penalty nine times since the U.S.

THE VIRGINIAN-PILOT

Unlike a lot of other papers, the *Virginian-Pilot* didn't come to public journalism looking for a new angle on a big story such as an election, the redevelopment of a city, or tension over race. It came because its beat structure was in trouble. The *Pilot* covers five cities around Norfolk, Va., and had traditionally assigned a separate politics-and-government reporter to each. By 1992 this was producing not only uneven journalism, but unimaginative journalism as well. So editor Cole Campbell borrowed an idea from "total quality management" theory, lumped the five reporters together into a team, and told them to reinvent their coverage from scratch.

This got team editor Tom Warhover and his colleagues thinking about why they were covering government at all. After some groping, they drafted a mission statement (reprinted in Chapter Six) declaring their aim to "show how the community works or could work" and to "portray democracy in the fullest sense of the word, whether in a council chamber or a cul-de-sac." They renamed themselves the "Public Life Team." One early test of their inventiveness involved a rezoning controversy covered at length in Chapter Four. Looking for ways to "show how the community could work," the team brought eight citizens together and reprinted verbatim excerpts from their deliberation. Surprisingly, what had looked first and foremost like a race issue ended up looking not only more complex but more manageable as well.

But Warhover and Campbell still felt that they were misreading citizens. In the rezoning story and others, people didn't seem to be coming from where the reporters had initially imagined. The *Pilot* hired Richard Harwood (author of *Meaningful Chaos*) to train the team more formally in public listening and to talk over with them how to use it in their work. "Now that we have radically altered the way reporters and editors work," Campbell said, "we want to change the way they think."

In fact, the team does only a few outwardly "radical" things: For instance, it meets with panels of citizens regularly to tap their thoughts and dreams for the region's future. What really changed journalism at the *Pilot* was the willingness to experiment itself, and the opportunity given to formerly isolated reporters to brainstorm ideas together. They haven't done any large, lasting projects, but they have tried out innumerable notions in small stories to improve the

(cont.)

THE VIRGINIAN-PILOT (*cont.*)

tone of public discourse. They changed tougher criminal sentencing from a polarized issue to something advocates of rehabilitation could support (see pp. 41–45). They opened a sense of possibility for the Hall Place neighborhood. In one October 1994 story, as the U.S. Justice Department was preparing to force ward voting on a town it thought hopelessly cleaved by race, the *Pilot* got black and white residents to talk freely about the plan. They were skeptical. Race relations weren't so bad, and dividing the city council into black and white fiefdoms might well make them worse. The issue, they said, ought to be what was good for the city as a whole.

Supreme Court declared it constitutional in 1976.) Under the bold headline "Facing a Decision: Weighing All Sides of the Death Penalty Debate," the paper ran five quick-read sections, none more than two paragraphs long. One section presented "The Arguments" about capital punishment, moral, deterrent, and economic. Another offered "Other Resources": nine books and two movies. The third suggested ways to get involved, listing pro- and anti-capital punishment groups beside the comment, "In addition to studying the issue, making your own decision about it and contacting your state senator and representative, you may want to contact groups pro and con that will provide you with information and enlist you in their causes." Then, just above quotations from three Wichitans with divergent views, the paper set out one-paragraph summaries of the core values at stake, under three headings: "Should Society Kill?," "Should Society Punish or Rehabilitate?," and "How Should Democracy Work?" In a header to this section, the paper asked readers: "What are your values on the capital punishment issue? Are you at one of the extremes or somewhere in between? Are there places you can compromise?"

In deepening a one-shot story, simply asking "What would be most useful to citizens?" can suggest a better approach to reporting and writing. The habit many papers have gotten into of providing names and phone numbers for volunteer agencies or charities when reporting on a disaster is one example. In war coverage, the trick might be asking Serb, Croat, and Muslim partisans in Bosnia not why they are fighting but what would make them stop. By relying heavily on *Meaningful Chaos, the Virginian-Pilot* (see box, above) has turned writing the one-shot public journalism story into a virtual science.

A paper should be alert to the fact that one-shot stories aren't always what they seem. If breaking news relates in some way to the top public agenda issues, it can be tied into the "master narrative" with as little as a logo and a slight twist in story angle. Thus "What shall we do about race?" is a bedrock issue in most American cities, and when charges of racism flew around the closing of a public park in Charlotte and a rezoning issue in a Norfolk neighborhood, editors were canny enough to convene deliberative conversations among residents and reprint portions of them in the paper. (The details are presented in Chapter Four.) The resulting copy both stood alone as good daily newswriting and kept people thinking about a much larger issue, between projects.

One thing ought to be absolutely clear: Whether doing it daily or doing a project, a newspaper can apply public journalism to every article it prints.

✦ PUSHING THE ENVELOPE

1. "Doing it daily" shouldn't mean taking a short sighted view. One of a journalist's major roles, of course, is raising people's consciousness about newly breaking issues: making them seem important and dramatic. But a newspaper's *way* of raising consciousness can have a dramatic effect on the eventual working through. For instance, aggressive and emotional breaking-news coverage often gets the public overhyped, convincing people that urban crime, school decline, or Social Security underfunding is worse than it actually is; this may make it harder for people to find common ground when the time comes. Instead papers could actually *soften* the ground for the working-through phase during the consciousness-raising phase. The *New York Times*, for example, began running panoramic, insightful and background-heavy "periodic reports" on Vietnam in 1994 as United States–Vietnam relations began to thaw. They weren't intended to lead into a project, but it was clear that Washington would be dealing with Hanoi again soon, and problems would have to be worked through.

2. Editors could decide what routines they would like to learn from a major project even as they're designing it—how they'd like the project to translate out, in the end, into day-to-day practice. The *Democrat* started running a periodic public agenda page (see Chapter Five for a facsimile) at the same time it launched its huge public agenda project. The two aren't directly related; the page only borrows a few of the project's ideas and, more generally, draws on its popularity and momentum. By the time the two-year project has wrapped up, the editors intend to have developed an

audience and a workable style for the public agenda page that will keep it going into the indefinite future.

3. Another way of making public journalism habitual is to replace the Journalism 101 rules every beginning reporter learns with new and better ones. At one Project on Public Life and the Press conference, two dozen editors and reporters tried to come up with a "who, what, when, where, why, and how" for public journalism. Conventionally, a reporter asks those questions *about an event*: who did what to whom; at what location; at what time; for what reason; and by what means? Public reporters have other reasons to ask them. *About the problem or issue*: What is the problem; who does it affect; how and where does it affect them; when and why did it arise; and why won't it go away? *About the public dialogue on the issue*: Who ought to be talking; what about; when, where, and how can people get involved in the deliberation; and why is it going well or poorly? *About public action*: Who needs to be involved if the problem's really to be solved; what do they need to do; when, where, and how will they do it; and why are (or aren't) they taking action? Three hours weren't enough for the conferees to nail down a good set of questions—but everybody thought the idea was a fertile one, worth taking back to their newspapers to work out in daily practice.

✦

CHAPTER FOUR

Public Judgment

A Particular Kind of Talk

One thing has been missing so far from these notes on the decision-making cycle, something that takes place outside the newspaper. Kettering Foundation president David Mathews likes to say that the basic unit of politics is a conversation. Whether for psychological or intellectual reasons, people tend to form their most responsible judgments not in the privacy of their own minds but by talking things out with other people. American life, however, doesn't make this easy. Again and again, Kettering's studies of ordinary citizens, including *Citizens and Politics: A View from Main Street America* and *Meaningful Chaos*, show how isolated people feel, how unsure of their own ability to meet and connect. The swift, overwhelming ascendancy of town hall meetings and talk shows are just two signs of people's hunger for conversation about public affairs; the warm response to public journalists who convene forums and study circles is another.

The previous two chapters have dealt with how to figure out what issues the public wants to discuss, and how to supply the information readers need to discuss them. Now we will turn to the discussions themselves. People feel strongly that a problem like racism can't be solved without blacks and whites sitting down together; nor welfare without rich, middle-class, and poor at a common table; nor anything much at all without politicians and the voters who elected them really hearing each other out. Not in any abstract sense (such as the journalist's "national debate") but in very commonsense, concrete terms, they want the chance to bring "the community" together regularly to talk. The initiative for convening these conversations ought perhaps to rest with politicians or private citizens rather than the news media, but—even if you feel this way—the facts are that politicians and private citizens are doing an inadequate job of it, and that newspapers, as one of the few American institutions that still address people from all demographic groups within a city or state, are well positioned to do better. Journalists willing to take the step could help democracy work.

But this requires a clearheaded effort. It's not any, unstructured sort of conversation the media need to help people convene. What citizens want is to work through their differences and arrive at common ground, and this doesn't seem to happen at town meetings, press conferences, public hearings, or presidential debates. Daniel Yankelovich in *Coming to Public Judgment,* David Mathews in *Politics for People*, and Frances Moore Lappé and Paul Martin Du Bois in *The Quickening of America*—among many others—argue that working through or deliberation requires a very particular type of conversation, bound by strict if not always formalized rules of interpersonal etiquette. It's a type of talking that people—even journalists—are familiar with in their everyday lives, when they face a family or community problem they are really dedicated to solving, but one that has become so alien in the media and legislatures and political campaigns that it doesn't seem like the natural way people should talk when they talk about politics. Any of those books would be an excellent primer on taking this style of conversation public, as would participating in a National Issues Forum or study circle discussion.

As a first pass at the idea, Mathews relates an incident from a National Issues Forum discussion of affirmative action. It was late. Half the meeting had already gone by, and the multiracial audience had gotten exactly nowhere; blacks and whites trotted out the standard arguments pro-and-con that had been stated many times in the news media. Finally, a black woman said, "I guess if I were a white man . . . and somebody came along and said that there are scarce resources and everybody won't be able to get the same if we give so-and-so the chance, I would think that I might be one of those people [who] might not get a chance." There was a moment when the reaction from the white men might easily have become "You see!"—but it passed. Instead several opened up to say that if they had been victims of color prejudice they might insist on a strong remedy too. They were beginning, as Mathews likes to put it, to struggle *within* themselves as much as *between* themselves over the nature of this problem. From that point onward, the people in the room became partners trying to devise a solution all of them could live with.

The Study Circles Resource Center fleshes out the difference in attitude between deliberation (here called dialogue) and the debates journalists usually stage like this:

Dialogue is collaborative: two or more sides work together to achieve common understanding. Debate is oppositional: two sides oppose each other and attempt to prove each other wrong.

In dialogue, finding common ground is the goal. In debate, winning is the goal.

In dialogue, one searches for strengths in the other positions. In debate, one searches for flaws.

Dialogue reveals assumptions for reevaluation. Debate defends assumptions as truth.

In dialogue, one submits one's best thinking, knowing that other people's reflections will help improve it rather than destroy it. In debate, one submits one's best thinking and defends it against challenge to show that it is right.

Dialogue opens the possibility of reaching a better solution than any of the original solutions. Debate defends one's own positions as the best solutions and excludes other solutions.

Dialogue assumes that many people have pieces of the answer and that together they can put them into a workable solution. Debate assumes there is a right answer and someone has it.

Dialogue involves a real concern for the other person and seeks not to alienate or offend. Debate involves a countering of the other position without focusing on feelings or relationship.[*]

Kettering Foundation researcher Michael Briand adapted a comparison of negotiation styles from Roger Fisher and William Ury's *Getting to Yes* to make the same point in a different way. In the box below, he distinguishes *two* conventional approaches to political discourse (one aimed at getting a quick solution, the other at coming away with the best of the deal) from what he calls deliberative democratic discourse.

The Newspaper and Community Forums

In recent years, many newspapers have sponsored laudable efforts to bring political, social, and business leaders together to work out solutions for public agenda issues. No doubt things would get done much

---

[*]Adapted with permission from *The Study Circle Handbook* (adapted from the original work by the Boston Area Educators for Social Responsibility Dialogue Group).

CONVENTIONAL VERSUS DELIBERATIVE POLITICAL DISCOURSE

Conventional political discourse		Deliberative political discourse
"Easy" approach:	*"Tough" approach:*	

I view the problem as:

My responsibility	Your responsibility	Our (shared) responsibility

We treat other citizens as:

Friends	Adversaries	Fellow problem solvers

The goal is:

Agreement	Winning	A public judgment about what's best, all things considered, to do; and a public choice that everyone can go along with

In order to achieve this goal I try to:

Be easy on other people and on the problem	Be tough on the problem and on other people	Be easy on other people but tough on the problem
Trust others	Not trust others	Focus on the problem—mutual confidence will develop
Give up my opinion or position	Dig in and defend my opinion and position	Dig down until I find what really concerns me, what motivates my attitudes and actions

(cont.)

CONVENTIONAL VERSUS DELIBERATIVE POLITICAL DISCOURSE *(cont.)*

Conventional political discourse		Deliberative political discourse
"Easy" approach	*"Tough"* approach	**Deliberative** **political discourse**
		Ask myself what I really need
		Explain these [needs] to others in a way they can relate to
		Try to comprehend— i.e., understand and appreciate what my fellow citizens believe, feel, and need
Search for the single solution others will accept right away	Search for the single solution I will accept right away	Consider all the options together— weigh the pros and cons—the good and bad consequences
Yield to pressure	Exert pressure	Work toward a choice everyone can go along with because it addresses everyone's most important concerns and needs
Compromise and accept sacrifices	Don't compromise and don't accept sacrifices	Invent new options consistent with the choice that everyone can go along with

Reprinted with permission from "Understanding Deliberation: A Guide for Journalists," a Project on Public Life and the Press working paper.

more quickly and better if these people met more often and deliberated more thoughtfully—but this isn't public journalism. Economic summits, town meetings in which ordinary citizens sit and watch a discussion among local educators, closed-door sessions between business leaders: These all reflect a view of politics in which experts and elected officials do things, and citizens merely monitor (or complain).

For the past two or three years, public journalists have set out to provide ordinary people with the same kinds of opportunities to meet and talk that these other papers provide officials. Sometimes this has led to what should probably be called *citizen* summits: traditional bargaining sessions composed either of citizens by themselves or of experts and citizens together. Washington State's *Bremerton Sun*, facing regional concern over the preservation of open space in 1991, convened 47 town meetings attended by 1,500 local residents; 200 went on to hammer out a rank-ordered plan of action. As described elsewhere, the *Wisconsin State Journal* invented mock legislative sessions and grand juries, staffed by citizens, to help resolve problems like deficit spending and health care reform. More and more, though, public newspapers have been striving to break the old molds of public talk in favor of more self-consciously "deliberative" forums.

It's easiest to understand the course they've taken by going back to the test of realism. For an entire community to work through a public problem—realistically speaking—large numbers of citizens would have to be involved. Collectively, they had better represent all the diverse ethnic, religious, and socioeconomic groups on hand. They would have to meet in groups small enough that deliberative conversation was possible, and they might well have to meet many times in order to make real progress. Perhaps most important, they would all have to agree to talk about the same problem, the same choices, and the same facts at the same time. From the beginning, public journalists have seen only one obvious way to do this: Citizens would meet in small community forums throughout the state or city, and the newspaper would link them up with a common framing, "facts," and "narrative."

At first a few papers tried to do this single-handedly. The Minneapolis–St. Paul *Star Tribune*'s roundtables, described in Chapter Three, started out as almost entirely the paper's creature. Columnist Jeremy Iggers helped individual volunteers arrange enough meetings around the Twin Cities that any citizen who wanted could easily attend; he published rudimentary instruction in the study circle method to whet people's appetite. But to keep the project manageable, he had to restrict the issues discussed during the first year and a half to those for which the Study Circles Resource Center or the National Issues Forums had low-cost study guides in print; this way, the *Star Tribune* itself had to do only a limited amount of supplemental reporting. And still the project probably involved more time on logistics than on journalism. Ordinary citizens took the ball and ran with it—one month, for example, when the topic was race relations, people from the suburbs drove to meetings in the city to break across race and class lines, and a few groups set up extra sessions to go into the issue more deeply; they went well beyond what the *Star Tribune* had intended—but the project didn't necessarily play to the newspaper's strengths, and it didn't integrate into the decision-making cycle discussed in Chapter Three.

Gradually, public journalists discovered that they really didn't have to go it alone. Many cities already have active deliberative forums, though they may not appear on the typical editor's Rolodex. Or else there are civic groups that would be eager to organize deliberative forums if only they could get a little training.

While the largest, most familiar civic organizations don't typically work through issues according to the public journalist's sense of the term, scattered forums may well exist, connected to one of several national clearinghouses for deliberative groups—among them the NIF, the SCRC, and the *Utne Reader*'s Neighborhood Salon Association. Annually, more than 5,000 schools, churches, prisons, libraries, and other groups buy NIF issue books alone (though the network doesn't track how many use them in forums). Other national organizations that make deliberation their house style sponsor grassroots conversations in a less systematic way; among these are the Industrial Areas Foundation, Public Agenda, the National Civic League, and Search for Common Ground. The Rockefeller Foundation's October 1994 report *Communications as Engagement*, compiled by Marsha Sharp and Ann Beaudry, includes 50 pages of listings naming many more (though not all) groups of this type. Locally, councils of churches, university-based conflict resolution centers, and human relations commissions sometimes organize deliberative meetings on their own.

Public newspapers have come more and more to see the virtue of collaboration. By handing over the forum business to groups such as these, they can devote their own resources to the "facts" and the "narrative." The *Dayton Daily News*'s "Kids in Chaos" may be the archetype (see Chapter Three): At the start its editors sought out a grab bag of community groups willing to organize events and forums, made TV and radio partners who agreed to broadcast the deliberations, brought in the Kettering Foundation to train everybody (*Daily News* staff included) in the nature of deliberation, and then—freed of all that—went out and did the kind of journalism essential to making the forums work. Everyone in Dayton played from (or at least knew about) the same game plan; yet the paper paid only for the journalism, declined responsibility for the rest, and always maintained its independence and editorial control. Nor do journalists necessarily have to put such coalitions together; in Maine, the state council of churches approached the Portland Newspapers about a collaboration, an integrated forums-and-coverage project on the perennial issue of education (see box, below).

Whatever a newspaper feels its role to be in helping citizens come together there's a wide range of resources available to make the job easier:

MAINE'S PORTLAND NEWSPAPERS

Lou Ureneck, the editor of the *Maine Sunday Telegram* and *Portland Press Herald*, was hunting for his own style of public journalism when Sarah Campbell of the Maine Council of Churches phoned him with a proposal. The Council had been trying for the past few years to help congregants talk through their ambivalence over thorny public issues, beginning with the Gulf War in 1991. It had recently scored a success with a series of forums on abortion, using a method being promoted by an upstart foundation in Connecticut, the Study Circles Resource Center. What if the newspapers and the Council together could make study circles available to everyone in the state?

Ureneck and Campbell spent months on the idea, trying to figure out, if they were to collaborate, what the proper role for each of their organizations would be. Eventually they hit on a deal. The SCRC volunteered to send facilitator training manuals and, on one occasion, a trainer. Campbell agreed to organize meetings at locations throughout Maine and do the bulk of moderator training. The paper would promote the meetings through house ads and a sign-up coupon, and then just do whatever journalism it thought appropriate to help the discussions along. "The newspaper had sole control over editorial content," Campbell says. "They wouldn't have it any other way, nor would we." Only toward the end of their talks did they settle on a topic: education reform, then being talked about in a number of Maine communities.

In fact, the Council did influence the paper's coverage in one substantial way. The study circle method, like the National Issues Forum method, revolves around "core value" choices; Campbell thought it would help people keep their bearings if during each week of the four-week series of forums the paper focused coverage on that week's particular choice. Ureneck agreed, but—feeling that the

(cont.)

MAINE'S PORTLAND NEWSPAPERS (*cont.*)

choices in published study guides were too academic—he, Campbell, and local educators drafted four perspectives of their own: "The primary goal of education is to prepare you for a job," or ". . . to develop lifelong learning," or ". . . to develop good citizens," or ". . . to teach the basics." Ureneck asked reporters to give readers lots of background on each perspective and to write in an expository rather than conventional he-said/she-said style.

Seven hundred Mainers took part in the reader roundtables, even though January 1994 had unusually bad weather. (In line with the nonpartisan intent, neither participants nor moderators had any particular affiliation with the Council of Churches; they were religious and secular, Christian and Jew.) Each Sunday before the forums Ureneck ran more than 100 inches of factual reporting on education in Maine and elsewhere, op-ed pieces advocating the perspective of the week, and summary reports on what opponents of that perspective said. Revealingly, the conventional journalists on public broadcasting's *Media Watch* complained that the Portland papers' coverage was mostly old news, as if it were more important to be immediate than to be useful. But among ordinary citizens the forums were popular enough to bring 500 out for a second series in October. "The program worked," Campbell says simply, "because [Lou Ureneck] was open to it—because he was willing to look at this peculiar marriage of churches and newspaper."

Study Guides and Supplements

The SCRC publishes a free, regularly updated bibliography of study guides (called the "clearinghouse") with well over 100 public issue titles. All are ready for community forums to use. Included among them are the excellent and detailed NIF issue books, of which two dozen are in print with three new titles appearing each year. As stated previously, the *Dayton Daily News* and the *Pottsville Republican* successfully used the NIF books as cornerstones for their projects. Public Agenda meanwhile organizes nationwide, integrated multimedia and grassroots campaigns to jump-start deliberation on selected issues (most recently the "Condition Critical" campaign on health care and the "Help Wanted" campaign on education and employment), supplying not only citizen study guides, research reports, and instructions on joining the campaign, but predesigned newspaper supplements as well. The *Wichita Eagle*, the *Topeka Capital-Journal*, *Orange County* (Calif.) *Register*, the *Atlanta Constitution*, and *Columbus* (Ga.) *Ledger-Enquirer* were among more than 40 press organizations that participated in "Condition Critical."

Readings on Deliberation

How-to booklets on deliberative talk, organizing forums, and preparing study materials are legion. It's worth noting that different sources will advocate different sorts of forums: NIF-style (single meetings with an emphasis on actually making choices; ask the Kettering Foundation); study-circle style (multiple meetings that go progressively deeper into a subject, with no pressure to come to a decision; ask the SCRC); salon-style (more free-form still; ask the Neighborhood Salon Association); council-style (based on Native American custom, with strict rules for listening and speaking; ask the Ojai Foundation); negotiation-style (consult the newsletter *Consensus* or *Getting to Yes*); or some other style altogether. All are deliberative in the sense described in the chapter introduction.

Training and Organization

Increasingly, to get a firmer grip on this particular style of talk, public newspapers are inviting deliberative organizations to become full partners in their projects. The SCRC has volunteered advice and moderator training not only to the Portland Newspapers but to roundtable projects at the New London (Conn.) *Day*, the *Hartford Courant*, and the *St. Petersburg* (Fla.) *Times*. Kettering has done the same in Dayton (see the box in Chapter Three), Tallahassee, St. Petersburg, and elsewhere. Conflict resolution groups such as Search for Common Ground have accepted invitations to train or moderate local discussion groups too, though so far not in the context of a public newspaper project. Local forum sponsors have by and large welcomed the intervention; they've typically got the personnel and enthusiasm to get their communities talking, but are rightly aware that they don't have all the necessary skills.

✦ PUSHING THE ENVELOPE

1. So far most meetings organized by newspapers have been strictly segregated, with summits for leaders, and roundtables for ordinary citizens. If leaders and citizens met at all, the leaders were treated as experts answering questions or hearing comments from the crowd. It would be

possible, however, to convene meetings in which the two groups deliberated together. (This embodies the ideal of full-time and part-time citizens talking together as equals. However, veteran moderators warn that the ideal really has to be hammered home; otherwise leaders are quick to dominate mixed forums, and citizens to defer.)

2. Locally organized forums usually have their own agendas and discussions, wholly separate from the paper's. They are among the places where issues, trends, and options first bubble up in a community—far in advance of their appearance on the general radar. A paper could intermittently report on what local deliberative forums are talking about, under a logo or standing label such as "Problems to Keep an Eye On."

Journalists shouldn't look too narrowly at their relationship with deliberative forums. The ultimate prize isn't a temporary partnership between outside groups and the newspaper on a particular agenda issue, but a community of men and women who resort to deliberation naturally, who have gotten into the habit. Jay Rosen of the Project on Public Life and the Press argues that the ideal way for forums to arise in a city is the same way Alcoholics Anonymous chapters arise: wholly uncoordinated from any center, and so not dependent on anyone but the participants. There are several ways a public newspaper can help this come about:

3. Publish something analogous to "the 12 steps of deliberative forums." The Neighborhood Salon Association already hands out a pithy leaflet called *The Salon-Keeper's Companion*; public journalists could prepare a special newspaper section to serve much the same purpose.

4. Invent columns and features to support citizen groups in their deliberations—whether they're deliberating over issues on the paper's agenda or not. Frequently, for example, forums get stalled on disagreements over fact. (At NIF health care forums, somebody usually asserts that Medicare has the lowest administrative costs of any health delivery system in the United States, and somebody else says it isn't so.) The paper might run a column to which local forums could send brief but urgent questions of fact; it would print answers quickly enough that readers could use them in their next forum. Another columnist might offer advice in a "your auto doctor" style, "looking under the hood" of any forum that invited her and analyzing the formula that's fueling either the group's success or its frustration.

5. Map out "where people talk (or don't talk) in City X," perhaps in a weekend feature. Profile the different kinds of conversations going on in the community (e.g., "over the lunch counter," "in the senior center," "in the complaints room at City Hall," "on the job," and so forth). Encourage citizens to think of themselves as ticket holders in a huge,

communal conversation; show how diverse or how narrow that conversation really is.

6. Suggest "conversation topics" in the community calendar. This might be a short list of questions spurred by the day's events, or else curiosities pulled straight from overheard conversation, interviews, and so forth. The paper would nudge citizens to talk about public life topics such as these in quick encounters with strangers or neighbors in place of forgettable small talk; the topics themselves might be no more than ice breakers. In the hands of a good writer, ideas of the day might become as popular with readers as quotations- or jokes-of-the-day are in many papers.

7. Also in the community calendar, run a "Crossing the Lines" logo next to upcoming events that provide citizens with a good opportunity to meet across ethnic, gender, or (to borrow a term from Chapter Six) life-style-cluster lines.

8. Run a matchmaking service for organizations that don't habitually interact, for example, religious and secular social clubs, study circles and bowling leagues, or black and white churches. This has been one of the most successful parts of the *Akron Beacon Journal's* "Coming Together" initiative.

9. Adapting another idea from Akron, solicit pledges from citizens to "talk about the public agenda with five acquaintances or strangers" in the coming month.

10. Cross the lines that divide the media themselves. As Chapter Six will say again, daily newspapers never reach everyone in a metropolitan area; different citizens inevitably get their news from a variety of different sources. A public newspaper might run a column on "How Issue X Is Seen on Radio Station Y," introducing people who are conversing through one mass medium to those who are conversing through another. It would be fascinating to compare how black or Spanish-language radio, conservative talk radio, MTV, and the tabloid across town talk about, say, school prayer, right on the pages of the major metropolitan daily.

How Do You Put Working Through on the News Pages?

Deliberation is active, face to face; reading a newspaper is passive. Deliberation takes a lot of time, words, and gestures; newspapers don't have a lot of space. Conceptually, then, it's very hard to fit deliberation into a newspaper—yet it's essential, because the paper itself is the one forum all citizens have in common. The editors who have done it most successfully have tried to bring, instead of the words themselves, the *attitudes* of deliberation onto the page. If you believe readers' thoughts are as important as those of mayors and police chiefs, then you will print readers' thoughts in your paper. If you believe it's only rational to feel ambivalent about topics like abortion or crime's links to poverty, then you'll feature interviews with ambivalent people, to take advantage of their rationality. If it's truly essential to face the consequences of your choices, then your reporters will raise consequences each time they ask someone questions. Letters editors and op-ed editors especially should ponder how to get the message across—as the black woman did in David Mathews's anecdote at the beginning of this chapter—that the place people are entering is a deliberative space.

When the Mecklenburg County parks director closed Charlotte's Freedom Park to Sunday car traffic in mid-1993 in response to complaints from nearby residents, the *Charlotte Observer* could easily have written a standard what-the-two-sides-say story on the strained feelings of white homeowners and black teenage drivers; as with much breaking-news coverage of local affairs, this would have brought it home that emotions were high and the issue important—in Daniel Yankelovich's terms, it would have raised consciousness about the issue but gone no farther. Instead, the *Observer* lured its 13 interviewees (residents, cruisers, and community leaders) into talking about the root values at stake in Freedom Park. "We sought to draw out the best ideas," the editor said. "What should be done?" Independently, nearly all of them said the same things: City parks shouldn't just be closed, recreational cruising should be moved to nonresidential areas, drivers should turn down their radios, and a fee for parking might solve the problem. A long-festering issue that seemed to revolve around race relations became more concrete and manageable.

Following Charlotte's lead, the *Virginian-Pilot* tried a similar approach when controversy arose late in 1993 over the rezoning of farm-market land for a mostly black church that planned to expand into a television ministry. The paper gathered eight concerned local residents, four in favor of and four opposing the rezoning, and sat them together for a lengthy discussion. It started things off simply by asking what had brought each of them to take such a personal interest in the issue; in short order, their answers made it clear that questions of neighborhood overload and city council high-handedness probably played at least as great a role in the controversy as racism and property tax losses, which had been the focus of most news coverage until then. The next step after drawing on citizen voices for ideas was actually putting them together in deliberation. The taped discussions were edited down and grouped into six topic areas, among them, "Can the city afford for this property to be tax-exempt?" and the hot button "Is race an issue?" Partial transcripts ran alongside a more traditional news piece on the accusations and denials of racism.

Sometimes journalists are given the chance to nurture a fragile spirit of deliberation that has developed outside the paper. In 1994, for the first time in decades, black and white South Carolinian legislators seemed eager to compromise on whether the Confederate battle flag should continue to fly over the state capitol. Editors at the *State* realized that if they covered the debates in the standard he-said-then-she-said manner, they would never convey the unusual understanding being born between children of the civil rights movement and the grandchildren of Confederate veterans. So they emphasized the conciliatory language and downplayed the harsh. When readers suggested the paper was missing an important side to the story—that of Southerners who honored the flag but were not white supremacists—the *State* decided to do extensive and sympathetic coverage of the upcoming Confederate Memorial Day, an event that was usually relegated to an inside photo and whose participants were seen as pariahs. Thanks in part to the paper's big-tent spirit of respect, before the spring was over a Sons of Confederate Veterans commander had dramatically switched from insisting on tradition to insisting on compromise, and polls showed public support for flying the flag to have dropped from 55 percent to 40 percent.

These translations of deliberation to the page have been fairly literal, but you can be more imaginative with the idea too. The *Oregonian*, for example, kicked off its 1994 election coverage by looking at the qualities that contribute to good leadership. A small, irregularly published New York magazine called *New Combat*, meanwhile, hit on the idea of deliberative letters to the editor called "dialogues." When a thoughtful response to a thoughtful article came in, before publishing it the editors would ask the article's author for a counterresponse; they would go back and forth between author and reader, asking for progressively shorter and more pithy replies, then publish the "conversation" in its entirety. *New Combat* called these dialogues "a somewhat serious game that readers and editors play," but when it worked the result was sharper, more on the mark than any real-time conversation could be.

✦ PUSHING THE ENVELOPE

1. The *State*'s Confederate flag coverage is worth a bit more attention because it dispels several myths about the nature of deliberation. The comparison chart at the beginning of this chapter may have left the impression that deliberation is genteel, rational, and politically correct, but that isn't the case. Deliberation is *honest*, which means it's often

uncomfortable for everyone involved, full of emotion, and marked by as many refusals to budge as handshakes of agreement. This was the case in South Carolina. The dialogue there differed from debate principally in that people struggled to keep their talk constructive in spite of the tension. Deliberation may also sound at first hearing like splitting the difference, rushing to the midpoint between (say) Confederate flag supporters and opponents. That, of course, is *not* what happened in South Carolina. Sometimes deliberation does end in compromise. At other times it may uncover a common-ground solution nobody had thought of before, and if that happens it's wonderful. But there are many times when people on both sides just wake up to the fact that one group's concerns trump the other's. Many white people who had defended the statehouse flag for years and years came to believe in 1994 that the banner did them less good than it did harm to their black neighbors—and so, paradoxically, as more respect was shown to the Sons of Confederate Veterans, respondents in polls moved steadily toward the traditionally African-American position.

2. A deliberation column might explore why deliberation did (or did not) take place at a given town meeting, congressional session, press conference, or the like. Currently, the style of a meeting becomes newsworthy only when it's unusually nasty ("Senators hurled insults at each other") or rare ("Ordinary Americans were finally given a chance to ask the questions at the second presidential debate, and they asked good ones"); even then, it's reported more as a novelty than as a lesson in what to do or what not to do. A deliberative column could get citizens and officeholders thinking how public meetings ought to work if deliberation is the goal.

3. Papers could trace the consequences of *not* working through an issue with the same sort of "the events that led to" narrative they usually reserve for the aftermaths of disasters or diplomatic walks in the woods. After Congress's 1988 catastrophic health care legislation went down in flames late in 1989, it would have been easy to describe how senators and representatives, trying to be efficient, had pushed through the bill; and how groups that were going to be affected by it, not having been consulted or given time to think through the issues, rushed to defeat it in fear that something was being put over on them.

4. Deliberation begins in ambivalence; editorial pages tend to make absolute certainty into a house style. Frequently a little ambivalence would be both more honest and more helpful to readers. Editorial writers can, for instance, make useful observations about a thorny issue even if they can't come down hard for a specific position (occasionally the "Notebook" feature of the *New York Times* editorial page takes a step in this direction). Or, editorial pages—rather than opining on three issues a day, six or seven days a week—could treat three truly vexing issues for several days each, weighing the various choices, positions, or sides one at a time, fairly and carefully, before offering a considered judgment on the final day. This would mimic the NIF style of weighing choices almost to a T.

5. A newspaper could self-consciously look for ways to turn divisive events into constructive ones. The aftermath of elections and legislative victories, for example, is usually seen in terms of winners and losers, but if a community is to maintain its bonds, it's essential that those on the losing side feel their views will still count. A newspaper could make a "what the other side says" column a standard day-after feature. In it, partisans of, say, a losing presidential candidate could specify which of the things they fought for they most hope the winning candidate will keep in mind. This could replace the substanceless "we'll win next time" or "gracious in defeat" box that merely encourages people to continue feeling like adversaries.

6. One of the thorniest problems newspapers have yet to face is how to put a truly national deliberation into a newspaper. Past public journalism projects have tended to focus either on purely local issues (such as open space in Bremerton, Wash.), or else on national issues for which local citizens could take effective action by themselves (such as race relations in Akron and juvenile violence in Dayton). Federal deficit reduction, job flight to developing countries, the Pentagon's future role, global warming, and many of the other pressing problems of this age simply can't be worked through in Bremerton or Akron or Peoria alone; Americans have to work them out together. But how? How do you conduct community forums across a *national* community? What context do you give, to make Brooklynites feel it's important to hear the ideas of people in Tulsa? Most important, how can reporters be "experts on the community's public life" when the community is 3,000 miles wide? (In part it's owing to questions like these that public journalism has few devotees in either the wire services or the national press corps.) A few organizations have proposed interesting answers. Nationwide deliberative polls (such as the one in Manchester, England; see "Sidebar: Using Polls and Focus Groups" in Chapter Two) are one approach; they create a proxy deliberation among a small number of representative citizens. National Public Radio tried a different tack during its 1994 election project. Its local affiliates conducted forums and on-air reports in much the same way as a metropolitan public newspaper, then fed portions of their coverage onto national programs such as "Morning Edition" and "All Things Considered" for the larger listenership to share. A national coordinator helped the affiliates to work out a common template for their coverage and to receive training in deliberation. Following still another model, six Florida newspapers (including the *Miami Herald* and the *St. Petersburg Times*) and more than twice that number of broadcast partners coordinated and pooled statewide campaign coverage, also during the 1994 season; a few of the individual papers conducted community conversations or forums as part of the effort. (See Chapter Six's box on media partnerships for more information on how such things work.)

✦

In many of his writings, Daniel Yankelovich stubbornly warns that people will, if given the chance, squirm out of the hard work of making choices for as long as they can. They "wait for the perfect solution" to a problem by shooting down every imperfect solution the moment its shortcomings become obvious; meanwhile, the problem worsens. You can sympathize with the reason we all do this (it's painful to accept that universal health care *must mean* higher premiums, or that affordable health care *must mean* no heart transplants for people over 50), but it's a destructive habit all the same. Public newspapers can make it harder for people to duck the real world's trade-offs. A few ideas:

7. When sources, letter writers, or forum participants cite costs in a proposed solution to an agenda issue, reporters can ask them—not rhetorically, but fully expecting an answer—"Are those costs worse than the costs of doing nothing? Are they worse than the costs of alternatives A or B?" The letters editor could announce that, after a certain point is reached in the public debate, the paper will no longer print letters that don't address these questions head-on.

8. The two excuses people give themselves to justify waiting for the perfect solution are that doing nothing isn't so bad, and that some as-yet-unseen solution will arise that's better than anything now on the table. Face these excuses head-on. Each time the choices on an issue are discussed within the paper, present them side by side—advantages, costs, consequences, and so forth—with a description of the status quo. Interview experts on the prospects for coming up with choices that have fewer costs and consequences than the ones presented here.

9. Run an informal survey—"Either/Or" or "You Can't Have Both" —in which experts offer their judgments on the trade-offs to be made between two things citizens seem to want (say, stable or growing entitlements and deficit reduction). Citizens would phone or write in to vote on which alternative they choose.

10. To make the same idea more elaborate and whimsical at the same time, turn hard choices into a game. Maxis, the California-based creator of the intricate yet popular SimCity software series, also produces Sim-Health, a sort of civically earnest computer game which (in the words of its advertising copy) "turns you into an elected official charged with designing a national health care system. You make the tough decisions—

and live with the consequences." Try as you might, on SimHealth you can't opt for a benefit without receiving a bill for the costs. Translated to a newspaper, a choice-making game might be featured on the center spread of a major reporting project, designed by the art department and reporters together, and perhaps peppered with sidebars explaining why experts believe particular constraints and trade-offs are realistic. Taken in the right spirit it could be a pleasant diversion for news staff and citizens alike.

Making Sources More Deliberative

Ultimately the deliberative flavor of a newspaper derives less from what editors do on the page than from what reporters do on the street; they are the ones who catch, or don't catch, their sources in a deliberative mood. (The same goes for moderators of public forums and town halls.) Fortunately, a diverse lot of thinkers—particularly labor negotiators, mediators, and diplomats—have studied the twin skills of putting people in deliberative moods and nudging them toward consensus, and many of their ideas can be appropriated by journalists.

This key idea has been stated a half-dozen times already. It was John Marks, president of the conflict resolution group Search for Common Ground, who first summarized mediation's lesson for journalists by noting that, if you ask your sources different questions, you'll get different answers; the style of question defines the story. Asking "Where do you agree?" produces a different story than "Where do you disagree?"; the same with "Where could you and your opponent work together?" versus "Why do you think your opponent is wrong?" It isn't just the focus of the stories that will differ when you change the style of questions; the questions also put the sources in different frames of mind. Marks has applied this insight in media settings himself, most notably in 10 public television "debates" between opposing sides of the country's most intractable issues. In one half-hour, he steered the heads of the National Right to Life Committee and the National Abortion Rights Action League to identify five areas of common ground on which they had the potential to act together. (Watching this tape is enough to convince anyone that no problem is so divided, so intractable, so "stuck" that it can't be moved forward by asking the right questions.)

Many organizations have pet questions to deflect both citizens and experts from sterile or divisive speech toward the kind of speech a deliberative forum uses to build judgment, mutual understanding, and consensus. A few examples:

SOME DELIBERATIVE QUESTIONS

"What brought you into this issue?" (The *Virginian-Pilot*). This question gets people right to the emotional core of their positions; it promotes understanding in group interviews because opponents can usually empathize with each other's personal stories more easily than with each other's arguments.

"What experiences or beliefs might lead decent and caring people to support that point of view?" (The Study Circles Resource Center). The reporter asks this of, say, pro-choice advocates about the anti-abortion point of view. It asks people to look sympathetically at points of view they've rejected and at the opponents themselves.

"Is that where the disagreement lies?" (John Marks of Search for Common Ground). When a source explains how two sides in an issue disagree, the reporter might restate what's been said in very concrete terms and ask this question. It often prods the source into saying, "Well, it's not exactly that way," and then redefining the disagreement more carefully and narrowly.

"What's your underlying interest?" "Is that something you personally believe?" "What's your reason for saying that?" (John Marks). Provocative questions to get behind opponents' views to the aims and beliefs that motivate them.

"Describe the other side's position to me." (John Marks). The reporter insists on getting a description, not a caricature, then follows up by asking the opponent if it's fair. This forces the source to reason for a few moments from within the opponent's terms.

"What point that the other side makes, makes the most sense to you?" "What trade-offs would you be willing to live with?" "What sacrifices are you unwilling to accept?" "What alternative is the least persuasive?" "What makes this issue so difficult?" (Lisa Austin of the Project on Public Life and the Press). Such questions help define where common ground is more or less likely to be found.

This isn't what most people expect when interviewed by the press; reporters need to seek out sources who'll respond well to this style of questioning. Marks says it's partly a matter of temperament, partly a matter of position. Some people are natural common-grounders, while others find it impossible to break out of an adversarial tone; if two sources are available, go to the one who doesn't flinch when asked, "Where do both sides agree?" Often journalists gravitate to lobbyists and officeholders for quotable comment, but these are a class of people whose jobs virtually force them to be rigid: They're paid to represent constituents, not to speak for themselves. Marks says an ideal source is a respected man or woman who's associated with one side of an issue (say, "pro-life" or "pro-choice"), has the respect of people on that side, but thinks independently and doesn't hold a position of authority. Go outside the PACs and look for retired elder statesmen and creative mavericks.

To a lesser extent, the location of an interview; whether it's done one on one or as part of a panel; whether it's done immediately after a breaking news event, or a few hours or days later; and the reporters' own frame of mind (whether they're out to "get" a source, like Sam Donaldson, or to learn from the source, like Bill Moyers)—all these things help determine the source's willingness to be deliberative. Speaking to an interest-group spokesperson at the office, or an elected official at the legislature, to take one example, frequently provokes a more rigid, conventional response than meeting such a person at an unfamiliar cafe, park, or library. One of the best places to meet officials may be at a regularly scheduled deliberative forum or study circle meeting somewhere in the community.

✦ PUSHING THE ENVELOPE

1. Public journalists can also study deliberative questioning more formally. The National Issues Forums and the Study Circles Resource Center publish moderator guides, with explicit instruction on how to steer people in group settings toward constructive conversation. Ideas from professional negotiators can be tapped through such national or international organizations as Search for Common Ground, Partners for Democratic Change, the MIT–Harvard Public Disputes Program, and the International Healthy Cities Foundation. University-based conflict resolution centers often stage training courses for people who wish to moderate deliberative forums. (So do more than a dozen regional NIF institutes.) Newspaper staff could take an abbreviated training course, or arrange with a local center to tailor a training session to their needs.

2. Newspapers can invent ways to help *citizens* think more deliberatively too. In early 1994, the *Spokane Spokesman-Review* named two "interactive editors" to its editorial pages. Their job was to help citizens write cogent opinion pieces (titled "Your Turn") to fill two weekly slots.

They trained the writers in many stylistic conventions (don't pontificate, speak in personal terms, use declarative sentences, etc.); there's no reason they couldn't train them in the convention of deliberative writing as well. Alternatively, a paper could do a straightforward project on "asking the right questions"—how to constructively talk with experts, officials, other citizens—incorporating, for example, material from the Rural Southern Voice for Peace training manual from Chapter Two, or the deliberative question box above. Or it could invite mediators to explain their business in the paper. Any training that's good for reporters is probably good for citizens too.

3. Even sources who are temperamentally common-grounders may not be able to see a familiar problem in a new and constructive light. E. J. Dionne's *Why Americans Hate Politics* argues that if an issue has well-defined "sides" (pro-choice and anti-abortion; free trade and America-first) it's a good indicator of sterile thinking; the partisans are out of fresh ideas, and the public finds neither the extremes nor a simple compromise among them particularly attractive. Public reporters could consciously reduce their reliance on "sides" when hunting for sources, seeking out the unorthodox as well. In some fields, longtime sources may be able to point out unusual (or "radical" or "innovative" or "kooky") schools of thinking. A 1995 *New Yorker* article profiled a well-established "truth school" of lawyers and judges who favor neither the "strong" evidence-exclusion rule of civil libertarians nor the "weak" rule of law-and-order conservatives; the media radar had missed them because they don't fall cleanly onto either "side." Alternatively, people who have thought long and hard about a public issue but are not professionally related to it frequently write letters to the editor, or contribute to specialized magazines, on-line bulletin boards, phone-in shows, and the like. Reporters might phone up the psychologist or foreign-exchange student who wrote about affirmative action, or the small business owner with a new take on juvenile crime. They may have the brilliant insight everybody's been waiting for. Recall that it was Heinrich Schliemann (a businessman) who found the ruins of Troy by studying *The Iliad* when archaeologists thought Troy was nothing but a myth.

✦ SIDEBAR: TRAINING DELIBERATIVE REPORTERS

Sources aren't the only people whose frame of mind makes a difference to public journalism. Reporters themselves are called upon to do a number of things normal journalists don't: To hold informal, open-ended conversations with citizens. To act consciously as the public's representative when meeting with experts, officeholders, and candidates. To know how every segment of the community feels about their common problems and one another.

✦ To boil down information into what citizens need to know right now. To be patient about pacing and tentative about conclusions. To write to readers' deepest civic motivations. To collaborate with other reporters. And, of course, to ask deliberative questions. Altogether this amounts to a thorough deprogramming of everything they learned in journalism school.

Pioneering public journalists have typically found it harder than they ever expected to win colleagues over to this style of reporting—or even to make it comprehensible to them. This has turned a handful of newsrooms into subtle tugs-of-war, in which a few people (usually top editors or specialty reporters) face off against a majority to whom these ideas are strange, suspect, or else stamped with all the hallmarks of one more fad imposed from on high. A newspaper will always do itself a favor if it sets aside time and plans a strategy to introduce the staff to public journalism. Here are a few strategies that have succeeded so far:

Just Talk It Out

Public journalists often say that their colleagues have to pass through an "Ah, *now* I get it" phase before they can develop any enthusiasm for the deliberative style. Plenty of editors have short-circuited this process by beginning their staffs on public journalism just by announcing superficial changes in routine and then handing out story assignments. A good skim through theory should precede launching into practice, and a staff bull session is a good environment to take one.

Provide Formal Training

More and more papers have hired consultants from deliberative organizations to work with their staffs (most notably the *Dayton Daily News* and the Norfolk *Virginian-Pilot*). Among the organizations that do this kind of thing are the Study Circles Resource Center, the Kettering Foundation, and the Harwood Group.

Let Peers Train Peers

An essential stage in the *Virginian-Pilot*'s training plan has been to let members of its intensively trained "public life team" spread the lessons they're learning from experience and Richard Harwood throughout the newsroom—reporter to reporter, story editor to

✦　story editor. This makes sense not only because the teachers will better understand the students' point of view. Very often class tensions in a newspaper add a needless complication to learning public journalism.

Make Experience the Teacher

As part of the *Detroit Free Press*'s ongoing "Children First" campaign, reporters are allowed two paid hours each week to volunteer at local schools or in other community organizations that help kids. If seeing citizens in a new light is an essential part of the "Ah, *now* I get it" experience, then working with citizens must be one of the quickest ways to get there. The idea of providing paid time for nonreporting work may prove seminal in other ways too. Reporters could be given time to study the books on democracy and citizen attitudes referred to in this book, or else to participate in deliberative forums as private citizens.

Piggyback on the New Media

One broadcaster sees on-line newspapers as a natural arena to train public journalists, simply because they can't be written the same way as conventional newspapers. For the moment, all on-line journalists are at sea; this makes them more receptive to trying something new. He suggests editors should be on constant lookout for such "routine-destroying opportunities."

Stuff Public Journalism with Prestige

Editors such as Chris Peck of the *Spokane Spokesman-Review* are of the conviction that reporters learn what they're awarded for. Several now make a point of running public journalism stories more prominently, often on page one. Peck has proposed that someone invent a Pulitzer Prize of public journalism. What journalists first do for glory, they may gradually learn to do for love.

Pick the Natural Public Journalists and Leave the Rest

As John Marks says, some people are natural common-grounders and some aren't. Some take quite naturally to public listening and deliberation; others take naturally to investigative reporting and

✦ "gotcha" Q&As. Each has a place even in a public journalism newsroom. Many editors begin by separating beats that require the skills of public journalism from those that require the skills of Woodward and Bernstein, then they assign staff to whichever beats make them most comfortable and productive.

✦

CHAPTER FIVE

Helping
Citizens Act

"Civic Virtue Is Not Its Own Reward"

Citizens express many frustrations with American democracy, but if for some reason one had to be singled out it would be an easy choice to make: They resent to their core that problems don't ever get solved. In the language of *Meaningful Chaos*, "People are seeking a sense of possibility—that action might occur on a public concern, and that they might play a personal role in it . . . so that discussion on public concerns does not seem so isolated from action." When they find instead that political involvement doesn't get them anywhere, they simply tune-out, stop voting, grow cynical, or keep their eyes focused close to home, acting on a neighborhood scale where they feel they can make a difference. Journalist E. J. Dionne's bestseller makes this point in the plainest possible terms: Why do Americans hate politics? Because politics doesn't work.

So far, this book has talked about how journalists can make public judgment easier and more accessible to citizens—how it can give them the information they need and the opportunities for discussion they want. And this is all well and good. But citizens will lose interest in journalism, too, if it does no better than politics in getting their judgment acted upon. As Jeremy Iggers of the Minneapolis–St. Paul *Star Tribune* phrases it, "Civic virtue is not its own reward."

Most editors (even public journalists) are reluctant to face what this means. They would like to believe that whoever may be responsible for civic action, it's certainly not the press. So intensely concerned are they about crossing the line into advocacy, they end up stopping well short of it—and rarely consider the impossible expectations they're throwing on citizens as a result. Not long ago at a Project on Public Life and the Press conference, the editor of a major public-journalism-oriented daily described where *his* paper was going to draw the line: He would publish lengthy, in-depth, value-centered coverage on public agenda issues, collaborate with civic groups to convene forums and report on them as a public service . . . then he would step back, wash his hands, and "let citizens act." He explained that going any farther would compromise his editorial stance as an independent, unbiased, critical voice, willing to tell things as they are and to champion unpopular causes (like free speech or affirmative action) if and when the majority turned against them. Other editors in the room assented. This makes perfect sense from the newspaper's own point of view; it's both ethical and consistent.

But then someone asked exactly *how* citizens were supposed to act. Put yourself in the shoes of an ordinary man or woman: not Ralph Nader or Kate Michelman, but a busy Los Angeles truck driver or Cincinnati schoolteacher. How would you—a private citizen—bring your neighborhood forum into conversation with the 50 or 60 others in your community? (Alternatively, who would you trust to do it for you?) On what authority would *you* identify the community's common ground? How would you publicize the "will of the people" you'd heard, and how would you make it the standard against which public action would from then on be measured? How would *you* hold the feet of public officials and other citizens to the fire? The press and public figures talk fast and loose about Americans "sending messages" to Washington or the state capital, but how as a practical matter are they supposed even to put those messages together, without some central, trusted, neutral organization such as a newspaper to help them? (The editor said that this was a good point and, revealingly, one that had never crossed his mind.)

This chapter's premise is a natural extension of the whole premise of public journalism: Acts of citizenship (besides voting) are unnecessarily hard for ordinary Americans to perform, and so, just as one ought to expect, they don't perform them often or well. They don't find common ground, draft clear messages, or act in concert to solve their problems. Journalists should always be on the lookout for ways to make those acts easier. The examples on the next several pages demonstrate that there are indeed lines that newspapers can draw—still well this side of bias, advocacy, and subjectivity—within which public journalists can do much more to help citizens act. But first it's worthwhile to go back to the test of realism and consider what "acting on the public's judgment" ought to mean.

Chapter One made the case that journalists too often equate action with the things officials do; ordinary people, on the other hand, see problems as too big and intricate for governments, bureaucracies, or think tanks alone to solve. People want results, not activity. Congress can pass a wonderful crime bill, but thrown into a vacuum it won't solve the problem of crime. Neighborhoods can set up creative block-watches and antidrug programs, but without the appropriate laws, policies, budgets, and regulations to back them up, their grasp will fall woefully short of their reach. Truly successful action can only mean coordinating the action of groups starting with the family and ending with the state or federal administration. To complicate an already daunting task, Chapters Two and Three insisted that people see such problems as "schools," "drugs," "youth violence," "jobs," and "family" as so interwoven that they must be addressed all at the same time. How can a community—let alone its newspaper—transform something so large and ill-defined into a concrete, practical task (without retreating into the kinds of narrow, partial, Beltway-centered solutions and debates people are so dissatisfied with)? How can it succeed?

The key may be a concept that David Mathews of the Kettering Foundation calls "complementary action." Most social problems *are* too big to solve all at once, but even so we get less for our efforts than we might just because we so often head in contradictory directions. What schools are doing to help troubled kids doesn't jibe with what the police are doing. Voluntary organizations embrace one solution for urban poverty, while city hall embraces its opposite. Employers' family-leave policies don't mesh with Washington's economic, trade, or welfare incentives. (And often an unconsulted public balks at policies invented by their elected and unelected bosses.) Activity waters down other activity, and leaves us with less than the sum of the parts. If, on the other hand, a community's varied and independent groups could all work from the same basic credo—a well-defined public judgment on the given issue, broad in scope even if slight in detail—their actions could reinforce one another, leaving us with more than the sum of the parts. Look around for precedents. Religious charities, Alcoholics Anonymous chapters, environment groups, yellow-ribbon campaigns—in all these cases independent groups enhance each other's work not through explicit coordination but simply through a shared understanding of their goals.

This chapter therefore proposes three roles for journalists: First, *hearing the public's consensus* on a given issue, and stating it in a way that's as precise and unambiguous as possible. Second, *acting as a watchdog*, to make sure officials (as well as individuals, neighborhoods, and private organizations) act according to its lights. And third, *maintaining people's awareness of the public's voice* after the special sections and big projects hit the recycling bin—over the long haul—so that complementary action continues. As the chapter develops it ought to become clear that this is a more pragmatic and promising program than it might seem at first blush.

How Do You Spot—and Spotlight— an Evolving Public Consensus?

To be honest, public newspapers haven't bothered with hearing consensuses so far. Saying "X is the solution people want, and so the mayor/legislature/Congress must enact X" seems to smack of an especially great arrogance (although, perversely, saying "X is the solution our editorial board wants on the public's behalf" does not). As the boxed examples in the next sections indicate, newspapers have tended so far to go straight from forums to action: They've helped people volunteer, network, give aid to kids in trouble, and express good will across racial or economic lines—all of which has unleashed enormous energy in supposedly apathetic citizens. Put in Chapter Three's terms, they have treated "the narrative" as everything and "the facts" as unimportant, and in some cases that's fine. Everyone agrees that kids in trouble need adults to give them support; everyone agrees neighbor should help out neighbor; nearly everyone agrees that people shouldn't judge one another based on skin color alone. Projects focused on straightforward problems such as these don't need a lot of working through; citizens are straining at the bit to get involved, and the newspaper can set them to work simply by helping them coordinate. But that isn't the case on health care, criminal justice, welfare reform, affirmative action, or most of the other stagnant, persistent, thorny issues that people are most deeply troubled by. Here everyone doesn't agree. Here volunteering by itself can't solve the problem. Here, in other words, the emotionally satisfying work won't accomplish much if the hard work of nailing down agreed guidelines isn't done first.

"Consensus" may be a misleading word here—more an obstacle than an aid—because obviously large publics seldom if ever zero in on a single agreed solution to a problem. Deliberation is no magic wand in this regard; the experience of organizations like the National Issues Forums and the Study Circles Resource Center, with long histories of organizing public forums, is that diverse groups of Americans, even after meeting half a dozen times on an issue over long periods of time, will still disagree on even some of the broadest aspects of public policy. To get around the semantic confusion, NIF avoids the term "consensus" and says that in deliberation it's looking for something it calls "a public voice." Journalists at a 1994 public journalism seminar came up with what's perhaps a more immediately vivid term: "a new ledge to stand on."

Recall the cycle of decision making from Chapter Three. When a community first addresses a social problem, it has a starting point—some general way of seeing the decision it has to make, defining its limits, sensing what's truly important to resolve and what's less important, which trade-offs will be hard and which will be easy. Regarding health care, people started off worried both about escalating out-of-pocket costs and about the millions of Americans who either weren't insured or were in danger of losing their insurance. Any "solution to the health care crisis" would have to resolve those worries first. Technology, ethics, and any number of other might-be issues were of peripheral importance at best.

As the community grapples with the problem over time, however, its starting point shifts: the limits change, convictions about what's truly important and what trade-offs are possible evolve. Concerning health care, by mid-1994 Americans had pretty clearly decided that medical insurance and treatment should *not* be entangled in yet another layer of bureaucracy, whether it be a statewide insurance pool or the federal government itself. The "national debate" would continue—but if some kind of action had to be taken *now*, whatever Washington did or statehouses did or hospitals, employers, and charitable institutions did would have to fit within that common goal. Thus, in a partial though extremely significant way for policy, the "public voice" had spoken; the health care agenda had "a new ledge to stand on" in its climb toward a solution, one narrower, more certain, and better defined than the old ledge.

So, instead of spotlighting a detailed consensus, camera-ready and in legal language, it is this subtler "new ledge to stand on" that public journalists must try to hear and to express. In some cases it may be an exact answer ("Yes to Proposition A"); in others it may be an outline ("You can't do this, and you must do *at least* that"). In Search for Common Ground's public television dialogues (see pp. 118–119), it was a set of areas where people who couldn't agree on fundamentals could still do shared work (e.g., for Right to Life and the National Abortion Rights Action League, it included stronger prenatal and adoption programs). In rare cases it may be nothing but the recognition that a community is hopelessly divided. (Often the new ledge may be just short of unanimous and yet invisible to watchdog journalists all the same. Public Agenda cites attempts to fix public education. For a decade big majorities have told pollsters that the foremost goals should be safety, enforcing personal discipline, and hammering home "the basics." On this point African-American parents concur with white parents, born-again parents with secular parents, Des Moines parents with Philadelphia parents—even parents as a group with *non*parents. Yet school reformers keep drafting brilliant plans centered on multicultural curricula and higher order skills—which frustrated citizens shoot down—and journalists devote the education pages to administrative disputes, church–state cases, and the distribution of condoms, on none of which the public has a coherent voice.) Hopefully as a result of public deliberation any "new ledge" people come to will at least be broader based and better defined than it otherwise would have been.

In and of itself, there's nothing arrogant about a newspaper identifying a "new ledge" defined in these terms; unlike a full-blown "answer," a "solution," or a "consensus," it's something that's really there in the community, something it's possible to get nearly everyone to agree upon. The issue is a purely practical one of how to read the "new ledge" through a process citizens can trust. Once again, success depends on a newspaper staff's expertise about its own community, its ability to hear citizens' talk constructively and subtly—its grasp of the whole range of public listening techniques elaborated since Chapter Two.

At least two organizations, NIF and Search for Common Ground, have been identifying "new ledges" at either the small-group or the national level for many years. NIF's Public Voice program, for example, tries to sum up the common sense of all the thousands of forum groups that discuss the network's three chosen topics each year. To do this, NIF inserts ballots into every discussion guide. Participants fill out one ballot before a forum and another one afterward, offering their opinions on the three or four choices in which the issue is framed and answering questions of the form "Would you support . . . even if it means . . ." and "Do you agree with statements X, Y, and Z?" The ballots are tabulated both to measure public opinion outright and to see how it's moved as a result of deliberation. As a qualitative check, moderators send in descriptions of their forums, including participants' statements that seemed to strike a chord with the group. Finally, NIF convenes six special forums on each issue each year, involving about 200 people; videotapes and transcribes them; and boils the whole mass of information down into the outlines—sometimes sharp, but often rough, partial, or only suggestive—of a "public voice." Every spring it presents the findings to a panel of politicians and journalists at the National Press Club, broadcasts their discussion on PBS, and compiles a brief report that's made available to the public.

A newspaper could mimic this formal approach exactly, or else, benefiting from its more intimate long-term contact with readers, it could adapt the less rigid methods moderators use in individual forums. There it's possible to go back and forth with participants until the "new ledge" is stated in terms everybody agrees to. For example, NIF discussion leaders will often tentatively state aspects of the group's public voice as they arise, while the forum is still going on; participants can either agree, disagree, or try to sharpen the wording through careful discussion. Similarly, John Marks patiently built two lists—"areas of common ground" and "areas of disagreement"—during each of Search for Common Ground's televised dialogues on abortion, gun control, and other issues. He would intermittently announce to his panelists, "You both seem to be saying . . ." and propose that something be added to one of the lists. Doggedly, he would prod them to put the addition into their own words, to narrow and refine it, slicing partial agreements off of disagreements wherever it was possible. The lists became a case of "if you build it, they will come"; long-time adversaries whose last intention had been to spell out their mutual agreements did so because Marks made it an essential part of the show.

A newspaper could do much the same thing by, for example, making a "What's the Public Voice on Issue X?" box a standard feature of its editorial page. Each week or month (depending on the intensity of public deliberation on an issue) the reporters, editors, and community leaders who have devoted the most effort to public listening could meet to suggest statements to go in the box. A box on public schools might include, "Safety, discipline and basic skills are the topmost priority." Other statements could be less definite. "Most people favor Y as a first step, and most others don't strongly object." Or, "The real debate seems to be over question Z; everything else is trivial in comparison." The paper could then invite the public to respond. Phone-in lines might tally how many readers agreed with each statement in the box so far. Letters could be published; if the paper had TV or radio partners, phone calls could be broadcast. Editors could put a premium on publishing responses that offered a more concise, unambiguous proposal for the "public voice" box, or else a clear explanation of why a particular statement already in it was wrong. Then the next time the paper published "What's the Public Voice on Issue X?" it could correct and refine the community's new ledge. Gradually, the box would become full enough, precise enough—and attain broad enough consent—to provide real guidance for public policy.

✦ PUSHING THE ENVELOPE

1. Public-opinion scholars Benjamin Page and Robert Shapiro have written an exhaustive defense of ordinary citizens, *The Rational Public*, in which they argue that, on policy question after policy question, Americans have come to reasonable and stable collective judgments over time. Their working model of judgment isn't as pluralist or as purely descriptive as the "new ledge to stand on" (they write mostly about what majorities do or don't believe), but it is nuanced enough to give readers a grasp of what practical consensuses amount to, how long they take to develop, and how

they've shaped public action throughout most of this century. A journalist might read it as a kind of Dr. Spock guide to what's normal in working through, and for clues as to where intelligent journalism can improve on the process.

✦

The skeleton idea of spelling out a new ledge by talking back and forth through the newspaper can be adapted in a lot of ways. Among them:

2. To ensure the new ledge is rational, experts can be invited to add a second column to the paper's public voice box. It would offer the best informed guesses (where in dispute, an assortment of them) of the costs and consequences of each common ground statement the public had agreed to.

3. Sometimes citizens assume there's a common ground when in fact there is not. Many Americans read about the dozen-plus polls showing strong support for universal health care in 1994 and assumed there was a consensus; yet Daniel Yankelovich was able to show through more careful polling (see "Using Polls and Focus Groups" in Chapter Two) that there wasn't. The newspaper could keep things clear by occasionally reporting on "what's not yet a consensus, and why."

4. While gradually building up common ground through deliberation, the paper could borrow John Marks's idea and publish a separate list—perhaps a detailed one, just like the needs list in the *Charlotte Observer*'s neighborhoods project (see box, below)—of "where we can already act together."

5. A paper could even step back and let citizens build all these public-voice and common-action boxes themselves. Editors would invite community forums to send in *their* comprehensive proposals for each box and then print two or three of them in the paper. (This would have a tonic effect on the forums themselves, where despite the best efforts of moderators people often talk around a tough issue to avoid the work of making choices. Getting their work in the paper would concentrate a lot of minds.) Readers could write, phone, or fax, participate in surveys, even vote, to select which of the public voice boxes they'd like the newspaper to watchdog.

Facilitator and Watchdog

Compared with pinning down "the public voice," playing the watchdog probably seems like journalism at its most traditional. But public journalism sees the role in an unusual light. As Chapter One argued, uncovering scandal and throwing the rascals out of office—though honorable work—doesn't build roads, fix schools, or make black Americans feel comfortable with white Americans and vice versa. If newspapers are to play a truly useful watchdog role in the future, it has to come down to making sure that the public voice is the basis for public action.

Once a newspaper has found a way to hear the public voice and to flag it, this mission more or less reduces itself to two broad classes of tasks, carrots and sticks—that is, *making it easier* for officials, volunteer groups, neighborhoods, and families to act together in complementary ways, and then *holding them responsible* for acting consistently with the public voice.

Making It Easier to Act

Journalists tend to assume that, if officials or citizens aren't acting toward the public good, it's because they're unwilling to do it. Not enough after-hours volunteers at public schools? People are selfish. No movement on the crime bill? The legislature is stalling. As a consequence, the press falls naturally into the role of moral conscience, alternately berating and exhorting the community about what it ought to do. Public journalism assumes (at least at first pass) that unwillingness probably isn't the problem. Citizens, institutions, and officeholders may well want to act together on a public issue but for some reason—inertia, ignorance, bad communication, lack of coordination—can't get the ball rolling. The press will accomplish more by playing the facilitator than by playing the critic.

Any number of things, grand or trivial, may be blocking a particular community at a particular time. When the Bergen County *Record* undertook a major project to reexamine juvenile justice, editor Glenn Ritt was amazed to learn that local judges, prosecutors, and family services workers didn't even know one another; they had to introduce themselves at meetings arranged by the paper. "If it was not for the newspaper, there would be no chemistry that could lead to the kinds of solutions that we proposed." Residents in a depressed Fort Wayne, Ind., neighborhood were living with unrepaired sewer lines because they couldn't figure out how to work the city bureaucracy; so the *News-Sentinel* detailed the process by which the city planned and budgeted its repairs. People who had begun by asking the paper to pressure officials ended up contacting officials and getting the problem solved themselves.

In many places, lawmakers won't pay attention to citizens' ideas; the *Tallahassee Democrat* felt that part of its public agenda mission was getting policymakers to understand what they could learn from ordinary people. Public journalism, said executive editor Lou Heldman, is "really

THE *CHARLOTTE OBSERVER*

By mid-1994, when Charlotte's crime rate rose to 18th nationwide, the *Observer* had already pioneered more techniques of public journalism than any other single newspaper. Editors quite naturally turned their creativity to the hot topic of the day. "Virtually every poll in America puts crime at the top of citizens' concerns," wrote executive editor Jennie Buckner, yet news coverage got them nowhere, tending to "frighten and depress readers, pulling them away from neighborhood life and leaving them pessimistic about their community's future."

Residents of high-crime areas struggled by themselves against worsening odds, while residents of safer areas read about it anxiously in the *Observer*. What if instead the paper could get the whole city mobilized on behalf of the most troubled neighborhoods? "We would invite readers to help these neighborhoods help themselves. There would be no question but that we were all in this together, working to understand what we could do about a problem." Armed with that idea, some grant money from the Pew Center for Civic Journalism and a few media and charitable partners, the paper launched "Taking Back Our Neighborhoods," a one-and-a-half-year project that would focus all of Charlotte's attention on 10 target areas, each for six weeks at a time.

The June 5 kickoff explored the city's crime problem in general terms, drawing on an unusual, intensive poll of high-crime-area residents themselves. The first specific target would be Seversville, a section in the northwest. Reporters held a long, candid meeting at midmonth with an advisory panel of neighborhood leaders, who detailed problems including crack cocaine, high unemployment, and overwhelmed parents; this shaped all the coverage that was to follow. On June 26 the *Observer* began running an investigative series on the links between crack houses and absentee landlords on nearby Cummings Avenue, and two days later held a massive community meeting in a Seversville church. At a United Way resource fair immediately after the meeting, scores of residents signed up for previously understaffed neighborhood crime watches, Big Brother programs, and the like.

The project's real test came on July 17, when the paper and its radio and TV partners introduced the entire city to Seversville, its problems, and struggles in a daylong media blitz. The coverage

(cont.)

THE CHARLOTTE OBSERVER *(cont.)*

included an itemized list of needs in the neighborhood. By September, more than 200 organizations, individuals, and agencies—from private law firms to the YMCA—had offered their support, answering virtually every need on the list. A special *Observer* liaison officer helped coordinate these efforts with those of local residents, while still more Charlotteans phoned a voice-mail line offering tips to Seversville leaders on other ways to solve their problems. The mayor and police stepped up city programs to complement the private activity.

By then the *Observer* had turned to its next target, Commonwealth-Morningside, and showed the city that each unhappy neighborhood is unhappy in its own way. The culprit here wasn't poverty so much as busy arterial avenues cutting off one section from another, allowing burglars easy escape and defeating any sense of community. Response from outside was strong for this neighborhood too—but came from entirely different civic groups, in response to the entirely different problems it was facing.

---

about changing the way people think and act. If those now calling themselves 'residents' or 'taxpayers' begin thinking of themselves as 'citizens,' and acting in intelligently empowered ways, it follows that public officials will begin to think differently about citizens and their own responsibilities." In Akron, Ohio, the barriers to working on race relations were partly just barriers of opportunity. When the *Beacon Journal* hired two facilitators to help community groups coordinate race relations projects, 140 eventually got involved, comprising between 10,000 and 15,000 people; when it provided readers with a clip-out coupon on which they could pledge to fight racial discrimination in the coming year, 22,000 made the pledge (see box in the next section).

What's necessary and appropriate for any given community depends on the community itself. Journalists must be expert enough in seeing the strengths and weaknesses of their particular officials, religious institutions, police, schools, citizens, and systems to tailor the patch to the leak. But there's at least one thing that every community seems to need, and the news media, being a daily part of most citizens' lives, are perfectly positioned to produce it: momentum. Look at Akron, Dayton, Huntington, Wichita, or Charlotte; they are all fine examples. As a result of the *Charlotte Observer's* focus on the impoverished Seversville neighborhood (see box, above), a YMCA found free day-camp places for 41 local children, volunteers came forward to renovate housing and tutor the out of work, a sign company donated entrance signs as a mark of community pride, a bank pledged $50,000 to build a new recreation center, and politicians started coming to community meetings to discuss what government could do to help—among many more things. Any of the initiatives that erupted from across the city in 1994 could have been launched in 1993 or 1990, without any help from the paper; none of the ideas were especially new, or required great coordination. But they *weren't* launched. Despite central Charlotte's well-known problems, they weren't even suggested or thought of. The fact is, citizens probably get the bulk of their motivation from working in a common enterprise. They need to see that things are happening, that their own contributions are adding on to those of others. They like to be swept up in the tide of a great cause. And this is precisely what the *Observer* gave them. It spelled out the final act of Chapter Three's "master narrative": the community coming together. And the community leapt in to make it happen.

Holding Everyone Responsible

This kind of common enterprise—unlike everyday politics—puts responsibilities not just on officeholders and other public figures but on citizens as well, and it only succeeds if a great number of people perform. This adds immeasurably to the press's scope for fair comment. A good newspaper ought to know from its public listening whether all segments of the community are taking the time to discuss a public issue; whether they're truly deliberating or merely talking at one another; whether citizens, political leaders, and experts are taking account of one another's views; whether they're facing the consequences of their choices; and finally whether lawmakers and citizens are passing the bills and doing the work necessary to bring off the public's consensus judgment. Conventional reporting has nothing like these objective benchmarks by which to judge popular and official behavior; if the governor and the senator haven't committed actual crimes, the worst they can be accused of is showing what the newspaper thinks is poor judgment on a bill or not passing a bill at all. A public journalist can frankly say after a bad city council session that "the meeting was entirely irrelevant, because members talked at one another instead of with one another, and their resolutions lay outside the boundaries of the 'public voice.' " This is a wonderfully powerful tool. (The *Observer* demonstrated some of its power during a 1992 senatorial election, when it warned one recalcitrant candidate that if he didn't address citizens' foremost concerns it would simply print white space beneath his picture and alongside their questions. The paper followed through. Soon afterward, the candidate changed his campaign plan and answered the questions.)

It's no harder in principle to watchdog citizens; the trick is to expect from the beginning that they show responsibility. In Bremerton, Wash., the *Sun* insisted that citizens, not experts, write a proposal for preserving the region's open space; the paper organized community meetings and provided background materials to those willing to hash out a draft. (The proposal eventually failed as a ballot initiative, and many of the participating citizens regrouped into a nonprofit advocacy group for the open-space cause.) The *Dayton Daily News* showed its expectations in a wider range of ways: It insisted that groups outside the paper organize forums. It invited volunteers to be trained as forum moderators. It asked for more detail than the *Beacon Journal* had in pledges made by citizens, which leaves it the leeway to go back at a later date and see whether people did all that they promised. Davis Merritt of the *Wichita Eagle*, of course, made expectations explicit in his introduction to the "People Project" (see "Telling the Narrative" in Chapter Three): "At the end of [this project], we'll know an important thing about ourselves: whether we have the will, given the opportunity, to take responsibility for our lives and our community." All this is fair warning that the newspaper will compare citizens' performance, in the same ways as officeholders', against the benchmarks of democratic practice and the public voice.

✦ PUSHING THE ENVELOPE

1. Tone is crucial. Thomas Patterson's *Out of Order* piles up evidence for the destructive effect of conventional journalism's relentlessly skeptical voice. Trust and optimism erode beneath it like flesh beneath acid. Watchdogging ordinary citizens should not mean extending to everybody the harsh treatment now reserved for public figures, but unfortunately a skeptical (or just mean) watchdog is the only kind of watchdog many reporters and editors know how to be. A good newspaper might try to invent a different voice. *Asking* citizens and officials if a particular judgment is really rational, rather than *accusing* them of being irrational; writing frequent success stories about mayors and legislators who deliberate well as a way of putting pressure on those who deliberate poorly; editorializing a bit more ruefully (e.g., using Davis Merritt's tone of voice) when the community falls short—these are straightforward approaches. To spur your creativity, ask: What if we don't assume malice, intolerance, or selfishness? What other factors could explain why people haven't deliberated, acted on the public voice, and so forth? And how can we write about those factors in an honest and constructive way?

2. Chris Peck of the *Spokane Spokesman-Review* has suggested that one way to put officials and citizens on the spot to act on the "public voice" is to ask them at the end of a major news-and-forum project, "What should we do now?" Are we prepared to continue talking? (If so, the newspaper will help organize more forums.) Are we ready to act? (If so, the newspaper will solicit pledges.) Or are we simply going to put the matter aside, file away the public voice, and use it as our starting point on another day? And if that's our choice, on *what* other day? Don't let precious momentum drag off without a comment. Make it clear that, if nothing is done, it's the public's choice and not the newspaper's.

3. Newspapers may still be reluctant to give up their traditional editorial independence in order to champion a "public voice." What if the community is divided over racial justice? Who will unequivocally insist that action is necessary? Frank Denton of the *Wisconsin State Journal* proposes splitting editorial functions in two: One editorial page would be the paper's, the other "John and Jane Public's." On the first, the editorial board could champion whatever it regarded as the right viewpoint (just as ed boards do today); the second would help citizens frame their new ledges and press officials to respect them.

4. David Mathews and Daniel Yankelovich assert that one of the main problems with American democracy is impatience: We act too soon, before workable solutions have emerged, or before deliberation has fleshed out a common ground among ordinary people. (Mathews often cites the catastrophic health care bill, passed with lightning speed by Congress in 1988 without popular debate and then repealed with lightning speed in the face of intensive protest.) Following the test of realism, an editorial page might insist that officials *refrain* from acting whenever it appears the public isn't ready.

5. Public newspapers such as the *Beacon Journal* and the *Eagle* have received some of their warmest praise just by acting as a coordination point for volunteers. Citizens have frequently commented, though, that they'd be more likely to do something if they could more easily match up with organizations that needed their skills. Three ideas for making this so: (a) *Public-participation coupons.* Readers could mail in vouchers saying, for example, "I owe you two hours of volunteering, and my skills include (check boxes below)." The paper could then make the coupons available to community groups in need of people. (b) A *help wanted/available page*. Its only differences from the standard page would be that ads could be placed free of charge, and they would be themed according to needs required to fulfill the public voice. (c) *How-to-help boxes.* At periodic intervals, the paper could publish a box explaining, for example, "What Retirees Can Do" to help on the top public agenda issues. The next time it would explain "What Small Business Can Do" or "What Students Can Do" or "What People with a Foreign Language Can Do."

6. Similarly, a newspaper could regularly explain how basic functions of government, law, economics, or social services work, on periodic "How It Works" pages. Citizens can be easily intimidated by processes most reporters find straightforward, for example, writing a city budget or submitting ideas to a state senator. They need to know at what points their input is welcome, what form it should take, who they should talk to, and how they should prepare. A paper might, for instance, map the budgeting season out visually, with arrows marking exactly where citizens can intervene.

7. Most Americans don't really understand why their political leaders won't act more effectively; they assume cowardice, self-interest, or ineptitude by default. A newspaper could convene a roundtable of local or state officials to explicitly discuss what newspapers and citizens could do to help them act decisively on public agenda issues. What, for example, is the matter with the way the public voice is expressed now, that officials feel more reluctant to alienate a minority of voters than to do what the majority favor? How could the press and readers depolarize an issue in order to help politicians confidently take the middle ground? What do citizens have to say to convince officials that their opinions are responsible? A transcript could be printed and perhaps used as a discussion topic in citizens' forums.

Acting for the Long Haul

There will still be teen violence in Dayton, Ohio, long after the *Daily News* wraps up its "Fixing Our Families" project. The *Beacon Journal's* 10-month-long "A Question of Color" project did not shove race relations off Akron's agenda; nor will the social problems being raised right now in the *Tallahassee Democrat's* public agenda surveys be resolved when the final survey is completed a few years hence. Even the longest and most ambitious public journalism projects are too short to take a community all the way from consciousness raising to peace and harmony. What papers like the *Daily News*, the *Beacon Journal*, and West Virginia's *Huntington Herald-Dispatch* (see boxes, below) have done so remarkably well isn't to lead citizens all the way to a solution, but to be forceful and canny enough to make the momentum they've created self-sustaining. They've been planning to hand off the leadership role from the very beginning. They've let readers know this in no uncertain terms. And they have made it an integral part of the project to encourage

THE AKRON BEACON JOURNAL

... and for the excellence of its "A Question of Color" series on race relations, the *Beacon Journal* won the 1994 Pulitzer Prize for public service.

That's how journalism's hero stories typically end, but it's where this one begins. It was about five months after the 10-month-long project started running that editor Dale Allen and his colleagues began to ask themselves, "If we're just reporting on stories, and they just disappear into the ether as so many investigative pieces do, what will that accomplish?" The "Question of Color" reports had identified people's isolation as the first barrier to improving race relations; not enough whites and blacks had close personal relationships. So the *Beacon Journal* started running coupons asking citizens "What can we do?" It hired two part-time facilitators—a white retired minister and a black retired principal—to help organizations that wrote in learn about one another and integrate their efforts. "We said, 'well, hell, if we can bring a dozen groups together to talk about race relations, then that's a success, because it's more than what's transpiring in the community today.' " In fact, 85 organizations signed on right away, rising to 140 by the end of the year.

In December, the paper ended the "Question of Color" project by asking Akron residents to mail in a coupon for New Year's pledging to work at improving race relations in 1994; 22,000 did. "There are only a certain number of things you can write without being repetitious," Allen says; the newsroom returned to its old habit of reporting on race relations only as newsworthy events arose. The *Beacon Journal* organization, however, remained on the scene as a rallying point for the burgeoning civic activity outside.

The paper had 10,000 T-shirts, lapel pins, and caps made up bearing the logo "Coming Together," which it also authorized for community projects considered worthwhile by the two facilitators. It hosted meetings for businesses collaborating on diversity in the workplace and student groups interested in promoting racial harmony. In February, it sponsored a Kent State sociologist's seminar where 200 people deliberated over how to get past racial barriers. The facilitators continued to help white churches pair with black churches, students at one high school organize with students at another. Gradually, in these ways, between 10,000 and 15,000 people were drawn into the loose network.

(cont.)

THE AKRON BEACON JOURNAL *(cont.)*

Allen feels his journalists have stepped onto the sidelines grace-fully. "One of the reasons we hired the facilitators was to maintain the separation between the newsroom efforts and the community efforts. The newsroom staff are still free to report on the successes and failures of this program as they transpire, just like any other story."

---

the formation of private groups and citizen–government coalitions, to keep the ball rolling when the paper turns to something else or steps back to being a watchdog.

In Huntington, the *Herald-Dispatch* saw its opportunity when, at the huge town meeting it sponsored, citizens decided to form six task forces to study the city's economic options. The paper ran coupons to help the task forces recruit additional volunteers, but from that point on Huntington's redevelopment efforts rolled forward in the citizens' own hands. Executive editor Randy Hammer was able to scale back his coverage without diminishing the momentum, resuming the paper's more traditional role as reporter and critic. He insisted, "We're a newspaper and it's our job to find things out. We are not a public relations tool. I tell [citizens], 'We may have brought y'all together, but we're not your sponsor.' "

The *Daily News* insisted that civic groups do most of the work on teen violence from day one, while the *Beacon Journal*, by keeping on its two facilitators, has continued as a major catalyst in Akron race rela-tions long after "A Question of Color" wrapped up, but these differences are superficial. In essence, these papers have done the same thing the *Herald-Dispatch* did. In Dayton and Akron both, civic groups are ener-getic, active, well-staffed, and integrated enough to carry on with or without the paper's further involvement.

Once it's out, and for years thereafter, a public newspaper can help to ensure the momentum will remain strong by coming back to a public agenda issue in smaller, less demanding ways. For example:

Progress Reports

The *Charlotte Observer* periodically goes back to targeted neighborhoods like Seversville to report on how they are doing; the *Herald-Dispatch* runs updates on the six Huntington task forces whenever it seems appropriate. Progress reports of this sort don't have to be laundry lists of

THE *HUNTINGTON HERALD-DISPATCH*

In the early 1990s, Huntington was a city avoiding its problems. About 70,000 mining and manufacturing jobs had left West Virginia over the years, 10,000 of them from Cabell County. Yet the state had no economic development agency and the city government hadn't updated its strategic plan for more than a decade. The *Herald-Dispatch*'s new executive editor, Randy Hammer, began groping in 1993 for a way to change all that. He convened a discussion with 20 local leaders to figure out how the paper should deal with the jobs issue, and sent reporters out to interview hundreds of citizens about their visions for the future. This led to a 12-page special section in November 1993, called "Our Jobs, Our Children, Our Future."

Hammer was eager for ordinary people to get involved, so he structured the whole project around citizens' ideas. The November section included a clip-out coupon asking "What one thing should be done to bring jobs to the area?"; it drew several hundred responses. Then in January, the *Herald-Dispatch*, an NBC-TV affiliate, and a local university sponsored a town meeting, attended by 900 citizens as well as the governor, to hammer out a new strategy for Huntington's future. Remarkably, the citizens didn't expect the city, the state, or the newspaper to do the hard work for them. They divided themselves into six task forces, each themed on a different approach to renewal, and set to planning. The paper ran coupons asking other citizens to volunteer; other citizens did. And from that time to date the task forces have driven the city's unprecedented rush of activity.

They are consulting with the National Park Service on building a national museum of the Underground Railroad, on which Huntington was a major stop. They're renovating historic homes. To attract industry, they lobbied the state legislature to reform workers' compensation laws, and applied to HUD for a $3-million enterprise grant to pay for daycare centers and other social infrastructure. After HUD approved the grant in December 1994, the governor agreed to kick in $1 million more. In the meantime the city has updated its old strategic plan, and the county put a $1.5-million development tax levy on the November ballot. All of which has brought 400 new telemarketing jobs to Huntington, with several other companies on the way.

The *Herald-Dispatch* has stepped in at intervals to help keep enthusiasm high. It reports on task-force meetings as regular hard-

(cont.)

THE *HUNTINGTON HERALD-DISPATCH* (cont.)

news events. It sponsored a second town meeting in March and a visit to the West Virginia legislature on closing day, to pressure lawmakers not to ram through last-minute work without proper scrutiny. (As usual in this project, the effort worked; a special session was called to give the legislature more time.) But the paper's activism is limited. Says Mickey Johnson, the content editor, "I like to think the task forces can keep the ball rolling on their own."

---

landmark events, or to mark anniversaries. It may seem in hard-news terms that public efforts on an issue haven't shown sufficient success, failure, or even movement to make people read a substantial story, but that isn't usually the case. Remember the dramatic power of the master narrative: "the community's struggle to solve issue X." Public journalism at its best involves us intimately in our neighbors' lives. Once, in mid-1994, PBS's *MacNeil/Lehrer NewsHour* went back to Los Angeles to check on the progress of an athletic-shoe store that gang members had opened in the aftermath of the south-central LA riots. Nothing much had happened; the store was neither flourishing nor going under. And yet the reflections of one of the gang members on learning business skills, earning his first legal paychecks, and helping neighborhood kids were fascinating, because it was impossible not to want this young man to succeed. One human being's story, well told and often revisited, is inherently fascinating.

Public Agenda Pages

The *Democrat* has institutionalized the public agenda on a periodic page. One Sunday a month, its editorial front (see box, below) becomes a forum for updating and discussing issues that may already have had their period of community forums and intensive coverage. One feature, "Tallahassee's Talking About . . ." reprints lengthy viewpoints from citizens about a selected public issue (here, children) "that keeps turning up in the community dialogue." "Where Things Stand" updates public agenda projects, identifies groups working on the issues, announces when hearings or planning sessions will be held, and tells how citizens can make an input. "Citizens Want Answers On" gives a reader's question followed by verbatim replies from officials or experts, and finally "Feed Your Mind" offers short digests of books, articles, movies, or other sources containing important information for public discussion or action. As a whole, the page is quick, efficient, diverse, and refreshing—a sort of once-a-month tonic to keep people invigorated about their agenda.

Special Reports

Sometimes it's only boredom, lack of focus, or uncertainty about what to do next that makes public activity lose steam. People need a small jolt of the purpose that public journalism gave them initially. After Huntington voters rejected the ballot initiative drawn up by its citizen task forces, the *Herald-Dispatch* ran a four-day series discussing the different directions economic redevelopment might take from there. It wasn't a terribly original idea, but it was just the spur necessary to draw the task forces and readers back into facing the problem. As a generalization, any newspaper that sees public interest in an issue falling off can revisit "the facts" in a way that invites new deliberation. Based on the new ledge the community's standing on, what do citizens need to do next or to decide next? What aspect of the issue haven't they talked about in a while? What strategic facts will get them talking about it constructively? Journalists can restore focus in all sorts of different ways: with an investigation, a one-time forum, or a special series as in Huntington.

The Ethics of Public Journalism

This is a good place to discuss ethics, because helping citizens to act is the final straw for many critics of public journalism. They object to the innovations discussed in this book not so much on the grounds that they're time-consuming or ineffective but in the belief that they're dangerously unrestrained. If a newspaper starts setting agendas, framing issues, forcing candidates and experts to explain themselves in different ways, promoting forums, and spelling out what "the public" wants, it may think it's speaking for ordinary citizens but it will really end up speaking only for itself. Journalism's one protection against arrogance—its one claim on the public trust—is its refusal to get involved. Giving that up, it will inevitably career down the same slippery slope as demagogues and spin doctors. It will end up speaking only for citizens it agrees with, and cheerleading civic action in which it's improperly involved.

Actually, public journalism has a golden rule—an ethical line—every bit as sharp as mainstream journalism's rule, and just as easy to

A PUBLIC AGENDA PAGE

SUNDAY, NOVEMBER 20, 1994   TALLAHASSEE DEMOCRAT

Comment

editorials, letters, columnists, viewpoints

SPECIALS

POLITICS: Even back when he wasn't a star, he was 100 percent Newt Gingrich **3F**

HILLARY: A remarkable interview hardly got noticed **5F**

ALSO INSIDE:
Cal Thomas, 3
Letters, 5, 6, 7

WHERE THINGS STAND:

TALLAHASSEE'S TALKING ABOUT:

Children

"What can the community do to make Tallahassee a better place for children?" That question keeps turning up in the community dialogue. Here's what some of you have to say.

LIZZ HOLMES, 29, communications specialist for Kidd & Driscoll Public Relations: I don't think that we are providing our populations with enough family activities that are both educational and entertaining.

Because most families are dual income, the weekends are the only time parents can spend quality time with their children. In Tallahassee, parents are visiting play areas or visiting restaurants or pizzerias just to have an activity to share with their families! As a community, we need to support cultural and learning organizations to fill this void.

DONNA BLANTON, mother, attorney: If we think of trying to solve all the huge problems, we become overwhelmed. I tend to think of doing something tangible, something you can accomplish relatively easily.

For instance, it would be enormously helpful to have sidewalks and bike paths. It would add to our quality of life and give us more of a sense of community. Children could ride their bikes to school.

The children, parents feel comfortable letting their children ride in the neighborhood, they have to feel we have a safe community."

KIMBALL THOMAS, father of three and principal at Riccards: I think there needs to be a multicultural task force that looks at how kids are responding to use different entertainment and recreation offerings out there. We need to try and come up with some common strains that incorporate what's going on in the community calendar.

We need to talk to, and listen to, kids from every sector of the community to see what it is they need and like.

ANDREA MITCHELL, 34, a mother of three who works at the Humane Society's regional office: The root problem is what's happening to our children. Sometimes it's parenting. Sometimes it's just rebellious kids.

For the most part, thinking about my relationship with my kids and parents I know, if you're hungry you're not going to worry about a tree or traffic. I think our first responsibility is to make certain a lot of things being addressed are aimed directly at the poor, making sure no one goes hungry. If emotional and physical needs aren't met, people can't see a higher calling or purpose. I think focusing on education and parenting should be top priorities. For example, we need to start something like FSU's lecture series, where we could offer parents free courses.

CHRISTIE KOONTZ, a mother of two, community activist and FSU faculty member: To make Tallahassee a better place for children, you need to make Tallahassee a better place for parents. Provide local government funding so community and school activities can be available and accessible to all, not just the diminishing few who can go to the library once an hour, can go to the baseball field, can go on expensive school field trips, or can go to a family doctor. Instead, bring the library to the housing development, transport the housing-development children to the baseball fields. Support people who are parents, and children all over town will benefit.

KIAMBE TUNSIL, 22, public-relations major at Florida A&M University: It's going to have to start at home. Parents are going to have to instill the knowledge of right and wrong, good moral values, discipline and just love for yourself and one another. I think we can help parents by having some kind of community counseling available for parents, especially young parents who might come from broken families.

those who may not have had that mother or father figure in the home to teach them about parenting.

JERRY FUENTES, pastor, Tallahassee Seventh-day Adventist Church: It's easy for us to look to community resources to make up for our deficiencies in the family. But when we do that, it potentially enables our denial of the changes we need to make in our own lives.

If anything, the community should focus its resources on rehabilitating and habilitating — families, on rebuilding and building family ties. It is unrealistic to expect the community to miraculously heal the social deficiencies of the home. I think the community, the church and the schools can — and should — work in cooperation with families, but not instead of them.

PAMELA DAVIS, executive director, Big Bend Coordinated Child Care: We need to establish a value system that tells children: "We love you, we appreciate you, and we know you're our future."

We spend a lot of time and energy conserving our natural resources, but we don't do a lot to conserve and preserve our children. I know we care about our own children, but I don't get the sense that people care anymore about our community's children.

I'd rather pay a few dollars more a year to be sure the children who don't have the advantages I can provide my children, get them. I want to pay it now. I don't want to pay it when they go to jail."

RUSSELL McGUFF, psychological resident, Eastwood Clinic: We have to give our children the love they need in their prenatal and early-childhood care.

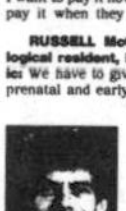

When we do that, we get kids who are smarter, who learn to pay attention, who do well in school and who have a much better shot at making it in life.

And people need to turn off their TVs and start taking to their neighbors about what the needs are of families and our community.

Voices of the people

If you read the *Tallahassee Democrat* last week or watched WCTV, you know about the creation of The Public Agenda project. Today's Comment begins carrying material under The Public Agenda heading to encourage participation in all aspects of public policy.

Encouraging democratic participation has always been part of the newspaper's mission. What's new is the structure The Public Agenda provides for seeking active citizen involvement that goes beyond voting or writing letters to the editor. That structure includes small discussions groups, in addition to this page, news stories and the larger community dialogues. If you are interested in setting up a group of your own, we will help and will train a discussion leader.

To the degree that print can be interactive, we want this page to have that quality. So we'll use quotes from forums, material gathered by reporters, dialogue from Tallahassee Free-Net and your input to illuminate what's on the minds of people in the Big Bend.

This Public Agenda page will also provide a sort of citizen action line, with the *Democrat* helping you get answers from public officials. Please send us your questions, and we'll track the officials down for answers.

We pledge to be undeterred by buffers that often separate taxpayers and their employees.

We'll also use this page to point you toward books, articles and other thought-provoking material. (We'd like your suggestions, too.)

The Public Agenda has no political or ideological intent. It aims to establish a new structure for public discussion, a way for Tallahasseeans to meet, talk and seek solutions on issues of broad concern. Our Tallahassee project is based on the work of Public Agenda, a nonprofit, nonpartisan research and education organization founded 20 years ago by Daniel Yankelovich and Cyrus Vance.

Their goal is to improve on our system of competing special interests and citizen disenfranchisement by enhancing citizen deliberation and encouraging public judgment.

"Public judgment," as Yankelovich describes it, "is the state of highly developed public opinion that exists once people have engaged an issue, considered it from all sides, understood the choices it leads to, and accepted the full consequences of the choices they make."

The initial sponsors of the local project are the *Tallahassee Democrat*, WCTV, FSU and FAMU, with financial underwriting by the Pew Charitable Trusts. For information, call 644-7555 and leave a message.

Lou Heldman
Lou Heldman, Executive Editor

N.E. Parkway

■ **UPDATE:** Recent negotiations between City Hall and large landowners have renewed talk about construction of the Northeast Parkway.

■ **PUBLIC HEARINGS:** There will be a decision Monday, after asked-for study. That's because the Leon County Commission has asked for at least two more public hearings probably for early December. Barring delays, the Metropolitan Planning Commission could reach a decision on the corridor study in January.

■ **CITIZENS GROUP:** CURRE — Citizens Urging Responsible Road Building — opposes the Northeast Parkway, fearing high costs, environmental damage and dramatic effects on neighborhoods. You can read the group's information paper at the reference desk of the Leon County Public Library (downtown and branches) or buy copies at Pichard Printing, 1660 N. Monroe St. For information, call Bob Fulford, president of the Council of Neighborhood Associations, 576-1617.

Traffic

■ **UPDATE:** Traffic is a big community concern. A city-funded study, conducted by citizens, will look at the problems and recommend solutions. It is not too late to get involved.

■ **21ST CENTURY COUNCIL:** The council conducts intensive studies of Leon County issues, using committees that reflect the community at large. The idea is to work toward solutions through consensus. Last year, the council studied juvenile crime. Now, it is turning to transportation.

■ **GETTING INVOLVED:** You can help the 21st Century Council sort out this and other issues. Membership is open to anyone (the $25 membership fee is optional). For information, call Tom Keating, executive director, at 668-5734.

Life Flight crashed Nov. 4

Life Flight

■ **UPDATE:** What is the future of Life Flight in the aftermath of the Nov. 4 crash?

■ **DECISION MADE:** Tallahassee Memorial Regional Medical Center officials aren't certain when the helicopter service will resume flight, but a decision could be reached within days. The new helicopter still needs special life-saving equipment.

■ **INJURED CREW MEMBER:** Life Flight nurse-paramedic Trent Robinson remains at Shands Hospital in Gainesville in fair condition.

■ **MEMORIAL:** A scholarship fund has been set up in memory of pilot Jimmy Tucker and paramedic Rich and Thompson. For information, call 681-5085. A permanent memorial is under discussion.

CITIZENS WANT ANSWERS ON:

Pensacola Street

"Citizens Want Answers" is where we ask public officials to answer your questions about issues of community concern. Send your questions to: The Public Agenda, Tallahassee Democrat, P.O. Box Tallahassee 32302 (or send Internet e-mail to agenda@freenet.fsu.edu).

DAVID WINIALSKI works for the Legislature and has taken an interest in transportation issues. He asks: I am not an FSU alumnus, so perhaps I am lacking the perspective that would make the closing Pensacola Street at Doak Campbell Stadium, forming a T-intersection, logical.

What I see, though, is a resident of this city who has experienced all of the problems we have with real traffic. There are so many road projects that could be undertaken that I cannot imagine why the Metropolitan Planning Commission did this. Well, actually, I do know why: FSU and its powerful friends in state government wanted it done.

I just wish the FSU administration had revealed their entire plan back when they announced the University Center project. If they had told, nobody would have gone along with them. Why can't this pedestrian and traffic access be revamped so it wouldn't overpasses?

MARK BERTOLAMI, associate director of facilities planning for FSU, responds: This project, when it reaches fruition, will create a safe, aesthetically pleasing green area where Pensacola Street now threatens student safety. An estimated 15,000 pedestrians, bicyclists and mobility-impaired people making their way to the University Center daily will be safe from highway traffic. If this section of Pensacola Street remains open, these same people would be forced to cross a highway that carries

30,000 vehicles a day.

Not only is this the best solution for safety, but it gets rid of the collapsing Pensacola Street bridge, which would have to be replaced at great cost if this segment were not closed. Overpasses aren't conducive for the mobility impaired, and our analyses have shown that most pedestrians don't use them.

The 1989 Legislature provided FSU with the first planning money for the University Center, with the initial construction funds provided in 1990. It was not until 1991, after construction began, that we first considered relocating Pensacola Street. As a result of a study conducted by the Florida Department of Transportation at FSU's request, it was determined in 1993, and the city agreed, that the relocation was an option worth pursuing. We have communicated with city and state officials since the idea was conceived.

The project will be a community asset. It will be completed with out taking private property or removing many trees. In addition, the majority of the funds needed has been provided by the Legislature, so it shouldn't affect other local transportation projects.

FEED YOUR MIND:

"Feed Your Mind" is where we recommend thought-provoking books, articles, movies, videos or other sources of information. We'd like to pass along your recommendations, too. Send them to The Public Agenda, Tallahassee Democrat, P.O. Box 990 Tallahassee 32302 (or via Internet e-mail at agenda @ freenet.fsu.edu).

■ **SPIRIT OF COMMUNITY:** Restoring responsibility and curbing the expansion of personal rights is important: argues Amitai Etzioni. If "community" is to be more than a feel-good phrase. In his book "The Spirit of Community: Rights, Responsibilities and the Communitarian Agenda" (1993 Crown Publishers, New York), he argues that our society has so resettled people from personal responsibility that they no longer feel obligations to others. Etzioni's sometimes provocative book is available for checkout at the Leon

COUNTY COMMISSIONER GARY YORDON responds: There were aspects of the project I did not like, but after six months of negotiations I was convinced there were two prevailing reasons to vote yes. First was the issue of safety.

The second reason requires a longer view. For years, local government has been trying to convince the single FAMU and TCC to plan in partnership with our community. It became clear in this process that President D'Alemberte is committed to joining with the other institutions in establishing that planning partnership. It would have been disastrous to lose the university's joint-planning hand the first time FSU held it out.

Feed Your Mind Leon County Public Library

■ **SEX EDUCATION:** An often emotional issue in many communities is the question of sex education in schools. For a condemning critique of sex-education programs, see the October edition of *The Atlantic Monthly* in which Barbara Dafoe Whitehead of the Institute for American Values declares sex education a failure. Despite the claims of advocates, she argues, sex education has had little effect on the sexual behavior of teenagers.

■ **OUR NATIONAL PARKS:** Here's an issue for our larger national community to consider: the future of America's parks. How can such a legacy, beloved by millions, be so troubled by overuse, mismanagement and neglect? What can be done to turn things around? October's *National Geographic* has a comprehensive analysis. (*The Geographic* is not sold at newsstands, so check the library or borrow a copy from a friend.)

Reprinted with permission from the *Tallahassee Democrat*.

elaborate into a code book of professional norms: *Journalism should advocate democracy without advocating particular solutions*. This rule isn't so different from the conventional rule as it might seem at first glance.

Newspapers already recognize that certain democratic norms are essential for the news media to play their social role, and they feel no qualm about championing these norms, on the news pages or off. Take free speech, for example. No paper would hesitate to advocate the First Amendment, nor think twice about throwing its full resources into the First Amendment's defense. This is because, unlike abortion rights or aid to Russia or presidential candidate X or ballot initiative Y, the First Amendment is a sine qua non of informed public debate. Public journalists, looking at citizens' anger and apparent apathy, have simply asked themselves what other sine qua nons have gone unrecognized and unchampioned so far.

The evidence in this book shows that, if the news is truly to help people judge events wisely and exercise control over their government, then a number of things have to happen, both inside the newspaper and out. Candidates have to address the questions citizens want answers to. Expert opinions must speak to citizens' values. People must face the consequences of their choices. They must deliberate across social barriers like race, gender, geography, and class. The "public voice" must be the basis for governmental action. Private citizens must be given opportunities to act. And so on. Newspapers ought to advocate the spread of these practices as aggressively and with as little shame as they advocate the spread of free speech and a free press.

What keeps the press from sliding down the slippery slope here, in place of the rule of not getting involved, is good solid public listening. An editor knows as soon as significant numbers of people call an issue-framing wrong, a set of choices uninclusive, or a public agenda survey unfair that she's done something wrong, because agendas, issue framings, and "new ledges to stand on"—unlike majority opinions in a poll, or courageous stands on the editorial page—ought to command the consent of almost everyone in the community. What's more, if people do balk, reporters can engage them in fixing the problem rather than simply taking down their objections. If the issue isn't X, what should it be called that everyone would agree to? If the choices aren't inclusive, what other choice belongs? If our way of setting the public agenda is unfair, what would make the process fairer? This back and forth is built right into public journalism, as a permanent warning light against the arrogance, bias, and cheerleading critics are afraid of on the public's behalf. The fact that many public newspapers have actually seen complaints of bias decline, and public engagement improve, ought to speak for itself.

To turn the whole question around, public journalists could well argue that the mainstream's rule of noninvolvement is the one that realistically threatens the public. In cities such as Huntington, W. Va., and Dayton, Ohio, social problems were going largely unaddressed and citizens were growing ever more frustrated and angry until a newspaper broke tradition to advocate intelligent discourse and democratic process. Editors in such situations often come to see their new way of doing journalism not as an ethical minefield at all, but as far more natural and self-justifying than the old. (One executive editor now says, "I'd rather increase voter turnout than win a Pulitzer.") Which form of journalism is really more flawed and dangerous in a free society: the one that sits passively by while people grow divided, or the one that finds ways of bringing them together?

✦ PUSHING THE ENVELOPE

1. What public journalism hasn't had time to do yet is test its ethical boundaries. Editors could set up a "democracy wall" somewhere in their newsrooms on which colleagues could post clippings under two categories: "advocates democracy" and "advocates solutions." The first would be reserved for exemplary stories that—according to the man or woman who clipped them—stay within the bounds of public journalism ethics, the second to stories that cross the line into advocacy. Other journalists might leave their comments alongside to further the discussion.

Most journalists would probably agree that ethics policies are established for a pragmatic reason: to assure people that they can trust their newspapers; these policies are the Pure Food and Drug Acts of the journalism business. The best way to assess which policies are good and which bad, then, is to consult citizens themselves in a deliberative way. To do this:

2. Once a year the newspaper might publish its criteria for a good news story or series, along with an invitation something like this: "These are our guidelines for advocating democracy without advocating solutions. If we don't live up to these rules, write in and tell us when, where, how, and what we should have done." Newspapers now receive scores of complaints that don't lead anywhere; complaints on this model could lead to constructive dialogue.

3. The editor could hold a quarterly audit. Once a season, he or she would invite citizens to critique the paper's ethical performance and publish the results.

4. The paper could write an ethics policy for public journalism using the same collaborative give-and-take that it uses in setting an agenda or nailing down the public voice. At the formal extreme, it could print its existing policy alongside proposals for change, with brief arguments for and against as in those ballot supplements put together by the League of Women Voters. Through letters, calls, or forums, citizens could express their preferences among ethical standards. It's easy to understand why journalists might balk at the very notion—after all, doctors don't invite patients to redesign the Hippocratic Oath—but it's important to see the other side too. There is at the very least a logical flaw in any ethics policy that seeks to ensure public trust through rules that citizens won't endorse.

✦ SIDEBAR: MANAGING THE MARKETPLACE OF IDEAS

David Rubin, dean of Syracuse University's Newhouse School of Communications, came up with a good way of seeing where conventional ethics fall short. He suggests looking at the "marketplace of ideas" as if it were a real thing. He says he can no longer have faith that "if you have an open marketplace, a cacophony, and the left is speaking and the right is speaking and [ordinary] people from Kenosha are in the mix, then everything will come out okay." That may satisfy the ethicists of journalism, but it just isn't how real marketplaces work. Real marketplaces have *structure*.

Rubin is right. The New York Stock Exchange, for all its capitalist freedoms, tolerates nothing like the anarchy of the marketplace of ideas. It is a thoroughly regulated place, with rules, habits, traditions, and penalties to make sure that trading is fair, free, and open. An Exchange official can tell you the date and time of any sale and all the procedures that were followed. Market failures like insider trading, deals taking place after the closing bell, misleading statistics on prospectuses, and volatility that might lead to a crash are nailed down with vigor and corrected with legal rules. Similarly, in the marketplace of science, ideas don't make it past the laboratory door until they're expressed in standardized terms using mathematical language. Peers must review experimental work and be able to duplicate the results. All this rigor is in place because investors and scientists want their markets to *work*.

If the press wants the marketplace of ideas to function equally well, then it had better be just as relentlessly concrete. Are national debates (as we envision them) taking place? Then name the date, time, and place. If you can't, then they're imaginary, and you must help figure out how to make them real. Are "public voices" forming?

✦ Then write them down for me. If you can't, then they're imaginary too, and you must go out and find them by listening, and then help to cobble them together. Is this all somebody else's job? Then tell me whose. If you can't, do the job yourself. You are, for better or worse, the only manager the marketplace of ideas has.

Critics of public journalism may think this logic arrogant, but it's not. A manager is even necessary in groups of 20 or 30 people, gathered all in the same room, according to National Issues Forums veteran Bob Arroyo. Deliberation usually won't take place unless a moderator clears the channels, invites in the silent, chastises the domineering, suggests when to move on—in short, nails down the market failures and corrects them with vigor. A successful moderator, Arroyo says, is always "neutral but not passive." Traditional journalism's sense of objectivity has often led it to be passive; one might argue that public journalism is trying to discover how to be neutral instead.

✦

CHAPTER SIX

The Newspaper's Place

"A Fair-Minded Participant in a Community That Works"

At the end of all this, the newspaper is just one institution in a sea of institutions. Some of the people who shrink from public journalism suspect that it's trying to be everything to everybody: part church, part government, part schoolmarm, part social therapist. Taking the examples in this book at face value, that's far from being the case—but then what is a public newspaper trying to be? The *New York Times* is the paper of record; the *New York Daily News*, an aggressive, scrappy champion for the working stiff. The *Washington Post* tells the federal government's inside stories. Each has a niche that distinguishes and defines it. Davis Merritt of the *Wichita Eagle* has described the public newspaper's niche as being "a fair-minded participant in a community that works." What in the world does that mean?

When newspapers join the Project on Public Life and the Press network, they're asked to state the goals of their public journalism initiatives. Their replies typically give a partial, half-formed, but suggestive picture of the public newspaper's niche. The *Charlotte Observer* said that in its Freedom Park coverage it was trying to "create a forum for rational talk by providing a space in the newspaper where people could begin to discuss solutions, rather than focus only on the problem's emotional aspects." The *Dayton Daily News*'s "Kids in Chaos" project aimed "to establish a network of community-based approaches for saving our children." In Huntington, the *Herald-Dispatch* wanted "to bring a wider array of participants into the discussion about the community's economic future," while through a new "Quality of Life Project" the Bergen County *Record* hopes "to become THE unique institution in a region of disparate parts and common interests. . . . to strengthen [the paper's] image and identification as a glue to the community." The *New Orleans Times-Picayune* reported on race relations the way it did "to talk about [the condition we're in] in terms of action instead of in the passive way these things get talked about today."

These pictures all share a conviction that something essential is lacking in American life right now: rational talk, community-based approaches, participatory discussions, communal glue, a proper emphasis on activity. The two common strains come out clearest in statements from Gregory Favre, executive editor of the *Sacramento Bee,* and Tom Still, the *Wisconsin State Journal* associate editor who led the paper's "We the People" project. "Public life," Favre said, "is indeed disappearing, and if it does disappear then we will disappear along with it. So we have an obligation to try to keep the existence of that public life." To which Still added that simply bringing a divided citizenry together can't in itself make a public life; we need "to address the fact that we have democracy without deliberation": In other words, we have talk, but not the right kind of talk. Public newspapers are trying to create the as-yet-missing place where citizens can meet and talk with one another in a realistic and constructive way.

There simply aren't any other institutions that have a chance of doing this. Americans past high school age don't work, socialize, or worship in the same places. While a minority do make it a point to live in mixed neighborhoods, most travel in circles almost hermetically

---

MISSION STATEMENT OF THE
VIRGINIAN-PILOT'S PUBLIC LIFE TEAM

We will revitalize a democracy that has grown sick with disenchantment. We will lead the community to discover itself and act on what it has learned. We will show how the community works or could work, whether that means exposing corruption, telling citizens how to make their voices heard, holding up a fresh perspective or spotlighting people who do their jobs well. We will portray democracy in the fullest sense of the word, whether in a council chamber or cul-de-sac. We do this knowing that a lively, informed and most of all, engaged public is essential to a healthy community and to the health of these newspapers.

Reprinted with permission from the Norfolk *Virginian-Pilot*.

sealed off from one another. A fascinating 1988 book, Michael J. Weiss's *The Clustering of America*, brings this reality home especially well. It tells the story of how much better marketing firms understand the country's diversity than newspapers do. One such firm, Claritas Inc., decided in the 1970s to see if Americans could be clustered together, not by geography, race, or class, but by consumer life-style: the things they bought, read, ate, drove, liked, hated, and even thought, believed in, and voted for. It turned out that they could, and quite successfully too. Claritas was able to assign every neighborhood in America to one of 40 "life-style clusters," to each of which it gave a colorful name such as "the Urban Gold Coast" or "Shotguns & Pickups." The residents of a single cluster weren't uniform but were remarkably similar. Those in "the Urban Gold Coast" of Upper East Side Manhattan were apartment-rich and well-educated, rode trains and read the *Atlantic Monthly*, ate rye bread and avoided pork sausage at rates far above the national average; those in a "Shotguns & Pickups" town like Jewett, W.Va., by and large voted conservative and drove domestics.

When Weiss went out to report on an example of each cluster for his book, he found out two things of great importance: first, that their residents had been living in a few closely related clusters for most of their lives, even though they may have moved quite a lot in geographic terms: from hometown to college to suburb to retirement village. Second, that they didn't even know the other clusters existed. Having seen people like themselves wherever they went, they regarded their way of life as the *American* way. They were the middle class, middle America, the main-stream; most everyone had values and tastes fairly similar to their own. The wildly different people they saw on television were a minority of either rednecks, cultural snobs, or other dwellers on the fringe.

The point is, practically nothing in their lives brought these people together—not churches, not schools, not voting booths nor paying taxes. And yet, as it turned out, they were closer to one another than they seemed. According to Claritas, most of the variety found through-out the United States could also be found in any one of its major cities. During the 1980s, New York City's and Chicago's TV markets contained neighborhoods belonging to 37 of the 40 clusters; Cleveland's contained just under 30. America's subgroups could have held a national conver-sation without leaving home, but instead, as in the stereotypical New York apartment building, they kept entirely to themselves. Their social organizations did not cross lines. However, they still lived within reach of the same metropolitan dailies.

There are other institutions besides newspapers that link Ameri-cans to one another, but each has severe shortcomings as an avenue to public dialogue. People share federal, state, and city governments, but they don't connect up with public institutions every day, nor could they all meet together on the city hall lawn even if they wanted to. Governments do perform collective business, but they can't host a collective conversation. New technologies such as the Internet, "the 500-channel universe," and interactive television may soon reach everyone on a daily basis, but for now no town or city could deliberate on the Internet. The information superhighway is designed to let people select conversations tailored to their own interests, just as they select churches, magazines, and types of bread—the very thing that drove Americans apart in the first place. Computers link fly fishermen in Buffalo and Los Angeles, but they don't link Baptists and Rastafarians in Buffalo itself. And while it would be *possible* to get everybody in a town or city hooked up to a common bulletin board, and to arrange a time for them all to log on, and to set up ground rules for a conversation that would be deliberative (in Tom Still's words) and rational (in the *Charlotte Observer*'s), that would be a monumental job of reinventing the wheel—or more precisely, reinventing the *newspaper*.

Early on, public newspapers learned that if they linked themselves up with other papers or broadcast media that had a different demographic reach (see box, below), they could stage a coordinated conversation that included nearly everyone. All of Charlotte focused on the problems of Seversville through the *Observer*, WSOC-TV, and WPEG radio. All of Dayton deliberated on teen violence with the help of the *Daily News* and WHIO-TV. The mass media, alone among public institutions, can filter information so that everyone in a city is talking

---

RADIO, TELEVISION, AND OTHER MEDIA

Public newspapers now collaborate with other media almost as a reflex. Of the 11 projects this book describes in detail, all but two—the Bergen budget-cutting exercise and the *Virginian-Pilot*'s daily reporting—have involved TV, radio, on-line services, or other newspapers to a greater or lesser degree. Increasingly it's broadcast media who initiate the tie-ins. National Public Radio stations, for example, coordinated their 1994 "Election Project" coverage with newspapers in Boston, Dallas, San Francisco, Seattle, and Wichita. (Groups including the Pew Center for Civic Journalism and Public Agenda have helped collaborations along with funding or professional services.) There are three advantages to tie-ins:

(cont.)

RADIO, TELEVISION, AND OTHER MEDIA *(cont.)*

They Extend a Project's Reach

A community can't deliberate unless its various segments come together. Very often a newspaper with a skewed readership can lure other demographic groups into a project through radio and TV. In many cities, for example, black, Hispanic, and other ethnic listeners don't tune in to mainstream radio stations or buy mass-circulation dailies at all, but listen to (and trust) specialized black or Hispanic stations instead. Partnering up is the only way to do what public journalism promises. The point extends to nonmedia organizations as well. The *Dayton Daily News* teen-violence project has been so successful probably because it's reached citizens not only through print and broadcast, but through churches, synagogues, schools, and social clubs too.

They Reinforce Each Medium's Coverage

Some newspapers do tie-ins to benefit from the cross-promotion. The 1992 study *Common Knowledge: News and the Construction of Political Meaning* reported that most Americans get their news from both print and broadcast; journalists may be able—simply by covering the same issues at the same time—to synergistically increase people's attention to both media. Citizens who hear about a project on the radio may buy the newspaper to find out more. They may well also learn and retain more information.

They Allow Each Medium to Do What It Does Best

Collaborations typically result in a division of labor. While print and broadcast both do basic reporting and quote forum participants at some length, radio and TV concentrate more on the conversation— excerpts from town meetings, call-in shows, and the like—leaving newspapers to do the deeper digestion and interpretation of strategic facts. A few papers see a special place for computer networks too, where citizens can choose to go deeper into a subject if they've got the inclination and the time. The *Democrat*, for example, has established discussion boards on a free-access network in Tallahassee, while Glenn Ritt of the Bergen County *Record* proposes entering every letter to the editor verbatim on-line, to supplement the few edited letters that appear daily in the paper.

about the same strategic facts. They alone speak habitually with people every day. They have the resources to tap experts and officials. They can impose deliberative rules. And, as experience in Akron, Huntington, Portland, and elsewhere has made clear, they are the natural hub through which other organizations such as churches, civic groups, agencies, and even governments can hook into the conversation, make their presence known, and keep tabs with each other on a daily basis. People may have their *deepest* relationships through religious or neighborhood institutions, their *most formal* relationships through city hall or Washington, D.C., but they will have their *community* relationships—if at all—through public newspapers and the activities such as forums that reach out from them.

Why Public Journalism Makes Economic Sense

This unique position is also the key to a problem of more parochial interest. Everyone agrees that journalism as a business is in trouble, what with circulation declining, broadcast and interactive media gaining in popularity, and the habit of daily readership going the way of permanent job security, 9-to-5 and the single-earner family. Tabloidization; the creation of McPapers like *USA Today* with their emphasis on short, no-jump stories and beautiful color graphics; community connectedness; a call to revitalize old-fashioned hard-news excellence *and* public journalism—all of these are professional responses that have their champions and success stories. Public journalism, like the others, can show off an encouraging record of achievements to make its case as the one true solution (see box, below). But it also has something else that the tabloids and color-and-no-jumps people do not have: a strong, persuasive argument about *why* it should work in the long run—why this style of journalism should find and keep the central place in people's lives that mainstream journalism is now losing.

Jay Rosen, director of the Project on Public Life and the Press, likes to discuss declining readership in terms of the economic concept "added value." Over the long run, people will pay for a good or service only if it gives them something they wouldn't otherwise have gotten cheaper or better elsewhere. They won't pay for a Rolls Royce if all they want is transportation; they won't pay high boutique prices if they don't mind shopping at a Price Club or Office Depot. By and large, they won't buy rotary phones or stock tickers or vinyl records at all, because technology has moved beyond them; nor backyard air-raid shelters because the need they once answered no longer exists. Every successful company can point to a definable value added that makes people rush through its door

SOME EVIDENCE OF SUCCESS

Although public journalism has won awards, its practitioners are generally less interested in praise for praise's sake than in concrete evidence that readers need their work. Editor Glenn Ritt has said that when he came to the Bergen County *Record* he was disturbed to find in readership surveys that New Jerseyans "liked us and very much respected us, but did not feel passionate about the *Record* and did not really need us." This wasn't safe ground to stand on for the paper's long-term health. Fixing this problem was one of the catalysts that drove him to try public journalism. Here then is some of the evidence papers like his have picked up as they've moved forward in their work:

Increased Readership and Circulation

The data here is tentative and sparse. Some papers (such as the *Olympian*) have seen circulation rise; others (such as the *Charlotte Observer* during its 1992 election coverage) have seen subscribers actually read the paper more frequently. The typical trend is no trend, because public journalism is simply too young.

Unprecedented Response to Journalism

Complaints of bias, however, have fallen dramatically at papers such as the *Observer* and the *Wichita Eagle*. Reader-approval ratings have jumped at those two papers and at others, including the Columbia, S.C., *State* and the *Tallahassee Democrat*. And then there are individual cases of public journalism projects that drew unexpectedly high interest, from the *New Orleans Times-Picayune*'s massive and ambitious "Together Apart: The Myth of Race" (which prompted 6,500 phone calls) down to the *Record*'s simple reprinting of a forum transcript (which got 75; see Chapter Two). Many editors and reporters say citizens have started approaching them regularly to talk for the first time in their careers. "More than ever before, I felt I was out of the vacuum," said Judy Dolye, a *Democrat* editor.

Participation in Newspaper-Sponsored Events

Numbers can almost tell this story by themselves. Citizens have phoned or mailed in surveys in response to invitations from the

(cont.)

SOME EVIDENCE OF SUCCESS *(cont.)*

Eagle (more than 5,000), the *Oklahoman* (425),* the *Cape Cod Times* (700), and the *Boulder* (Col.) *Daily Camera* (more than 2,000). They have turned out for forums sponsored by the *Star Tribune* (500 to 3,000 a month), the *Dayton Daily News* (2,000), the Portland Newspapers (700), the *Spokane Spokesman-Review* (1,500), and the *Detroit Free Press* (1,100). They have participated at hunkered-down planning meetings for the *Huntington Herald-Dispatch* (900), the *Spokesman-Review* (400), and the *Bremerton Sun* (1,500). They have submitted pledges to the *Akron Beacon Journal* (22,000). Just how impressive these numbers are is hard to say. Perhaps most telling is the fact that there aren't any cases on record where major events were called and few people came. The norm is the Seversville town meeting in Charlotte, which 200 attended, standing room only, and the *Wisconsin State Journal* grand juries and mock legislatures, to which invariably more people apply than the 50 to 200 who can be accommodated.

Community Activity for Which the Paper Can Take Some Credit

In city after city, more people have voted than in recent years or have volunteered than *ever* before, from Tallahassee, Fla., to Huntington, W.Va., to Akron, to Charlotte; elections officials and civic leaders often attribute this directly to the local paper. The Columbia, S.C., *State's* sensitive treatment of the Confederate flag issue (see Chapter Four) helped bring the percentage of people who insisted on flying the flag over the statehouse down from 55 percent to 40 percent—the first significant change in many years. In Akron and Dayton, literally hundreds of formerly unaffiliated organizations have come together in networks for common work; the total membership of these groups in Akron lies somewhere between 10,000 and 15,000. Most impressively, as a direct result of public journalism coverage citizens have organized entirely new grassroots groups in Huntington (the six planning task forces), Oklahoma City (Central Oklahoma 2020), Bremerton (Kitsap Friends of Open Space), New Orleans (Eracism), Spokane (Vision Spokane), and elsewhere, many of which are now major forces for policymaking and public action.

---

*This number includes not only forms and essays written by 125 handpicked community leaders (of the 475 referred to in Chapter Two) but the submissions of 300 men and women from the general public as well.

rather than any other, from Federal Express (overnight delivery) to 7-11 (24-hour convenience). What, Rosen asks, is journalism's added value?

Most forms of the self-styled newer, better journalism don't have one. Newspapers that lean toward sensationalism can always be out-done by TV shows and supermarket tabloids that revel in it. If people truly want short, snappy news stories, they can get them through radio, "Headline News," and more and more on-line services—with anima-tion, audio, and video to boot. Sports, business, entertainment, and even political news arrives faster by cable and broadcast TV and is covered in more depth in specialized magazines and newsletters. Communities can connect, in social terms, through public access channels and electronic bulletin boards, as well as through a newspa-per. And as to good, old-fashioned, in-depth hard news: People have never wanted that just for its own sake. It has always answered some more basic human need—a need for entertainment; for a good read on a Sunday morning; for details on an event, law, or policy of significant personal interest; or for participation in a political com-munity—all of which needs already are or soon will be answered better by another, newer medium . . . except for one. The only advantage print–broadcast combinations have (and will continue to have) over all other media is their power to reach everyone at once, and the newspaper's particular ability to help that audience conduct an ongo-ing conversation in depth.

Postscript: Getting the Connections Right

Here, then, is what Davis Merritt meant by "a fair-minded participant in a community that works."* Communities that don't meet in political discourse are lacking something at their core, and usually know it; newspapers that bring them together (without also telling them what to decide) supply a need, and receive loyalty in return. This book began by proposing public journalism for purely task-oriented reasons, as a way to help citizens make wiser judgments; it will end with excerpts from a speech by Jay Rosen, asserting that newspapers play a vital role in forming a community that works. At a 1994 Project conference, Rosen contrasted how traditional journalists and public journalists see their relationship to public life:

"Two years ago I happened to be reading the *Washington Post* and I was struck by a column by Leonard Downie, the executive editor, who

---

*Merritt defines the concept more fully in his 1995 book *Public Journalism and Public Life*.

wanted to explain to his readers that the *Post's* recent endorsement of Bill Clinton would have no effect on the coverage of the campaign. Downie went on to say that he felt so strongly about this principle of separating the news pages from the editorial pages that he chose not to vote in the national election. I clipped this column because I felt there was something critically important about it. I felt viscerally that Downie was mistaken, but it has taken me two years to understand the mistake.

"Downie assumes, for one thing, that news judgment is best exercised at a safe distance from the political community. Getting the distance right is Downie's primary concern. He's willing to take an extreme step to remain properly detached. Not many journalists go to those lengths, but journalism in general shares Downie's approach. That is, it tries to remain properly detached. If you look carefully at the ethical structure of journalism, it's almost exclusively concerned with getting the separation right: Editorial functions are separated from the business side. The news pages are separated from the opinion pages. Facts are, of course, to be separated from values. Those who make the news are separated from those who cover the news. Even more basic, one day is separated from another because news is what we do today.

"But suppose that getting the separations right is not the right problem. This is where public journalism enters the conversation. What it says is, getting the *connections* right is our problem now. Public journalism worries about becoming properly *attached*. Now, the perspective I suggest is this: Traditional journalism tries to serve the public in essentially two ways. It seeks to inform on the one hand, and act as a watchdog over government on the other. Public journalism talks about something else. It tries to strengthen the community's capacity—the key word is *capacity*—to recognize itself, to converse well, and make choices. The guiding image behind public journalism is a vision of the well-connected community, where everything that should connect does connect. Where everyone who should be talking is, in fact, talking.

"Public journalism does not begin with information as the imperative. It does not even begin with the day's events. It begins with an act of imagination. Every day of the year public journalism is looking out at a community and imagining the following kinds of things: the missing-but-needed connections. The conversations that are not occurring because they are not embracing enough of the community to make a difference. The shrunken horizon. The community's growing inability to recognize what it is becoming as it changes. The avoidable but scheduled crisis. Finally, of course, the dwindling resource of hope. In public journalism, a community is well reported when these things are visible. This is the lens it offers on the world.

"But a good lens is not enough. As Buzz Merritt [of the *Wichita Eagle*] has said, public journalism is also about making the community a better place to live. He calls the public journalist 'a fair-minded participant in a community that works.' What's the nature of this participation? Well, first of all, public journalism participates at bringing the well-connected community about. It asks itself what new capacity the community needs [in order] to converse about making choices. Now, creating capacity may sound like an esoteric notion, but it is what [the] Akron [Beacon Journal] did in its racism project. It's what [the] Madison [State Journal] is doing [in 'We the People']. It is what [the] Bremerton [Sun] did in its economic summit. It is what Jeremy [Iggers of the Star Tribune] wants to do with his [proposal for a] 'neighborhood repair kit.'

"I do not believe journalists should be solving problems. I think they should be creating the capacity within the community to solve problems. If you look at the model of investigative reporting, the highest pleasure you can reap is when you expose some rotten state of affairs and there is an outcry about it, especially from the legislature. The legislature then changes some law or regulation, and it doesn't happen anymore. In that model of political action, the citizenry remains utterly uninvolved. They are mute spectators to the drama of the newspaper producing change. But the cycle of investigative reporting and reform leaves no new capacity—except maybe a diminished capacity, because of outrage.

"In committing an act of public journalism, you know you have succeeded when you have left behind something people continue to use, some added ability the community now possesses. The power of the press thus empowers others besides the press."

◆

References

Newspapers

Akron Beacon Journal: P.O. Box 640, Akron, Ohio 44309-0640. (216) 996-3000. Fax: (216) 376-9235. Glenn Guzzo, managing editor.

Bob Paynter was lead editor on the Pulitzer Prize–winning race-relations project "A Question of Color." Speak to editor Dale Allen about the ongoing initiative "Coming Together": (216) 996-3503.

Atlanta Constitution: 72 Marietta Street, Atlanta, Georgia 30303. (404) 526-5151. Fax: (404) 526-5746. Ron Martin, executive editor.

Bergen County Record: 150 River Street, Hackensack, New Jersey 07601. (201) 646-4100. Fax: (201) 646-4135. Glenn Ritt, editor.

Reporter Mary Amoroso can provide more detail on the citizens' panel that proposed cuts in the New Jersey budget.

Boston Globe: 135 Morrissey Boulevard, Boston, Massachusetts 02107-2378. (617) 929-3100. Fax: (617) 929-3186. Matthew Storin, editor.

Boston Herald: 1 Herald Square, Boston, Massachusetts 02106. (617) 426-3000. Fax: (617) 542-1315. Andrew Costello, editor in chief.

Boulder Daily Camera: P.O. Box 591, Boulder, Colorado 80306. (800) 783-1202 x349 or (303) 473-1349. Fax: (303) 449-9358. Barrie Hartman, executive editor.

Bradenton Herald: P.O. Box 921, Bradenton, Florida 34206. (813) 745-7000. Fax: (813) 745-7097. Wayne Poston, executive editor.

Bremerton Sun: P.O. Box 259, Bremerton, Washington 98337. (206) 377-3711. Fax: (206) 479-7681. Mike Phillips, editor.

Cape Cod Times: 319 Main Street, Hyannis, Massachusetts 02601. (508) 775-1200. Fax: (508) 771-3292. Timothy O. White, managing editor.

Editor Bill Breisky and senior staff writer Peggy Eastman were the journalists most intensively involved with the "Cape Cod Agenda."

Charlotte Observer: P.O. Box 30308, Charlotte, North Carolina 28230. (704) 358-5040. Fax: (704) 358-5036. Jennie Buckner, executive editor.

Assistant managing editors Cheryl Carpenter and Jim Walser can provide more detail about "Taking Back Our Neighborhoods." Speak to Rick Thames, assistant managing editor for news, about coverage of the Freedom Park dispute.

Columbus Ledger-Enquirer: P.O. Box 711, Columbus, Georgia 31902-0711. (706) 324-5526. Fax: (706) 576-6290. Al Johnson, executive editor.

Dayton Daily News: 45 S. Ludlow Street, Dayton, Ohio 45402. (513) 225-2211. Fax: (513) 225-2489. Steve Sidlo, managing editor.

Martha Steffens, the news manager for public life, led the "Kids in Chaos"/"Fixing Our Families" project; she is now managing editor of the Binghamton, N.Y., *Press* and *Sun-Bulletin*.

Des Moines Register: 715 Locust Street, P.O. Box 957, Des Moines, Iowa 50304. (515) 284-8000. Fax: (515) 286-2504. Dennis Ryerson, editor.

Detroit Free Press: 321 W. Lafayette Boulevard, Detroit, Michigan 48226. (313) 222-6600. Fax: (313) 222-5981. Heath Meriwether, executive editor. Jane Daugherty, associate editor for "Children First." (800) 685-4KID. Fax: (313) 222-6667.

Fort Wayne News-Sentinel: P.O. Box 102, Fort Wayne, Indiana 46801-0102. (219) 461-8222. Fax: (219) 461-8649. Joseph Weiler, executive editor.

Hartford Courant: 285 Broad Street, Hartford, Connecticut 06115. (203) 241-6200. Fax: (203) 241-3865. David Barrett, managing editor.

Huntington Herald-Dispatch: 946 Fifth Avenue, Huntington, West Virginia 25701. (304) 526-2799. Fax: (304) 526-2857.

Executive editor Randy Hammer, who drove the "Our Jobs, Our Children, Our Future" project, has left for the Springfield, Mo., *News-Leader*; Bob Gabordi is the new executive editor. For details on the project, speak with Mickey Johnson, content editor.

The Independent: 1 Canada Square, Canary Wharf, London E14 5DL, United Kingdom. (011-44-71) 293-2559. Fax: (011-44-71) 293-2022.

For information on the Manchester, England, deliberative opinion poll, speak with Colin Hughes, assistant editor.

Indianapolis Star: 307 N. Pennsylvania Street, Indianapolis, Indiana 46204. (317) 633-1240. Fax: (317) 633-9423. Frank Caperton, executive editor.

Miami Herald: 1 Herald Plaza, Miami, Florida 33132-1693. (800) 437-2535 or (305) 350-2111. Fax: (305) 376-2287. Doug Clifton, executive editor. Saundra Keyes, managing editor.

Retired managing editor Pete Weitzel shepherded the *Herald*'s community conversations through their early stages.

New London Day: P.O. Box 1231, New London, Connecticut 06320. (203) 442-2200 x349. Fax: (203) 442-5599. Lance C. Johnson, managing editor. Reid MacCluggage, editor and publisher.

New Orleans Times-Picayune: 3800 Howard Avenue, New Orleans, Louisiana 70140. (504) 826-3300. Fax: (504) 826-3007.

Editor Jim Amoss oversaw the paper's race relations project, "Together Apart: The Myth of Race."

New York Newsday: now the Manhattan bureau of *Long Island Newsday*. 2 Park Avenue, New York, New York 10016. (212) 725-3600. Fax: (212) 696-0487.

The Times Mirror Company closed *New York Newsday* in July 1995. At press time, the editors at *Long Island Newsday* (516-843-2700) had not yet decided whether to continue running "In the Subways" in their Queens County edition.

New York Times: 229 W. 43rd Street, New York, New York 10036. (212) 556-1234. Editorial dept. fax: (212) 556-3815. Foreign news dept. fax: (212) 556-7278. Joseph Lelyveld, executive editor.

Howell Raines is editor of the editorial page, on which "Editorial Notebook" is featured. Bernard Gwertzman runs the foreign news section, which produced the periodic reports on Vietnam. Isabel Wilkerson writes from the Chicago bureau: (312) 427-5275.

The Oklahoman: P.O. Box 25125, Oklahoma City, Oklahoma 73125. (405) 475-3311. Fax: (405) 475-3183. Ed Kelley, managing editor.

The Olympian: P.O. Box 407, Olympia, Washington 98507. (360) 754-5400. Fax: (360) 357-0202. Vikki Porter, executive editor.

Orange County Register: 625 N. Grand Avenue, Santa Ana, California 92701. (714) 953-7951. Fax: (714) 542-5037. Ken Brusic, managing editor.

The Oregonian: 1320 S.W. Broadway, Portland, Oregon 97201. (800) 826-0376 or (503) 221-8439. Fax: (503) 221-8557. Sandy Rowe, executive editor.

Philadelphia Inquirer: P.O. Box 8263, Philadelphia, Pennsylvania 19101. (215) 854-2000. Fax: (215) 854-5099. Max King, editor in chief. James Naughton, executive editor.

Donald Barlett and James Steele wrote the series "America: What Went Wrong?"

Portland Newspapers: *Portland Press Herald* and *Maine Sunday Telegram*. P.O. Box 1460, Portland, Maine 04104. (207) 780-9000. Fax: (207) 791-6920. Lou Ureneck, editor and vice-president.

About the reader roundtables on education, speak either to Ureneck or to Sarah Campbell at the Maine Council of Churches, 15 Pleasant Avenue, Portland, Maine 04101. (207) 772-1918. Fax: (207) 772-2947.

Pottsville Republican: 111 Mahantongo Street, Pottsville, Pennsylvania 17901. (717) 622-3456. Fax: (717) 628-6092. James C. Kevlin, editor.

Richmond Times-Dispatch: P.O. Box 85333, Richmond, Virginia 23293. (804) 649-6332. Fax: (804) 775-8059. William Millsaps, executive editor.

Sacramento Bee: P.O. Box 15779, Sacramento, California 95852. (916) 321-1000. Fax: (916) 321-1109. Gregory Favre, executive editor.

St. Paul Pioneer Press: 345 Cedar Street, St. Paul, Minnesota 55101-1057. (612) 228-5491. Fax: (612) 228-5500. Walker Lundy, executive editor.

St. Petersburg Times: 490 First Avenue South, St. Petersburg, Florida 33701. (813) 893-8215. Fax: (813) 893-8675. Paul Tash, executive editor.

Spokane Spokesman-Review: Review Tower, West 999 Riverside Avenue, Spokane, Washington 99201. (509) 459-5430. Fax: (509) 459-5482. Chris Peck, managing editor.

The Star Tribune: 425 Portland Avenue, Minneapolis, Minnesota 55488. (612) 673-4414. Fax: (612) 673-4359. Tim McGuire, editor. Jeremy Iggers, coordinator for "Minnesota's Talking." (612) 673-4524. Fax: (612) 673-7568.

The State: P.O. Box 1333, Columbia, South Carolina 29202. (803) 771-6161. Fax: (803) 771-8430. Gil Thelen, executive editor.

Governance reporter Nina Brook wrote much of the *State*'s coverage of the Confederate flag debates. Speak to Jane Sutter, the "Passages" editor, about the series "To Raise a Child."

Tallahassee Democrat: 277 N. Magnolia Drive, Tallahassee, Florida 32302-0990. (904) 599-2100. Fax: (904) 599-2295. Lou Heldman, executive editor. Phone: (904) 599-2150. Mimi Jones directs the paper's "Public Agenda" project. (904) 942-7199. Fax: (904) 942-6484.

Topeka Capital-Journal: 616 S.E. Jefferson Street, Topeka, Kansas 66607. (913) 295-1181. Fax: (913) 295-1230. Mark Nusbaum, managing editor.

The Virginian-Pilot and the *Ledger-Star:* P.O. Box 449, Norfolk, Virginia 23510-0449. (804) 446-2311. Fax: (804) 446-2414. Cole Campbell, editor.

The Public Life Team is located at 921 N. Battlefield Boulevard, Chesapeake, Virginia 23320. Phone: (804) 547-9763. Fax: (804) 436-2798. Tom Warhover, team editor.

Wichita Eagle: P.O. Box 820, Wichita, Kansas 67201. (800) 825-6397 or (316) 268-6240. Fax: (316) 268-6627. Davis "Buzz" Merritt, Jr. editor and senior vice president.

Wilmington News Journal: P.O. Box 15505, Wilmington, Delaware 19850. (302) 324-2500. Fax: (302) 324-5509. John Walston, executive editor.

Wisconsin State Journal: P.O. Box 8056, Madison, Wisconsin 53708. (608) 252-6000. Fax: (608) 252-6119. Frank Denton, editor. Tom Still, lead editor of "We the People."

Magazines and Journals

Consensus: Newsletter of the MIT–Harvard Public Disputes Program. Program on Negotiation, 516 Pound Hall, Harvard Law School, Cambridge, Massachusetts 02138. (617) 495-1684. Fax: (617) 495-7818. Lawrence E. Susskind, publisher. Paul Katzeff, editor.

Consensus, which comes out four times a year and goes mainly to federal, state, and local officials, recounts case histories of public-sector policy disputes that have been solved through creative mediation. (As styles of deliberative talk go, "mediation" involves an active moderator; the "negotiation" described in *Getting to Yes* does not.) The newsletter also lists conflict resolution practitioners across Canada and the United States and includes a separate section of shoptalk. It's full of ideas and resources, and not quite as dry as it may sound. For a more comprehensive presentation of some of the same ideas, see *Breaking the Impasse*, below under Books.

The New Combat: A Journal of Reason and Resistance. *New Combat* is published at 24 Ludlow Street, New York, New York 10002. (212) 529-8128. No fax. William Ney, editor and publisher.

This thoughtful, somewhat academic, political magazine addresses citizens rather than opinion makers. By going deeply into one or two subjects in each issue, it intends to give them enough information and argument to form reasoned judgments. *New Combat* comes out irregularly, on a shoestring budget, perhaps once a year.

Utne Reader: Fawkes Building, 1624 Harmon Place, Suite 330, Minneapolis, Minnesota 55403. (612) 338-5040. Fax: (612) 338-6043. Eric Utne, president and editor in chief. Jay Walljasper, editor.

Known as the *"Reader's Digest* of the alternative media," the *Utne Reader* reprints articles, brief reports, listings, memos, and items of all sorts on themes that range from pop culture and New Age life-styles to promoting public life and democracy in "the grand, populist midwestern tradition."

Other News Media Resources

MacNeil/Lehrer Productions: Producers of the *MacNeil/Lehrer NewsHour* (beginning Oct. 21, 1995, *The NewsHour with Jim Lehrer*).

For information on plans for a nationwide "deliberative opinion poll" to precede the 1996 presidential primaries, contact Dan Werner, vice president, MacNeil/Lehrer Productions, c/o WETA-TV, P.O. Box 2626, Washington DC 20013. (703) 998-2870. No fax.

National Public Radio: 635 Massachusetts Avenue NW, Washington, D.C. 20001. (202) 414-2000. Fax: (202) 414-3329.

For information on the 1994 Election Project and other radio–newspaper partnerships, speak with John Dinges, editorial director. (202) 414-2204. Fax: (202) 414-3027.

Pew Center for Civic Journalism: Suite 310 South, 601 13th Street N.W., Washington, D.C. 20005. (202) 331-3200. Fax: (202) 347-6440. Edward Fouhy, executive director.

The center gives grants to print–radio–TV alliances working on innovative public journalism projects; often the grants pay for surveys, town meeting programs, or other aspects of a project that might be unaffordable without outside financial help. Pew also cosponsors workshops, publishes a bimonthly newsletter and a manual of case studies in public journalism, and is developing a series of videos targeted to newsrooms, journalism schools, and the general public.

Poynter Institute for Media Studies: 801 Third St. South, St. Petersburg, Florida 33701. (813) 821-9494. Fax: (813) 821-0583. Robert J. Haiman, president and managing director. Dr. Karen Brown, dean.

An advanced school and research facility for print and broadcast journalists, its work touches aspects of the business from writing to graphics, video, ethics, and management. Poynter helped initiate tnd then studied the effects of citizen-centered election coverage in 1992 (at the *Charlotte Observer*) and 1994 (through National Public Radio) and plans to do the same in 1996. Advice, monographs, conferences, and a large library are available.

Project on Public Life and the Press: Department of Journalism, New York University, 10 Washington Place, New York, New York 10003. (212) 998-3793. Fax: (212) 388-0359. Jay Rosen, director: (212) 998-7965. Lisa Austin, research director: (207) 799-8918.

A networking point for print journalists, academics, and (increasingly) broadcasters interested in doing public journalism. The Project stages three workshops a year, at which participants share innovations, work through common problems, and advance the movement's "theory." Rosen and Austin travel widely both to observe innovative journalists at work and to speak, discuss, or debate public journalism. The Project provides, upon request, abstracts of interesting newspaper and broadcast work as well as occasional papers on useful concepts and tools.

Sources on Deliberation and Public Policy

Center for Living Democracy: RR #1, Black Fox Road, Brattleboro, Vermont 05301. (802) 254-1234. Fax: (802) 254-1227. Frances Moore Lappé and Paul Martin Du Bois, codirectors.

The Center is a clearinghouse for information on democratic innovations. It publishes the newsletter *Doing Democracy*.

The Communitarian Network: 2130 H Street NW, Suite 714J, Washington, D.C. 20052. (202) 994-7997. Fax: (202) 994-1606. Amitai Etzioni, chairman. David Seldin, communications director.

The Communitarians hold conferences, publish a platform and position papers, and give briefings on policy options they consider more consensual, community-minded and workable than those of Left or Right. The network promotes discussion of such ideas through a quarterly journal, *The Responsive Community*.

Prof. James Fishkin: inventor of the "deliberative opinion poll" (see Chapter Two). Department of Government, University of Texas at Austin, Austin, Texas 78712. (512) 471-5121. Fax: (512) 471-1061.

Prof. Doris Graber: author of *Processing the News: How People Tame the Information Tide* (see Chapter Three). Department of Political Science, University of Illinois at Chicago, 1007 W. Harrison Street, Chicago, Illinois 60607. (312) 996-3108. Fax: (312) 443-0440.

The Harwood Group: Suite 402, 4915 St. Elmo Avenue, Bethesda, Maryland 20814. (301) 656-3669. Fax: (301) 656-0533. Richard C. Harwood, president.

By means of focus groups and other qualitative techniques, Harwood researchers study the mechanics of social change, both on specific issues and more generally, for clients ranging from Georgia Health Decisions to Project Democracy. They work together with the clients to develop discussion booklets, programs, and strategies for improving those mechanics, as well. Harwood has consulted with or trained journalists at a number of public newspapers.

Industrial Areas Foundation: 220 W. Kinzie Street, 5th floor, Chicago, Illinois 60610. (312) 245-9211. Fax: (312) 245-9744. Edward T. Chambers, executive director.

The IAF organizes activist groups (particularly in low-income areas) that virtually become fully functional grassroots democracies, following ideas of the late Chicago sociologist Saul Alinsky; its "iron rule" is "Never do for others what they can do for themselves."

International Healthy Cities Foundation: 1 Kaiser Plaza, Suite 1930, Oakland, California 94612. (510) 271-2660. Fax: (510) 271-6814. Judy Mings, coordinator.

The Healthy Cities project is actually a network of very loosely coordinated regional and local projects in deliberative problem solving throughout the United States and the world; the Oakland office maintains a database. The best source of information about the network, however, is not an office but a single man, the Healthy Cities idea's inventor and leader emeritus, Prof. Leonard Duhl, MD, Warren Hall, Room 410, School of Public Health, University of California at Berkeley, Berkeley, California 94708. (510) 642-1715.

The Kettering Foundation: 200 Commons Road, Dayton, Ohio 45459-2799. (513) 434-7300. Fax: (513) 439-9804. David Mathews, president.

To order publications call (800) 600-4060. For Michael Briand, developer of the chart on conventional and deliberative discourse, call (719) 846-5240. On the surface, Kettering is a small research organization that examines democracy, education, and civil society around the globe—where, why, and how they work, and how they can be made to work better. Its influence, however, comes from a talent for leveraging: nurturing networks of independent scholars and practitioners who are facing these same issues from within particular fields, and letting them crossfertilize one another and the Foundation. Kettering has helped to organize, in addition to a network of journalists (the Project on Public Life and the Press), networks of philanthropic foundations (speak to Carol Farquhar), humanities scholars (speak to James Veninga, 512-440-1991), and political officeholders (speak to Maxine Thomas). It offers a variety of journals, books, articles, and advice, but no grants.

MIT–Harvard Public Disputes Program: c/o Program on Negotiations, 516 Pound Hall, Harvard Law School, Cambridge, Massachusetts 02138. (617) 495-1684. Fax: (617) 495-7818. Lawrence E. Susskind, director.

Students and staff help solve real public disputes through creative mediation, then use their experience to improve mediation theory and develop teaching materials. The program teaches its techniques at one-and-a-half-day courses throughout the year. Journalists interested in seeing how mediation has helped resolve conflicts over particular public issues can obtain case studies on those issues, as well as more general lists of books and articles on conflict resolution.

The National Civic League: 1445 Market Street, Suite 300, Denver, Colorado 80202-1728. (800) 223-6004 or (303) 571-4343. Fax: (303) 571-4404. John Parr, executive director.

The League aims to restore faith in the ability of different community segments (e.g., government, citizens, and business; or black, white, Hispanic, and Asian) to collaborate in solving problems; it does this through community intervention, partnerships with other national civic organizations, and the bestowing of annual "All America Cities" awards. It is currently helping organize an Alliance for National Renewal that will bring together more than 100 membership organizations, foundations, chambers of commerce, and other broad-based civic groups.

National Issues Forum Institute: 100 Commons Road, Dayton, Ohio 45459-2777. Within Ohio: (800) 433-4819. Outside Ohio: (800) 433-7834. Fax: (513) 439-9804.

NIF resists describing itself as an organization; it's more a loose web of schools, libraries, prisons, university departments, extension agents, ministers, and assorted others who each run their own programs employing a common discussion method. Most of the explanatory tools and issue books they use are, however, drafted by a core of people at the Kettering and Public Agenda foundations. Keith Melville, the most active editor of NIF issue books, works at Public Agenda, listed below. Each year, more than a dozen universities mount NIF training institutes. For general information about them, speak to Sharon Harden or Estus Smith at the numbers above. To order issue books call Kendall/Hunt Publishing at (800) 228-0810.

Utne Reader's **Neighborhood Salon Association:** c/o *Utne Reader*, The Fawkes Building, 1624 Harmon Place, Suite 330, Minneapolis, Minnesota 55403. (612) 338-5040. Fax: (612) 338-6043. Patricia Cich, salon coordinator.

The association is a sort of "salon placement service," putting members in touch with others in their geographic area who wish to form discussion clubs of one sort or another; it also tracks the 300-or-so ongoing salons and occasionally reports on what they're talking about in *Utne Reader*. Journalists frequently contact the NSA to find salons in their area. The association also offers a how-to booklet and resource guide, *The Salon-keeper's Companion*.

Ojai Foundation: P.O. Box 1620, Ojai, California 93024. (805) 646-8343. Fax: (805) 646-0902.

The Foundation hosts retreats and educational programs, which use council-style discussion as a method. To learn more about this method, speak to Leon Berg. The Foundation also distributes a brief guide, "The Practice of Council," which is full of extremely practical information though heavily overlaid with New Age language.

Partners for Democratic Change: 823 Ulloa Street, San Francisco, California 94127. (415) 665-0652. Fax: (415) 665-2732. Raymond Shonholtz, president.

Like Search for Common Ground and the Kettering Foundation, this group works to embed democratic decision making and conflict resolution in the emerging democracies of central and eastern Europe. It has staged training programs for journalists in Russia and Poland.

Project Vote Smart: Center for National Independence in Politics, 129 N.W. 4th Street #204, Corvallis, Oregon 97330. (503) 754-2746. Fax: (503) 754-2747. Richard Kimball, board president.

The project aims to provide citizens with free, easily accessible, and high-quality information on candidates, elected officials, and public affairs; as one route to this, it provides a range of services for journalists. A reporter's resource center maintains an extensive public affairs library and will do research for journalists at no cost: call (503) 737-4000. A project database can be tapped through the Internet. See also *The Reporter's Source Book*, listed under Books. Among services for nonjournalists is a voter research hotline that provides information on all elected federal officials: (800) 622-7627.

Public Agenda: formerly the Public Agenda Foundation. 6 East 39th Street, New York, New York 10016. (212) 686-6610. Fax: (212) 889-3461. Deborah Wadsworth, executive director. Founded by Dan Yankelovich and Cyrus Vance.

Public Agenda works to improve the quality of information available to officials about citizens, and to citizens themselves about public issues ranging from education to criminal justice to foreign policy. Its deep, carefully nuanced research into the public's starting points and evolving judgments relies on an expanded, seven-stage version of Yankelovich's process of coming to judgment. It has also coordinated nationwide multimedia "citizen education projects" among journalists, such as the "Help Wanted" project on education's role in the economy and "Condition Critical" on health care. Keith Melville, at Public Agenda, writes and edits many of the National Issues Forums issue books.

National Issues Forums' **Public Voice program:** Speak to Robert Kingston at
   the National Issues Forum Institute.

   Each spring the Public Voice program stages a roundtable at the
National Press Club involving national journalists and political leaders, in which they review deliberations from the previous year's NIF
forums and discuss the state of the "public voice." (Starting in 1995,
Public Voice has staged additional roundtables involving a different
mix of participants.) Each "A Public Voice" is broadcast widely on
public television; contact local stations for dates and times. A vide-
otape is usually available from PBS Video, (800) 344-3337. Contact
Ed Arnone at the NIF Institute for a printed summary of each year's
findings on the "public voice."

Rural Southern Voice for Peace: 1898 Hannah Branch Road, Burnsville,
   North Carolina 28714. (704) 675-5933. Jenifer Morgan, office manager.

   RSVP helps grassroots activist groups to better organize, network, and
connect with their wider communities. While it's achieved most of its
notoreity for Listening Projects in the rural South and abroad (see Chapter
Two), it also offers workshops on community organizing, nonviolence, and
other nuts-and-bolts skills.

Search for Common Ground: 1601 Connecticut Avenue N.W., Suite 200,
   Washington, D.C. 20009. (202) 265-4300. Fax: (202) 232-6718. John
   Marks, president.

   The organization works in the United States and abroad to find
collaborative solutions to seemingly intractable conflicts; it has brought
Marks's common-ground process, both in person and on TV, to South
Africa, Russia, and Macedonia as well as to many local American discussions of abortion. Videotapes of the "What's the Common Ground on
. . . ?" series from public television can be purchased from this office.

Study Circles Resource Center: Route 169, P.O. Box 203, Pomfret, Connecticut 06258. (203) 928-2616. Fax: (203) 928-3713. Martha McCoy and
   Phyllis Emigh, codirectors.

   The small but enthusiastic Center promotes study circle discussions
(and deliberation more generally) by offering how-to manuals, issue
guides, advice, training, and help in networking. It has hosted an on-site
gathering for public journalists who employ the study circle method.

Books

Barber, Benjamin R. **Strong Democracy: Participatory Politics for a New
   Age.** (Berkeley: University of California Press, 1984.)
   A philosopher's brief for participatory democracy—one of the many
recent books laying intellectual foundations for more practical work. Our
old liberal ideals of democracy are too "thin," Barber says; by emphasizing
private rights, nonjudgmental tolerance and a fear of collective action,

they have made us suspicious spectators in our own political lives, passive in the face of intractable social problems, image-based political campaigns, Wall Street greed, and so on. (One instance of this passivity is the detachment of the press.) Societies of this sort end up either falling apart or electing demagogues. A "strong" democracy, on the other hand—one that involves all of the people in making common choices and taking common action—puts muscle tone back in social, political, and communal impulses that liberalism has let atrophy.

Bellah, Robert N., Richard Madsen, William M. Sullivan, Ann Swidler, and Steven M. Tipton. **The Good Society.** (New York: Vintage Books, 1992.)

When Americans want to fix society, then tend to call for changes in individuals ("throw the rascals out") or specific organizations (corrupt S&Ls); they view institutions such as the family, religion, politics, and the market as either fixed in natural law or so complex as to be beyond our control. But these institutions set the benchmarks for what individuals and organizations can do: They form us as people, enable (or constrain) us in, for example, raising our children, participating in our communities, or using our talents. This wise, broad-ranging, and gracefully written book invites us to examine what we want from our social institutions, as a step toward remaking them. Although it doesn't specifically treat "reporting the news" as an institution, it's a fine defense of the spirit behind public journalism.

Dionne, E. J. Jr. **Why Americans Hate Politics.** (New York: Simon and Schuster, 1991.)

How false choices destroy public life. To Dionne, "liberalism" versus "conservatism" is a *deeply* false choice, and doesn't in any way reflect the pragmatic, consensual politics of which the great American middle is capable. He sketches a free-hand portrait of the values and instincts still widely shared in the United States and shows how Democrats and Republicans have drifted into choosing stiff, ideological positions outside the boundaries, blinded by the upper-middle-class social liberals who've taken over one party and the free-market conservatives who've taken over the other.

Etzioni, Amitai. **The Spirit of Community: Rights, Responsibilities, and the Communitarian Agenda.** (New York: Crown Publishers, 1993.)

A set of topical arguments in balancing rights and responsibilities, culminating in a manifesto. Etzioni is trying to stake out a new centrist American politics. Like E. J. Dionne, he indicts a lack of realism and imagination in conventional political arguments (both Great Society liberals and free-market conservatives assert absolute rights without sensible limits and responsibilities); unlike Dionne, he delivers very specific alternatives—mostly ex cathedra—that emphasize holding citizens responsible to one another both through law and through a reinvigorated moral voice of the community. He calls communitarianism "part change of heart, part renewal of social bonds, part reform of public life."

Fisher, Roger, William Ury, and Bruce Patton. **Getting to Yes: Negotiating Agreement without Giving In.** (New York: Penguin, 1991, 2nd ed.)

A simple, brilliantly written guide to the Harvard Negotiation Project's method of "interest-based" bargaining—one especially fertile style of deliberative talk. Negotiations often fail when parties see their initial positions, or some compromise among them, as the only possible choices; by talking instead about underlying interests (which bear some resemblance to this handbook's "core values"), they can usually invent better solutions, while at the same time reducing their reliance on secrecy, personality, arbitrary power, and splitting the difference.

Fishkin, James. **Democracy and Deliberation: New Directions for Democratic Reform.** (New Haven, Conn.: Yale University Press, 1991.)

On the whole, a thin, overly schematic treatment of the difficulty of practicing democracy in large nations, but with one ingenious and very practical idea thrown in: the deliberative opinion poll (treated in Chapter Two here under "Sidebar: Using Polls and Focus Groups"). "An ordinary opinion poll models what the public thinks, given how little it knows. A deliberative opinion poll models what the public *would* think, if it had a more adequate chance to think about the questions at issue. . . . This proposal is intended to adapt the deliberative possibilities of *small-scale* politics to . . . a large-scale nation-state"—the same thing that community forums, study circles, and several sane-to-fanciful proposals surveyed in the back of Fishkin's book try to do in different ways.

Gardner, John. **On Leadership.** (New York: Free Press, 1990.)

A warm, eloquent, humane examination of leadership as a concrete human activity—what it is, what qualities it requires, what it demands of followers and constituents, how to produce or destroy it. "In popular thinking . . . the mature need and the childlike fantasies [of leadership] interweave. One of the tasks of this book is to untangle them, and to sketch what is realistically possible." That includes recognizing that leadership is fluid—people lowly and great may lead in different times and circumstances, and in wholly different ways—and that good leaders don't so much command, proclaim, or manage as empower their constituents to work toward a common purpose: the very thing public journalists aim to do. Gardner invests the book with such scope and lucidity, it takes your breath away.

Graber, Doris. **Processing the News: How People Tame the Information Tide.** (New York: Longman, 1988.)

A well-conducted, influential case study in how ordinary people sift through the daily barrage of news, unfortunately mired in dense political-science jargon. The central idea—that people rely on existing pictures in their heads (here called "schemas") to interpret what they read about public affairs, and that they will either ignore new facts or struggle hard to fit them with these pictures before they'll alter the pictures themselves—identifies an important problem for journalists: how to present the news in a way that people will really *think* about it.

Harwood Group. **Citizens and Politics: A View from Main Street America.** (Dayton, Ohio: Kettering Foundation, 1991.)

Americans—far from being apathetic—participate in politics wherever they feel reasonably sure they can make a difference, this study concludes. Unfortunately they don't feel this way in most traditional political arenas, where discourse is shallow or arcane, and politicians, experts, and the press don't seem particularly interested in what ordinary people have to say. Harwood explores citizens' realistic views of the politics they would like and the politics they see, through the comments they made at 10 focus group sessions spread across the United States over the course of a year.

———. **Meaningful Chaos: How People Form Relationships with Public Concerns.** (Dayton, Ohio: Kettering Foundation, 1993.)

Short, pithy, essential reading. Harwood interviewed six panels of ordinary Americans as well as 13 noted journalists, scholars, marketers, and activists in order to identify factors that draw people into a public issue and sustain their engagement; it identified nine. (As the title hints, they are decidedly not the factors news programs put a premium on: People seek emotional involvement rather than detachment, ambivalence rather than certainty, big interconnected issues rather than narrow, easily digestible fragments—in short, an unwieldy but honest dialogue instead of a neat and tidy one.) Chapters Two and Three here describe the book in detail.

Kettering Foundation. **Framing Issues: Building a Structure for Public Discussions.** Michele Archie, writer. (Dayton, Ohio: Kettering Foundation, 1995.)

A 48-page workbook that retravels the path of Chapter Three's framing discussion but at a slower pace, with more time to mull over the subtleties. Some of the how-to sections will be old hat to journalists; the booklet is user-friendly to even the most inexperienced of community groups. But overall the exposition is simple, the advice practical, the examples and tips numerous—a good source to put shading and color on many ideas sketched quickly in this handbook.

Lappé, Frances Moore, and Paul Martin Du Bois. **The Quickening of America: Rebuilding Our Nation, Remaking Our Lives.** (San Francisco: Jossey-Bass, 1994.)

How Americans at the grass roots—inspired by democratic, egalitarian ideas currently in the air—are reshaping workplaces, schools, media, and other arenas of public life. Despite some sharply original ideas and analysis, *Quickening* isn't a treatise but an enthusiastic, vaguely countercultural self-help book, stuffed tight with anecdotes, exercises, tips, skills assessments, visual aids, and other tools geared to help readers apply the arts of democracy throughout their own lives. There is a lengthy resource list at the back.

Mathews, David. **Politics for People: Finding a Responsible Public Voice.**
(Urbana: University of Illinois Press, 1994.)

The "politics of government" leaves Americans cold: They feel officials have shut them out, while officials in their turn see the public as
uninterested, unrealistic, and ill-informed. Yet there is a "politics that is
not called politics"—citizens unaffectedly coming together to address
problems such as drugs in their neighborhood schools or decay in their
housing projects, pragmatically trying out solutions, and building personal
bonds along the way—that could be the template for a more successful
democratic life. Mathews draws on the Kettering Foundation's extensive
research and his own professional knowledge of history and political
philosophy to identify what officials, the press, and citizens themselves
have to do to make this happen.

Merritt, Davis. **Public Journalism and Public Life: Why Telling the News Is
Not Enough.** (Hillsdale, N.J.: Lawrence Erlbaum Associates, 1995.)

Part memoir, part argument. Buzz Merritt describes the heady, now
mythologized journalistic world in which he started his career—Charlotte
during the Civil Rights era, Washington during Watergate—and how its
blindspots, wrong turns, and long, steady decline in public trust drove him
to become one of the early inventors of public journalism. Along the way
he shines a different light on many of the arguments made in this
handbook.

Neuman, W. Russell, Marion R. Just, and Ann N. Crigler. **Common Knowledge: News and the Construction of Political Meaning.** (Chicago:
University of Chicago Press, 1992.)

How people learn differently from television, newsmagazines, and
newspapers. This book is a good complement to Doris Graber's. Instead
of cataloguing people's general tools for taming the information tide, this
study investigates whether it makes a difference what kind of issue they're
trying to learn about (e.g., AIDS vs. South Africa vs. a stock-market crash)
and what medium they're learning about it from. Unfortunately, it seems
that nearly everyone learns less from newspapers than from magazines or
TV, and that the style of newspaper journalism is to blame. There are fine
passages here on how very differently journalists and citizens frame issues
and make sense of the news (fleshing out a lot of what's said in Chapters
Two and Three here).

Page, Benjamin I., and Robert Y. Shapiro. **The Rational Public: Fifty Years
of Trends in Americans' Policy Preferences.** (Chicago: University of
Chicago Press, 1992.)

Bucking conventional wisdom about the American public's fickleness
and ignorance, the authors argue that collectively the public makes up its
mind pretty well: It forms stable opinions on political issues, changes them
sensibly in the face of new information, and roots them in its long-term
core values. This long volume methodically piles up supporting evidence,
public issue by public issue. If U.S. democracy doesn't work as well as it

might, "our research suggests that the American public should not be blamed. The fault is more likely to lie with officials and elites who fail to respond to the citizenry, and with defects in the system by which the public is provided with political information."

Patterson, Thomas. **Out of Order.** (New York: Knopf, 1993.)

How the values of the press undermine presidential elections, step by step. Patterson draws on recent history, social science and a wealth of press anecdotes to show how journalists—by treating elections as contests for office rather than deliberations over policy, by seeing all politicians as ethically suspect, by keeping the camera on themselves and off the would-be officeholders—make it impossible for candidates to get their ideas across and for citizens to evaluate them. Along the way the book clarifies what it means to say the press frames issues and sets the public's agenda.

Project Vote Smart. **The Reporter's Source Book.** (Corvallis, Ore.: Center for National Independence in Politics, 1994, 5th ed.)

Analyses of the public's starting point on half a dozen major issues, followed by issue briefs on each, and then more than a hundred well-indexed pages of expert sources—advocacy groups, think tanks, university professors, and on-line services. The briefs mimic the National Issues Forum format of breaking each issue down into choices, but then throw away the NIF spirit by contrasting very specific bills and policies ("The Clinton Plan," "The House Republican Plan") rather than more basic value-based or interest-based alternatives. Project Vote Smart updates the book twice during each federal election year, once during each off year.

Putnam, Robert D. **Making Democracy Work: Civic Traditions in Modern Italy.** (Princeton, N.J.: Princeton University Press, 1993.)

The premier source on the importance of civic capital (or social capital, as it's called here). When Italy created a new layer of regional government in 1970, Putnam tracked the success of each of the 15 new regional bodies—identical on paper, but vastly different in their social settings. After 20 years, the new governments had flourished in precisely those areas with the densest, most egalitarian, and honest civic associations. Putnam applies his conclusions to American life in "The Prosperous Community," in the spring 1993 *American Prospect*. In a later piece, "Bowling Alone: America's Declining Social Capital," in the January 1995 *Journal of Democracy*, he identifies which sorts of social organizations create the most productive social capital and speculates on why Americans participate in them less and less.

Rural Southern Voice for Peace. **Listening Project Training Manual.** (Burnsville, N.C.: RSVP, 1994.)

A step-by-step guide for community groups that wish to do public listening. Quite a lot of it is overly basic, repetitive, or "activist" for journalists. If you can see past the presentation, though, the ideas themselves are excellent: carefully tailored, with a consistent philosophy behind them. Chapter Two here boils down the important concepts; the manual itself contains several more examples of public-listening questionnaires.

Sharp, Marsha, and Ann Beaudry. **Communications as Engagement: A Communications Strategy for Revitalization.** The Millennium Report to the Rockefeller Foundation. (New York: Rockefeller Foundation, 1994.)

A road map to deliberative activity in the United States today—very broad although not very deep. The first half (a research paper) offers a taxonomy of deliberative groups while the second half (a resource list) gives a good sampling of each kind, ranging from block-by-block renewal ventures to "visioning" organizations such as the National Civic League. The overall picture may well be a big-screen version of what any journalist can find in his or her own city. The section on new media shows if you read between the lines what print newspapers are still good for, what they aren't, and where niches may exist for creative multimedia partnerships. Hard copies are available from Millennium Communications Group Inc., 1150 18th Street NW, 8th floor, Washington DC 20036, Attn: Liza Poinier. (202) 872-8800. Fax: (202) 872-8845. Updated versions can be downloaded from three on-line addresses: WWW URL (http://cdi-net.com/Millennium), Gopher (gopher.cdinet.com) and Anonymous FTP (ftp.cdinet.com).

Susskind, Lawrence, and Jeffrey Cruikshank. **Breaking the Impasse: Consensual Approaches to Resolving Public Disputes.** (New York: Basic Books, 1987.)

A mediator's procedural, aimed at a general audience. It offers food for thought on finding common ground. Many basic concepts of dispute settlement are better expressed in *Getting to Yes*, but this book gives a panorama of the field—describing different styles of negotiation (unassisted, aided by a facilitator, by a mediator, by an arbitrator), offering tips, and applying it all directly to the kinds of community issues a public newspaper would most likely want to deal with. The authors discuss when and how elected officials can join negotiations, and offer plenty of case studies.

Weiss, Michael J. **The Clustering of America.** (New York: Harper & Row, 1988.)

An extremely engaging, pop look at American diversity by way of the zip-code-based "life-style clusters" identified by Claritas Inc. in the 1970s. Weiss visited at least one example of each cluster and shows its flavor through statistics and residents' own words; he also trips, magazine-style, through the various ways in which Americans entertain themselves, consume, mate, vote, and work. The book draws no morals (except that the "average American" doesn't exist and that "you are where you live"), but a reader who's looking for them can draw dozens.

Yankelovich, Daniel. **Coming to Public Judgment: Making Democracy Work in a Complex World.** (Syracuse, N.Y.: Syracuse University Press, 1991.)

What it takes to move people from fickle "mass opinion" to responsible "public judgment." Chapter One here skims over the central themes and draws conclusions for public journalists, but the book itself goes in far more deeply, encompassing case studies, the psychology of choice, analysis of citizen behavior, rules for officials trying to help along public judgment, a general sketch of possible reforms—even a long detour into epistemology. In some ways, this is a model for democracy books—a simple idea seriously explored. Here Yankelovich divides coming to judgment into three major stages; in his more recent article "The Rules of Public Engagement" (cited below) he breaks the process down into a more nuanced list of seven.

Yankelovich, Daniel, and John Immerwahr. "The Rules of Public Engagement." In David Yankelovich and I. M. Destler, editors. **Beyond the Beltway: Engaging the Public in U.S. Foreign Policy.** (New York: W. W. Norton, 1994.)

An improved itinerary of the "mass opinion to public judgment" process. It spells out seven roughly sequential ways in which people wrestle with an issue before coming to a stable judgment, offering ideas to politicians and the media at each stage for making a two-way consultation more fruitful. Like the book's other 10 chapters (each a paper presented to Columbia University's American Assembly), the article's particular focus is on the public's role in forming post-cold war foreign policy.

Index

Note: Small capital letters indicate a key public journalism concept. Specialized guides are in bold, underlined type.